—A MAVERICK PUBLICATION—

Bombs Awry

Grover Ted Tate

cover illustration: Dan Gates

ISBN: 0-89288-093-7

Maverick Publications
Drawer 5007 • Bend, Oregon 97708

DEDICATION

For my instructors who helped me as I tried to be one of everything: pilot, navigator, bombardier, radio operator, gunner, electronic countermeasures equipment operator, flight engineer, mechanic, flight test engineer, and, finally, a graying passenger.

For Carl Hartley, Colonel Perrin, Hank Meyers, Deacon Cunningham, Freddy Verrips, Paul Diehl, Ray Fitzgerald, Don Siedhof, Jack Baldridge, Major Brightwell, Doug Coleman, C.T. Jones, Ray Tenhoff, Jack Ridley, Bill Bridgeman, Walt Simon, Spade Cooley, George Longworth, and the dozens of other close friends who perished in the pursuit of freedom and of aviation knowledge.

For all the many crew members who tolerated me.

For A.S. "Doc" Witchell Jr., the pilot who gave me the opportunity to fly the B-58 program and with whom I shared a few harrowing experiences.

For the many guys whom I loved who yielded up their lives in aircraft during the wars of my generation and to those who did the same in the war before my time.

For those who fought and won the wars that gave me the freedom to pursue a career of my choice.

And to God, who allowed me to survive the mistakes and tragedies of my lifetime of flying so that I could compose this bit of a memorial to those who survived and for those who were lost.

Pilot was one of 'best of breed'

Associated Press

JEFFERSON — T.D. "Doug" Benefield, the ace test pilot who died in the crash of a B-1 bomber prototype, was one of the "kids who've never stopped dreaming" about pushing machines to the "edge of ... endurance."

That dream, and a 34-year career piloting experimental aircraft including the supersonic Con-

BENEFIELD

corde, ended Wednesday when the $200 million bomber he was flying on low-level tests crashed in the Mojave Desert.

"We're flying every day because we're kids who've never stopped dreaming," said Benefield, 55, of Jefferson, in an interview this year. "We're always looking at another frontier ... the edge of human and technological endurance."

Wednesday, family members in this small East Texas town recounted his accomplishments.

"Doug was a very strong person of high intelligence," said his sister-in-law, Suzanne Benefield.

Benefield, the chief test pilot for the B-1 program of the aircraft's manufacturer, Rockwell International Corp., was a veteran of Air Force F-4C Phantom combat missions in Vietnam and the man who made all the early B-1 test flights.

Life magazine, in a profile in April, called Benefield and four others "the best of the breed" whose heroics in the early days of the Edwards test program were part of Tom Wolfe's novel The Right Stuff. He was one of the last active test pilots trained in the '50s.

Benefield logged more than 6,000 hours flying during the past 34 years.

TABLE OF CONTENTS

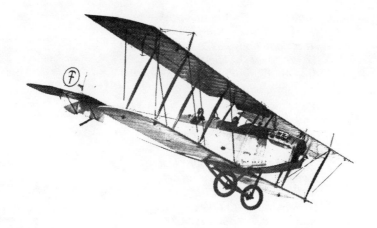

Curtiss Jenny   American Hall of Aviation History, Northrop Univ., Inglewood, CA.

TEST PILOT

So long as this is a free man's world,
Somebody has to lead.
Somebody has to carry the ball
In word and thought and deed.
Somebody's got to knock on doors
Which never have known a key.
Somebody's got to see the things
That the throng would never see.

Hotter than thrust when the boost is hit
Somebody's faith must burn.
And faster than mach when the rocket's lit
Somebody's mind must turn.
Somebody's got to get the proof
For what the designers plan;
And test the dreams that the prophets dream
In behalf of their fellow man.

Somebody's got to think of pay
In terms that are more than gold
And, somebody has to spend himself
To buy what the Heavens hold.
Somebody's got to leave the crowd
And walk with his fears alone.
Somebody's got to accept the thorns
And weave for himself a crown.

It is ever thus as the ages roll,
And the record's written clear.
Somebody has to give himself
As the price of each frontier.
Somebody has to take a course,
And climb to a rendezvous
Where a lonesome man with a will to learn
Can make the truth shine through.

Gill Robb Wilson

INTRODUCTION

About six years before Amelia Earhart wrote the book *For the Fun of It*, I went for my first airplane ride. It was in an open-cockpit biplane that was something from World War I surplus. I loved every curiosity-filled moment of that first thrust into the unknown, and since that bone-chilling first flight with the melodic sound of the wind whistling through the flying wires, I have been the classic aviation nut. Somewhere within the deep recesses of my mind, I always knew that my lifetime would be devoted to flying—and it was. I followed a pattern that kept me airborne in both reality and philosophy.

During the many years of hanging around airports, doing menial tasks for airplane people, learning to fly, working as a "rag-boy," performing wartime Air Force duty, flying in test programs, and growing into a juvenile maturity within the aviation environment, I have enjoyed a lifetime of doing what pleased me most. Flying was the vehicle that allowed me to touch all of the corners of the world and to walk with giants.

Flying, perhaps as no other profession in the world, is addictive because of the excitement and the adventure rather than because of any material gains. I was the confirmed addict and often worked at it for the minimum of compensation that barely covered my needs for minimum survival.

Flying, again as perhaps no other endeaver, has its extremes of happiness and of heartbreak. The very nature of flying dictates that it must be approached and practiced ser-

1

iously if one is to survive physically. The seriousness of flying and its inherent tragedies must be diluted with faith and a faint thread of humor that often provides the compelling inspiration to build and to fly again.

I was the romantic aviation nut and not the supreme realist of the nuts, bolts, and physical laws that made the whole thing possible. I had to fly in an airplane and it made no difference in what kind of a machine nor in what capacity. Grease monkey or pampered airline passenger, I loved it all. I flew in most everything, from machines so slow that angry kites could catch them to the multi-supersonics, and I have a continuing love affair with the memory of each one of them. The world beneath me could be crumbling and in tatters but I was always at peace in the sky. Never did I feel fear after that first flight, for it seemed that the sky, the flying machine, and I all shared a mutual respect. Although I touched base with tragedy and with hilarity many times, I feel that it was the best of all worlds. It was a world where I was among those who were privileged to fly high and fast and to walk a little above my fellow-man while doing the mundane tasks of the earthbound. I was one of those who was allowed to reach out and to truly "touch the face of God."

During 40 years of privileged flying, I participated in, or was witness to, many of the tragedies and much of the humor in flying. These incidents, like the aerial bombs that often went awry and failed to hit their targets, were the results of good intentions that failed to develop as planned. It seems suitable that this small collection of remembrances bears a title that is reminiscent of those errant bombs— *Bombs Awry.*

But whether on target or not, it was always as Miss Earhart wrote, *"for the fun of it."*

IN THE BEGINNING

For those of us who have spent a lifetime in the flying business, there is usually some particular memory that we feel started us on the road to ruin. My starting place is a bit shadowy in detail but very positive in its lasting effect. I was an eight-year-old in a sort of a rural boarding school that was actually the home of a shirttail relative who had taken me in while my parents were experiencing an assortment of personal problems. The home was out in the country near High Point, North Carolina, where we worked from dawn to dusk in the wheat, cotton, and tobacco fields. My host-bene-factor "uncle" worked in a feed mill in the city, and every now and then I would go along with him to help load feed in his old truck to bring home to feed the resident cows and other critters.

The matriarch of the household had a brother who had learned to fly airplanes in World War I and who owned some kind of an open-cockpit biplane that he used for barnstorming work. I assume that it was the classic barnstorming because he worked fairs, circuses, and special airplane shows. During one of the feed-gathering expeditions into the city, this renegade pilot asked if I would like to fly with him in his airplane. I think that I had never seen an airplane at that time, but I had heard a bit about "Lindy" in school and I thought that he was the neatest hero that we had going for us, so I eagerly accepted the promise of an airplane ride.

The airplane must have been a Jenny; at least I prefer to believe that it was, because that was the most romantic and legendary plane of that era. The pilot fitted me in some

3

vastly oversized flight clothing, and the helmet and goggles completely covered my head and shoulders. Regardless of the ridiculous fit, I flet that I was the exact image of the dashing hero Lindy. The ill-fitting flight clothing must have been an omen, for all flight clothing issued me ever since has always been oversized—or, perhaps more correctly, I have been undersized.

The cranky old airplane was hard to get started and I feared that I would be denied my ride, but it finally roared to life in a blue haze of smoke. The takeoff was a complete surprise since I had never even been in an elevator and had nothing with which to compare the escape from the ground. The closest thing I could think of was the feeling I experienced when I jumped from a barn roof on a dare. There was no means of communicating with the pilot, so I was completely at his mercy as we spiraled in a climb high over the city of High Point. We then flew out to the farm and the pilot pointed over the side of the airplane as we flew at house top level to wave to the matriarch who was boiling something or another in a big black pot in the back yard. We did all sorts of maneuvers and I don't recall a single moment of fear or apprehension, only the thrill and exhilaration of actually *flying*. It was cold and windy and the wind whistled its song all around me. I didn't realize it at the moment but I was hooked on flying! We must have had a smoke generator or some similar device attached (or else we were on fire and the pilot didn't tell me) because before we landed we flew low over the landing field and let out a long trail of smoke that was still visible when we turned to land. The landing was somewhat bouncy and I was chilled to the bone but a whole new world had opened her arms to me and I couldn't wait to grow up. The pilot carried me on his shoulders to the little office and we had a bottle of cream soda to celebrate. He promised to take me flying again but never did because the opportunity did not present itself. I don't know what ever happened to this great pilot, but I sincerely hope that he is still hanging around an airport somewhere and telling the new guys how they did it way back "then."

The day after the flight, I told all the guys at school about it and they all accused me of "dreaming again." The arguments got so heated that the teacher, a tough, tobacco-chewing old taskmaster, made me bring a note from home to verify that I had indeed flown in a real airplane. The note was provided and I was the recess hero for a while. Shortly thereafter, I was moved to another town and another school. In the new place, I didn't mention that I had flown in an airplane because there wasn't anyone at home to write a note.

The Depression was in full swing and, because of the maneuvering that was necessary for basic survival, there was a long dry spell before I got another airplane ride. To compensate, I dreamed and schemed and made crude wooden models of airplanes. At one time during this period, the rage among kids was to make a scooter using any kind of wheels that could be scrounged for an undercarriage. I used old roller skate wheels and made my scooter to resemble a classic "tail-dragging" airplane. Two sets of the wheels were mounted on the lower "wing" and one set of wheels at the rear of the platform floorboard. A broomstick was mounted spanwise across the upper "wing" and was used as a steering bar. This steering mechanism required a lot of "body English" to be effective. Power for the machine was the standard scooter "foot power" and the best acceleration was accomplished by running down a steep hill. Stability was lousy, acceleration and speed characteristics were a bit less than optimum, and steering was almost non-existent. At that time, a can of paint could be bought at the five-and-dime for a nickel, so I splurged and bought a can of bright red paint. I remember arguing with the clerk because the paint was identified as being vermilion and I had asked for red. The color turned out to be well-chosen for it was a perfect match for my blood that was spilled during frequent crashes of the machine. Time and maturity soon overtook both me and my "biplane" and I became affluent by selling newspapers, earning enough to buy a classy bicycle from a local junkyard for $3. It was often rumored that this particular junkyard acquired its merchandise through somewhat shady channels but that was of little concern as I had become

5

a devout student of the "end justifies the means" philosophy.

Circumstances had changed and I had been moving from North Carolina to Maryland, in a suburb of Baltimore close to the old Logan Field, home of the Maryland Air Guard and other assorted ragtag airplanes. The bicycle provided transportation from the house to the airport and I soon became the classic airport bum.

One bright day, Clarence Chamberlain brought his Fokker trimotor to Logan and sold rides for $2 a trip. He had a loudspeaker of some sort and would announce the points of interest as he flew over them, much as the modern-day airline pilot does. I was fascinated, and by selling empty pop bottles, intensifying my newspaper sales, and picking up a bit of other spare change by running errands, I bought a ride in the Fokker. I learned about how Colonel Chamberlain had flown his sponsor across the Atlantic Ocean to become the first passenger-carrying flight across the Atlantic. Colonel Chamberlain also told us about how he had refused to fly the airplane to London and of the non-pilot sponsor who then flew the airplane across the channel and managed to land it safely after watching other airplanes that were landing there. While Colonel Chamberlain was at Logan, I lived in his shadow, and whenever he didn't have a full load for his flight excursions, he would let me go along for free.

The National Guard had a fleet of what I remember to be O1 and O2 observation airplanes, and after I had been initiated and accepted by most of the pilots and mechanics, I was allowed to go along on some of the local flights. This privilege didn't come cheap because I worked my fanny off for those guys and was the perfect foil for their "bucket of propwash," "left-handed monkey wrench" and "Drink Lydia Pinkham's female remedy to gain weight" jokes. In the airplanes in which they let me fly, I sat in the belly of the fat machine with the rudder pedals and pilot's feet directly above my head, but it was *flying* and the circumstances were of no consequence.

The winters at Logan Field were bitter cold, and after the day's flying activities the oil would be drained from the engines and put near a stove overnight. The warm oil would then be put into the airplanes early the next morning so that the engine would have the benefit of preheated oil. (This procedure later gave way to wrap-around electric blankets and oil-dilution systems.) One of my most frequent tasks was the oil-draining process and as a result I always had oil-stained cuticles and fingernails. Parents, friends, and schoolteachers often remarked about the condition of my stained hands and seemed to be a bit repulsed by their always-grimy appearance. Their criticisms didn't bother me in the least because they served as a banner, a banner that said that I was a "flight mechanic," an unpaid but lofty position in that year of 1935 when I was a solid 13 years old.

SOLO

So much of our life is a group effort that it is really very seldom that we are faced with the individual "moment of truth," though it is perhaps those moments that are best remembered. When I fought my first boxing match in the Golden Gloves competition, it was the loneliest moment of my life up to that time. When the bell for the first round rang and my seconds left me alone in the corner, I was an empty shell of fear and desperation. I had but two choices: one was to run away and forget the whole matter, and the other was to waltz to the middle of the ring and do my best to win or at least to survive. I chose to fight and continued to do so for many years and many tournaments. The bouts were never as bad as I anticipated, but it was always a lonesome feeling of being left totally to one's own resources with nowhere to look for help. During those times, I thought that boxing was the loneliest of man's endeavors with soul, spirit, and courage exposed for all to see and evaluate. I was wrong, for I experienced a deeper feeling of the "moment of truth" when I first soloed an airplane.

Somehow my instructor, Nathan Traeger, and I wound up my training course in an old Aeronca C-2, a sort of a flying, fabric bathtub. Cockpit seating was so close to the ground that after each landing one was tempted to inspect his hindquarters to assure that he hadn't left part of it on the runway. Nathan had patiently tutored me through seven hours of dual instruction, had decided that he had given me all of the knowledge that he had to offer, and set me out on my own. It was 1941 on a soggy field in Barstow, Florida.

Although a failing memory of today can scarcely recall what I had for dinner last night, I can recall the smallest detail of that lonesome first flight.

Mentally, I tried to rationalize that the flight would be no different than those when Nathan was with me, that I had learned well, that the airplane wanted to fly, and that I knew what I was doing—but there was still the nagging tug of doubt. I lined up on the grass field and looked at Nathan as he watched in prayerful wonder and then, just as in that first boxing match, I advanced the power and took off to meet the challenge of the unknown. The takeoff was easy, everything worked just as it did when Nathan was aboard, and I left the pattern to do a bit of sky wandering. But the idea of the landing to come was a bit worrisome and colored the enjoyment of the free flying. I was filled with the euphoric thrill of actually being in an airplane alone in the "wild blue yonder" and I didn't want it to end with the spectacle of a lousy landing. There was no fear of bodily injury, only of the bruised ego and fear of doing it wrong. Each time that I would head toward the field to make the landing, I would think of some reason to delay it until I finally ran out of excuses and had to face the real bull in the arena. I reviewed all that I had been taught, assured myself that I could do it properly, and then promptly screwed up the approach to landing a couple of times before getting on the approved textbook final.

I flew directly over a surrounding orange grove, and the pungent smell of an adjacent orange juice processing plant masked the heavy smell of my own sweat as I neared the touchdown point. Over the threshold of the runway, I followed what I had been taught by Nathan and lo and behold it all worked quite well. I touched down, bounced a bit, and rolled to a neat stop near the spot where Nathan was waiting for me. I wanted to leap out of the airplane, turn cartwheels of joy and celebration, but Nathan gave me a sign to takeoff and do it again. Confidence was in charge now and I made five or six more takeoffs and landings before Nathan signaled me to stop for the day.

Nathan briefed me about my obvious errors, chastised me

for the more dangerous ones, and was somewhat noncommital about the fact that I had just accomplished one of the more important feats of man. He did look a bit smug when he entered my solo flight in my log book and signed it with a flourish. My own happiness could not be contained. I was no longer a student, I was *a pilot*, a pilot who had faced the unknowns of the sky alone. I had also faced the doubt within myself and I had won.

There are many "moments of truth" within our lives, but for me that one special moment is when one faces up to his own fears and doubts about his capabilities and ventures alone on that magic trip in an airplane that is called the first *solo*.

PART I

THE B-26 MARTIN MARAUDER

After working at the Glenn L. Martin Company as a flunky in most of the factory and airport disciplines, I got a lucky break and was allowed to fly as a flight mechanic. I had taken a flight release or a "first flight test" to Flight Operations and signed the airplane forms certifying the airplane as ready for flight. Mr. Thomas L. Taylor, a gray-maned magnificent son of the South, was the designated pilot and he signed the acceptance of the flight release. After signing, he asked about the relative condition of the airplane and I told him that it was 100 percent perfect.

"So perfect that you would go with me?" he asked.

I was stunned by this unusual question but then recovered somewhat, ran to draw the necessary flight equipment, and was suddenly and magically transformed from the greasy mechanic to the proud peacock of flight crew member.

Being a flight mechanic involved being a crew chief, getting the airplane ready to fly, and then flying the operational test flights to attend to some of the minor tasks in flight. These tasks included such things as cranking down the flaps, keeping the pilots informed of the mechanical condition of the equipment, and any other chores that might arise during flight *including* holding on to the cockpit canopy handles during the takeoff run because they had a nasty habit of flying open at this critical time.

The B-26 was a brand-new airplane, fraught with equally new equipment and ideas. We had been caught short in our preparations for war and were desperately trying to pick up the slack. As a result, the design-child of visionary Peyton B.

Magruder was hurried through its construction and operational test programs. The B-26 had a rendezvous with greatness as a warplane and precious little time to get on her way. As we hurried through the test program, we tolerated some things that would not have been done under normal circumstances and often paid dearly for that tolerance. The airplane acquired a reputation as being unsafe and was sometimes referred to by the ugly name of "The Widow Maker." Still others called it "The Flying Prostitute" because its short wings gave it no visible means of support. Such cruelties were not the fault of the airplane, rather of the system and of the urgencies of war. The B-26 went on to war where she flew 129,943 missions, dropped 169,382 tons of bombs, shot down 402 enemy aircraft, and lost 911 airplanes in the effort.

The B-26 was the fastest airplane in its class and it had a higher wing-loading (the weight-carrying load imposed on the wing of the airplane) than any other of the combat airplanes. She was a thoroughbred and she performed as one when handled properly but turned into a wild range mustang when abused. Whatever her performance, I loved that airplane, although as in lover's spats, I would often kick her tires in anger when she "done me wrong."

Although only a flight mechanic, the carrier of oily rags, and the target of abuse whenever things went wrong, I was Baron von Richthofen and Eddie Rickenbacker in the B-26. The monetary compensation for this lofty position was 50¢ an hour and a free pair of Ray Ban sun glasses.

ME AND THE MARS

During the B-26 manufacturing program at the Glenn L. Martin Company, shortages of parts and money were often encountered, so workers were temporarily shifted to other programs during these periods. These other programs were the Model 167 Maryland bomber, the Navy Patrol Bomber (PBM), and the huge experimental Martin MARS. During one of these B-26 parts shortage interruptions, I was briefly assigned to the construction phase of the MARS.

Aircraft work was not as highly specialized in those days as it is now, so I had several specialities such as sweeping floors, mowing the grass, riveting, cutting sheet metal, and whatever else that might be needed. In this particular instance, I was cutting and fitting an entrance door in the fuselage of the MARS. The procedure involved pinning the door in place, marking the edges, removing it, filing where needed, and repeating the process until the perfect fit was achieved. Each time that I had the door pinned in place, someone would need to get into the interior of the fuselage, so I would have to remove the door and start all over again. After a series of these oft-repeated interruptions, I grew a bit belligerent, and the next time that someone knocked for admittance I yelled at them.

"You'll have to wait until I get the door fitted," I hollered.

"After about ten minutes, the knock was repeated and I yelled back my little ultimatum. Finally, satisfied with the fitting, I removed the door and there on the platform was Mr. Glenn L. Martin, accompanied by the then-Secretary of the Navy Knox. I almost burst in tears for I feared that my impertinence had cost me my job.

Mr. Martin looked at the work that I was doing, sensed my fears, and was magnanimously sympathetic. After a short pause while he inspected my work, he said aloud and for all to hear, "Stay with it, son, you are the first one that I have encountered today who *wasn't* looking for an excuse to *stop* working."

From that day on, Mr. Martin always spoke to me by name whenever we passed in the factory or in the flight line and I walked a little bit taller.

A LITTLE BIT OF DIRT

The Martin B-26 had an hydraulic pressure bypass line in its system so that whenever the operating pressure had reached its maximum the fluid would bypass the pressure accumulator. When the pressure fell below the limit, the valve in the line would shuttle to one side and allow pressure to rebuild in the system. During one of the early test flights, we had the valve stick open in the bypass position and the hydraulic pressure fell to zero.

The wing flaps could be lowered manually, the brakes could be operated with emergency air pressure, and all of the other systems were okay except for the aggravating problem of not being able to lower the landing gear. The emergency air system for the gear would not operate the lowering mechanism since it would also be bypassed through the open shuttle valve, so we had a somewhat serious problem. Our choices were to bail out or to land with the gear retracted. We chose the gear-up route and after cranking the flaps down made several practice approaches but were reluctant to make the actual landing. As we got lower and lower on fuel and the day was fading into evening twilight, we were finally forced to make the landing.

As flight mechanic, I felt a personal responsibility for the situation and frantically tried to unstick the offending valve, but no matter what I tried it stayed stuck. When the fuel level became so low that we had to land, I took a desperate swing at the bypass valve with the flap crank. Whatever had been lodged in the valve broke loose, the hydraulic pressure soared to normal, the gear was lowered, and we made a neat and normal landing.

Mr. Glenn L. Martin met us as we got out of the airplane and was beaming with smiles, which was somewhat uncommon for him. He shook hands with each of us and asked how we had managed to save the aircraft at the eleventh hour. Without explaining the "hit it with the flap crank method," the pilot, Henry Myers, pointed to me and told Mr. Martin that it was my "mechanical expertise" that had accomplished the in-flight fix. Mr. Martin left the corrective measures to the engineers.

I got a nickel-an-hour raise but was denied overtime for the extended flight because the overtime had not been previously authorized.

THE BITTER WINE OF
VINDICTIVENESS

During the flight test program of the gigantic MARS navy patrol flying boat, a temporary false dorsal fin was attached to the vertical fin for some data-gathering flights. The installation was solid but of a temporary nature and did not have the structural integrity of the basic aircraft. The navy pilot who was flying the test mission was cautioned to "fly easy" and to avoid any exaggerated of violent maneuvers. Disregarding these instructions and those of a vinegar-mouthed flight test engineer aboard the aircraft, he banked too steeply and the test dorsal failed. The pieces lodged between the elevators and rudder, locking these control surfaces and causing the aircraft to enter a slow, spiraling, descending turn. As the aircraft spiraled toward the cold waters of the Chesapeake Bay below, the pilot and the flight engineer argued as to the best procedure to set engine power to offset the spiral and to somewhat control the impending impact. The hard-nosed pilot won the argument and the aircraft hit sideways and hard. The aircraft was totally destroyed.

Rescue boats picked up the crew, and the flight engineer, who had suffered some cuts from the impact, tried to console the distraught pilot. He told him that he had done an excellent job under extremely adverse circumstances and that his expertise had saved the lives of the crew.

"That lousy airplane belongs exactly where it is now," the pilot scowled, "about 20 fathoms under the water."

The flight engineer seethed but said no more. The incident was reviewed, the thousands of reports were completed, the crew's wounds healed, and the incident was apparently forgotten—but not quite.

Several years later, that same pilot was killed while flying a commercial airliner, one of the worst commercial accidents

15

of the time. The widow assembled a group of his old flying mates as pallbearers and the flight engineer from the MARS incident was one of them. After the service was completed and the casket lowered into the grave, one of the pallbearers remarked to the flight engineer that it was a shame that such a youthful pilot with a promising career had died so soon. The long arm of bitter memory choked out any compassion and the grizzled old flight test engineer gazed at the grave and answered, "No, no, it isn't too bad. He's right where he belongs, six feet under the ground!"

WITNESS TO TRAGEDY

The procedure for delivering a new B-26 airplane to the Army Air Corps was for the company flight crew to fly it until they were satisfied with its safety and performance. An Air Corps crew would then fly the airplane, and after they were satisfied with it, a Ferry Command crew would deliver the airplane to its designated base. This procedure has somehow endured through the years with other airplane programs and is still practiced in somewhat the same manner in modern programs.

Mr. Roland Sansbury, the Martin Company Chief Pilot, had completed his acceptance flight of an early B-26A and found that the airplane was okay except for an unusual stiffness in the aileron control system. My crew and I inspected the system, readjusted the aileron cable tensions, and sprayed graphite on the control quadrants. The ailerons smoothed out and operated within acceptable limits. It was a very hot day and the skin of the airplane was too hot to touch for any length of time so we were very careful while working on it and refueling it for the Air Corps flight. We released the airplane for the flight and noted that the fuel tanks were venting heavily, but assumed that it was because of the hot day and the expansion of the full load of fuel aboard. Mr. Sansbury sat on his parachute pack eating his lunch while we waited for the Air Corps crew to arrive.

Major Perrin, an Air Corps acceptance pilot, and Mr.

Bowman, a Civil Service inspector, were the crew members for the flight. After making a detailed preflight inspection, they accepted the airplane for flight, and after they completed their engine run I pulled the wheel chocks, gave them the "thumbs-up" signal, and they taxied to the active runway. I sat on a wheel chock at the edge of the ramp to observe the takeoff.

They took the engines to maximum power, released the brakes, and the airplane started its normal takeoff roll. Just at lift-off point, it was wracked with a horrendous explosion and plummeted to the ground, enveloped in fire. The airplane was destroyed and the two pilots were killed.

I stared at the spectable of horror in disbelief and soon felt salty tears falling into my mouth. I couldn't respond when my boss told me to go to Flight Operations to help find a reason for the accident and to assure that the airplane had been properly prepared for flight. I was physically and mentally numb because I was in an area of life and death where I had never been before. It was not real, only a specter of something that could happen. It was death and destruction before my very eyes—destruction of an airplane that I had verified as safe and airworthy, deaths of people who were my friends, and all of this only a few hundred feet away from where I had stood and watched in terror-filled fascination. It was tragedy at its worst.

When I recovered sufficiently to get to my feet and head for the operations office, the stark reality was brought even closer. There, only inches in front of me, was the handle from the crew compartment door and a few bits of twisted metal fragments. The ferocity of the explosion had blown the parts there. I picked up the parts and wearily carried them to the operations office, more pieces of evidence to be viewed in the investigation of the cause of the accident.

It was later determined that an error in design, or at least a poorly designed vent system for the fuel tanks, had allowed pressure to accumulate in the tanks to the point of explosion. This discrepancy was corrected and there was no more trouble in this area, but the one accident was one too many.

Late that same night while changing clothes by my hangar locker, I stared for a long time at the big legend painted on the hangar wall:
"FLYING IS NOT INHERENTLY DANGEROUS,
BUT LIKE THE SEA, IS TERRIBLY UNFORGIVING
OF MISTAKES"

HERO WORSHIP

One of the worst side effects of being an aviation nut is the worship of its heroes, or at least of those who were heroes in my eyes. One of my very particular heroes was Douglas Corrigan, the interped Irishman who flew across the Atlantic Ocean in an old Ryan airplane after having been denied permission to do so by the CAA (now FAA). He claimed that his compass had malfunctioned and that he had headed east when he had intended to fly west to California. He could hardly be blamed because a malfunctioning piece of equipment had caused him to end up in Ireland when he really wanted to fly to California. Because of this slight error in aerial navigation, he was dubbed "Wrong-Way" Corrigan and immediately became the darling of the world.

Shortly after this mission, Corrigan came to work at the Glenn L. Martin Company as a B-26 pilot and I was privileged to serve as his ground and flight mechanic during part of the time he was there. He had a few personal habits that I found myself adopting, but it became so obvious that I was copycatting him that I made a serious effort to avoid doing it. One thing he seemed to always do was to have a Clark's candy bar and a pint of milk for lunch. I soon became addicted to the same sparce diet and still keep a good supply of Clark bars on hand.

As a sort of a "show of power," we had several B-26's readied for delivery so that Pathe News and all those folks could film the awesome sight of a whole flock of airplanes being delivered and on their way to the Air Corps. Douglas Corrigan was the "star" of this operation and I was his crew chief. The whole show went well until Corrigan took off and his landing gear would not retract—I had forgotten to remove the manual gear locks! He landed at Bolling Field in Washington, D.C., and I was dispatched, along with others, to investigate and correct the problem with the gear, and I was surely the clown of the day when my mistake was discovered.

Shortly after that, I enlisted in the Air Corps, but my apparent burst of patriotism failed to evoke any forgiveness for that one monumental mistake—seen by most of the U.S. through the courtesy of Pathe, Paramount, and MGM.

B-26 FLY-BY

At some time early in the B-26 test program, a display of the United States' latest and developmental airplanes was staged at the Glenn L. Martin airport in Middle River, Maryland. Most of the aircraft were barely out of or still in the experimental stage and some of them still bore the "X" designation. The show was a rather low-key display rather than the "gee-whiz" shows of later years and the pilots were cautioned to fly-by conservatively. The P-40, P-39, XP-47, Brewster Buffalo, the Rainbow, the Airacuda, B-17, and B-23 were some of the outstanding participants.

A group of very highly ranked dignitaries was assembled in the control tower for clear viewing of the airplanes, and Mr. Glenn L. Martin with some Hollywood luminaries were the hosts.

While the show was in progress, the pilot of a test B-26 called in and asked for permission to join the show by making a low-level fly-by. His request was granted, but he was sternly cautioned to make only a non-spectacular, low-speed, routine pass. He acknowledged the instructions and stood by for clearance for his conservative buzz-job.

The Martin airport control tower was situated between two hangars and the structures formed a wide "V" with the tower as the vertex. Guy wires and antennae were strung from the top of the tower to the tops of the hangars. The clearance between each hangar and the tower was about 50 feet and the wingspan of the B-26 was 65 feet.

After he had been cleared for their "low-speed, with caution" pass, the B-26 pilot, crew, and airplane roared by at full power, shoestring-level, banked sharply, and aimed for the open space between the tower and one of the hangars. The observers in the tower fled, dignity giving way to basic survival. The down wing tip of the B-26 almost dragged the ground and the airplane cut sharply through the various wires that were strung between the buildings. Somehow, the pilot squeezed the airplane through the opening and then made a picture perfect landing, trailing wires and trash behind him. As the pilot crawled from the cockpit, the group from the tower streamed toward him like a swarm of angry bees. The airport manager assured Mr. Martin that he would fire the pilot immediately, but Mr. Martin assured him that it would not be necessary.

Reserving the privilege for himself, Mr. Glenn L. Martin fired the pilot on the spot.

The pilot of this incident enlisted in the Air Corps, did a good combat job, and later retired as a respected member of the Society of Experimental Test Pilots.

SHANGRI-LA

During the super-secret preparations for the first U.S. Air Corps raid on Tokyo during World War II, the B-26 and the B-25 airplanes were both considered for the mission. It was to be a daring thrust against the enemy and all of the details had to be worked out with extreme care. The B-26 was much heavier, required more runway, and carried a heavier bomb load than the B-25, but the B-25 was ultimately selected because of its takeoff characteristics from the short flight deck of the U.S. carrier *Hornet.*

While the evaluation was being made, both the B-26 and the B-25 were being flown from runways marked with transverse bright yellow lines. Takeoff performance under varying conditions was judged by observing the distance for the takeoff at the yellow marker at lift-off. For these performance evaluations, there were many people from many official agencies who clustered around the runway daily to evaluate the tests. Among the pilots who were performing the actual flight tests was Major Jimmy Doolittle, who was to command the actual mission.

After a spectacular takeoff where he literally "hung the B-26 on its props," Major Doolittle looked down at the throng of people on the ground and grinned at his young copilot.

"You know, son, about 90 percent of those people watching us thought that we weren't going to make it."

"Yes, sir, I certainly realize that," the shaken copilot answered, "and if *you* thought that we were going to make it, there was still 50 percent of those in the airplane who agreed with that 90 percent on the ground."

WHAT TO DO
UNTIL THE DOCTOR COMES

The B-26 airplane had horrible single-engine characteristics manifested at their worst during or immediately after takeoff. With the loss of an engine, the entire airplane wanted to rotate around the operating engine, and it was a man-sized chore to keep the airplane flying straight and level—or flying at all, for that matter. To compound the problem, the rudder trim selector handle was a small knob with a low mechanical advantage that required lots of turning to get a little bit of rudder tab movement. Typically, whenever an engine quit on takeoff, there was general chaos in the cockpit, the pilot trying to hold the rudder until the trim could be cranked in, the aileron control wheel turned to near maximum to keep the airplane from rolling, stick back to keep the airplane from diving to destruction, and juggling the power on the remaining good engine. It was early-day yoga with a bit of twist thrown in for effect and a prayer for recovery.

To prepare them for this emergency, the student pilots were subjected to a simulation of this horror chamber during their training. The instructor pilot in the right seat would pull back on the power on one engine and then sit back to evaluate the student's actions in handling this so-called simulated emergency. Many times during these little sadistic practice periods, things got really hairy and became real emergencies.

During one of these training periods at McDill Field in Florida, an instructor pulled back the power on the right engine during the takeoff and advised the student pilot that the right engine had been hit by flak. The startled young (we were all young then) student stretched to get in full rudder, twisted the wheel, and frantically reached for the rudder trim tab wheel.

"I can't hold the airplane," he pleaded.

"Hang in there, you're doing fine," the instructor advised.

"Help me, sir, I just can't handle it," the student begged.

"Can't do that," the instructor drawled. "The same flak that knocked out the engine killed me, so do exactly as you would if this was the actual situation in combat."

"The student looked unbelievingly at the cool customer in the right seat, evaluated his own terror-filled position, and turned to the wide-eyed flight mechanic who was looking over his shoulder.

"Sarge," he yelled, "get this dead dummy out of the cockpit and come hlep me hold this airplane until we can get it flying again."

He got things organized with the help of the mechanic and passed his flight check with flying colors, most of those colors being a pale white and sickly green. The instructor had a delightful time telling and retelling the story in the officer's club—properly embellished with more intense action and far more colorful language.

LIEUTENANT MIDDLEBROOK
AND THE
WASHINGTON-YOUREE

During the World War II years, the leading hotel in Shreveport, Louisiana, was the regal old Washington-Youree. The hotel was in the middle of downtown Shreveport on the side of a gently sloping hill. It was the focal point for downtown entertainment for the troops stationed at nearby Barksdale Field. In the club part of the hotel was the exotic Zephyr Room where we were often entertained by such first-class vocalists as Peggy Lee. Friends and relatives who came to visit from far away places usually stayed at the Washington-Youree.

One of our squadron pilots, Lieutenant Middlebrook, had a short history of flying a bit lower than the leaders desired, and it was rumored that he would often check out the program at the local drive-in movie by flying by to read the advertising on the theater marquee. He always knew what was playing, so I suppose that the story was true. When Lieutenant Middlebrook's fiancee and future mother-in-law came to visit him, they stayed at the favored Washington-Youree Hotel, and the eager young lieutenant was always restless to get his training flights completed so that he could be with his visitors. Others of us in the squadron always regarded Lieutenant Middlebrook as one of the best of the B-26 pilots, but we didn't stand in line to get on his crew as we weren't too eager to participate in his low-flying tactics and feared the exhibition that he was fate-bound to demonstrate for his fiancee. True to form, the lieutenant would make a low pass over the hotel to alert his visitors that his flight was completed and that they should make their way to Barksdale to meet him at the club. One afternoon he got a little lower than usual, flattened out the props so that they sang their unholy siren's song and whistled by the

Washington-Youree. After landing at Barksdale, he was arrested and charged with endangering life, government property, and the entire town of Shreveport, as well as violating almost all of the military regulations, regulations of the government, and of the basic Bill-of-Rights.

After an investigation, Lieutenant Middlebrook was brought to trial and the testimony of many indignant witnesses was overwhelmingly against him. One woman testified that he was so low that the propwash stripped her of her wig and of her loosely tied blouse, causing her great embarrassment. As the last witness, Leiutenant Middlebrook's potential mother-in-law was called to testify.

"And what is your version of this incident, madam?" she was asked.

"I think that the entire matter is ridiculous and a waste of time," she replied indignantly. "Here these magnificent young men are giving their very lives for their country and it seems that all you people do is to harass them with your silly rules and regulations. I say that he did no wrong—he only showed what an excellent pilot he really is."

"How low was the airplane that Lieutenant Middlebrook was flying when it passed by your hotel room balcony?" the prosecutor asked.

"Well, he was just below the balcony where we were standing and it seemed that we were up pretty high," she answered sincerely.

"And on what floor of the hotel is your room located?" the prosecutor continued.

The lady took her hotel room key from her purse, studied it for a moment, and somewhat shyly answered, "It is on the second floor, we have room 202."

Lieutenant Middlebrook was grounded for 30 days and fined $1500.

THE B-26 AND THE HUEY P.

To experience the real speed of an airplane, it is always more exciting and more fun to fly low and to "buzz" things.

Bridges always hold a special fascination and seem to have been built just so that airplanes could fly under them. The Huey P. Long bridge in New Orleans was a special challenge for those who liked to fly beneath bridges and always offered an inducement for us to do wrong and to accept the challenge. Another incentive perhaps was the fact that it was in New Orleans, the alleged "sin city," and that added a special touch of naughtiness. The speedy B-26 was a perfect airplane to meet the challenge of the bridge and it was only natural that the confrontation would come to pass.

I was flying as mechanic with an ex-veterinarian from Maryland who was an excellent pilot and had a boyish appetite for adventure. It seemed perfectly logical that we should fly under the Huey P. bridge, so we did just that. We approached it kind of easy and then poured on the power as we went under and then made a somewhat spectacular pull-up. Moments later, we received a cryptic order to return to our home base of Barksdale Field at once, without delay, without argument, and without deviation. We became a bit suspicious of the urgency of the order and instinctively knew that we were in deep, serious trouble.

"Barksdale Tower," the pilot called, "this is B-26 1234. Does that order to return have anything to do with a bridge?"

"Roger, it certainly has," the tower officer replied in clipped, precise, and very military tones.

"Well," drawled the pilot, "seeing as how we are already in a bit of difficulty and might have a fine to pay, I have an idea that might help us all. If you'll have the folks of New Orleans stand on the banks of the river at a dime apiece and on the bridge for a quarter apiece, I'll go under upside down," he offered.

"Knock off the chatter and get your butt back here," was the rather unkind answer to this exciting offer.

Back on the ground at Barksdale, we weren't even afforded the courtesies usually extended to prisoners of war but were herded into base headquarters like we had done something seriously wrong. I suppose that we were lucky to get away without being chained to the wall, as the attitude of some superior officer gents seemed to indicate that kind of punishment. At a subsequent hearing, all of the crew members claimed to be occupied with other duties and that they did not see the "under-the-bridge" incident. Offered immunity for damaging testimony, they all refused and were then privileged to share in a 30-day, no-pay grounding with the pilot.

Fortunately, we were not invited to share in the payment of the $1,500 fine that was levied against the pilot.

APOCALYPSE

It was inevitable that I witness death among my friends in the flying fraternity, and I certainly saw more than my normal share. But there is one tragedy worse than the others—the first one. I had seen one other such accident but never before had I been this close to the horror.

We were in number one position, waiting to take the active runway at Barksdale Field, holding for another B-26 that was on final approach. I had the upper navigator's hatch open and was sitting on top of the airplane watching the other B-26 as he approached for landing. The approach seemed normal but something happened before touchdown and the airplane hit the ground in a three-point attitude about 25 yards short of the runway. It slithered like a wounded animal to the end of the runway with parts flying in all directions. When it hit the concrete runway, it burst into violent flames, the fire enveloping the airplane in one awful whoosh. There was no sign of life or of anyone trying to escape the inferno, and I burst into uncontrollable tears. As I watched in horrible fascination, a head poked above the top fuselage hatch and I recognized it as that of a friend and barracks-mate. He desperately tried to raise himself to the top of the fuselage but soon gave up the death struggle and dropped out of sight. I could not, or did not want to, believe what I had just seen, but the roaring of the fire trucks, the screams of the ambulances, and the odor of seared flesh brought it all to reality.

The heat from the fire was so intense that it could be felt in our airplane, and since I was sitting on top of the airplane it actually burned my cheeks. I dropped back inside our airplane and found that the rest of the crew was as emotionally destroyed as I was. We were dumbfounded and we all sat in silence while our engines idled and the tower screamed at us to clear the area. In shock, we managed to taxi back to the parking area.

I didn't sleep that night and repeatedly condemned myself for not running to the other airplane to help the trapped crew. It would have been an impossible task, but perhaps. . . Thoughts like "Why didn't I?" and "If only. . ." prevailed. The smell of the wreckage and of the burned men permeated the base and it seemed that God was punishing all of us for some monstrous sin. I had great difficulty in accepting the reality of death. "So-and-so augured and bought the farm" was no longer just an abstract phrase, it was real and horrible. It really happened and it was terrible and ugly. It was a time for decision. It was a time to dilute the romance of flying with the reality. It was a time to grow up and to quit flying the harmless rubber-band airplanes. It was a time of fear and of questionable courage. It was time to bite the bullet or be bitten. It was a decision that didn't come easy.

The beds of the guys who were killed were stripped and their belongings were packed away. Only this morning they were here singing in the shower and bitching about the lousy food in the mess hall. Now they were bits of charcoal packed in a box with an empty uniform. Homecoming.

After a few days of grounded airplanes, while an investigation of the accident was conducted, we were cleared to fly again.

As we roared down the runway, I couldn't help but look at the spot where I had so closely witnessed death and destruction. I wondered if we would take turns and when my turn would come.

DAMN THE B-26

A test pilot named Carl Hartley who worked for the Glenn L. Martin Company was my hero. He was all of the things that went into the making of the Hollywood romantic version of the test pilot except that he was real and a truly excellent pilot. He was somewhat aware of his image and of his abilities so he did a little bit to enhance the picture. He was tall and handsome, he wore the leather jacket of the flier with a silk white scarf wrapped neatly around the throat. He wore the billowing, pleated silver-tans of the pilot and, as an added bonus, sported bright yellow pigskin flying gloves. I knew that if I could be somebody else that it would not be a president nor a millionaire—it would be Carl Hartley.

Unlike some of the other test pilots who were rather aloof, Carl asked that all of the mechanics call him by his first name, that they join him at lunch, and sit and talk with him during the smoke breaks. It was rumored that he had been "released" from the old Army Air Corps for bouncing the wheels of a fighter plane off of a rooftop when he buzzed his home town. True or not, it added more color and allure to the romantic pilot.

Whenever a B-26 was released for Carl to fly, he made only a cursory preflight inspection and let it be known that he had the utmost confidence in the abilities and dedication of the mechanics who had prepared the airplane for flight. As a result of this philosophy, Carl always got an airplane that was a bit better and cleaner than those readied for other pilots. Sometimes after a late flight, Carl would stop by our favorite beer joint and share a drink with us. Quite often, he would chide the bartender for serving beer to his "teenage" mechanics and then he would buy a round for those same "teenagers." We all truly loved this guy and came to worship him as the perfect hero and the epitome of courage and success. We vied for the privilege of flying with him and in many cases offered something "to boot" to trade flying

28

with another pilot for a flight with Carl. We were never disappointed, for he played the movie role to the hilt and we got some exciting "unmonitored" test rides.

When the war started and the need for airplanes grew severe, the Martin Company opened another B-26 manufacturing facility in Omaha, Nebraska. As a salute to the opening of the new plant and to let the employees get a look at what they would be building, Carl Hartley was selected to make a low-level fly-by with a B-26. At this time, the B-26 was suffering from a chronic problem that caused the cockpit overhead canopies or hatches to come open during the takeoff. Several engineering fixes had been made but the problem continued. The inside of the canopy was lined with one-quarter-inch armor plating and it was very difficult to hold it closed if the locks failed. When Carl made his takeoff and spectacular pull-up at the Omaha demonstration, the canopy unlocked and blew off its hinges. It impacted the horizontal tail, stuck there, and jammed both elevators and rudder. There was nothing to do but jump, so both Carl and copilot Henry Meyers bailed out. Unfortunately, they were too low for a successful parachute opening and neither one survived the jump.

When the news of Carl's death reached the Baltimore plant, the place was plunged into a deep gloom. Mechanics kicked the tires of the B-26 and cursed it. They refused to work on it and viewed it as a killer, a destroyer of heroes. The beer joint was quiet and the normally loud jukebox was silent. Glenn Miller and Tommy Dorsey were out of place at this moment.

The passage of time and the necessity for survival soon returned the flight line to its normal pace, and soon another, far less colorful test pilot replaced Carl in the flying ranks. Still, we all asked each other the eternal question, "Why him?" Cruelly, we added, "Why not one of these other dodoes?"

After all of these years and hundreds of other tragedies, I still ask that same question and, still, there is no answer.

SLOW-ROLLING AROUND THE COLONEL

During the time I was privileged to fly as instructor aerial engineer with the old Army Air Corps, I flew many maintenance test flights with young First Lieutenant Enoch George Longworth. He didn't particularly relish the Enoch bit, so we all called him George. George was a Van Johnson look-alike and the merriment of the Irish danced in his eyes continuously. He often roller-skated from his quarters to the flight line, forgot to wear rank on his uniform most of the time, and loved to recite a ragged version of "Dangerous Dan McGrew" in the Non-Commissioned Officer's Club— where he wasn't supposed to be in the first place. No matter how serious the nature of the flight of the in-flight emergencies we encountered, George and I always had a good time. Our attitudes and behavior were looked upon as somewhat "irresponsible" by some of the more dedicated types.

After completing the shakedown flight of a new airplane, a new model of the B-26, we spotted another B-26 cruising along at the same altitude. This was a special B-26, for it was not clad in the dull colors of war but was resplendent in bright and highly polished aluminum. We figured that it was a factory demonstration model of some sort so we eased in behind it for a closer look. It was very new, very sparkling, and had little in the way of armaments. George was sure that it was being flown by a civilian factory crew, so we decided to demonstrate to them that the military knew a little bit about flying this particular kind of airplane. We feathered the prop on our right engine, pulled abeam of the left side of the pretty airplane, and executed a lazy slow-roll in the direction of our dead engine, a thing totally prohibited by the flight handbook and the Bible. We passed over the top of the other airplane, stabilized on their right side, restarted the right engine, feathered the left, and repeated the slow-roll maneuver in the opposite direction. This ridiculous display of "Look, Ma, no hands" completed, we started the left engine and made fighter passes at the other airplane from all angles. We literally tore up the sky and at no time did we communicate with the pretty airplane. After we had our fill of the game, we did a full-roll in front of the other airplane, dipped the wings in farewell, and headed for the legal training area.

After we completed our flight and landed back at Barksdale, we were a bit startled to see the pretty silver airplane sitting on the ramp. The surprise got another shot of adrenalin when the military police drove up and put George under military arrest. George knew that he was in deep and serious trouble so he removed all rank insignia from his uniform and took the silver pilot's wings from above the breast pocket of his shirt. After he was escorted into the commanding officer's office, he saluted smartly and extended an open hand, offering to surrender all of the vestments of his position. Colonel Joe Kelly, the commander, waved them away and left George standing at stiff attention while he stared at him with cold eyes.

"Were you the pilot of B-26 number 1234?" he asked.

"Yes, sir, I was," George answered.

"That was quite a dangerous and irresponsible performance you put on for us, lieutenant. Were you aware of the risks you were taking and of the risks to your crew?" Colonel Kelly continued.

"Yes, sir, I was," George answered. "But there was no real risk involved. I know the airplane's capabilities and I know my own. I also know that I violated the handbook procedures and all that, but I also know that there was no risk because I had practiced those maneuvers many times and I was good at them."

"So this isn't the first time you have violated the rules?" Colonel observed.

"No, sir," George answered, and cast his eyes downward.

"Was your crew aware of your irresponsible barnstorming, lieutenant?" was the next question.

"Yes, sir, Matter of fact, they encouraged it," George parried.

"Well, lieutenant, regardless of your self-proclaimed proficiency and the apparent demonstration of those talents, you are aware that I will have to take disciplinary action, are you not?" said the colonel.

"The subdued lieutenant only nodded his head in understanding.

"The colonel continued. "The airplane you buzzed around this afternoon is my new personal transport, and I was getting some expert flight instructions from a company test pilot when you interrupted with your shenanigans. During the hour or so before your show, I had been warned against doing the very things that you so dramatically demonstrated. I was told that it was unsafe to do much of anything in that airplane except to fly straight and level. I was told to not even think about banking into a dead engine, much less doing it. You came along at a damned inappropiate time. It now happens that I need a copilot for that shiny, new airplane and it will be among one of the most miserable of jobs for a 'hot-rock' pilot who is itching for combat. It will involve the wearing of fresh, crisp uniforms, a hat that does not have the so-called '50 mission crush,' and a rather strict adherence to military regulations in all categories. You, my lieutenant, will be that copilot and you will not be relieved from that job until I feel so inclined to give you some other assignment. I wanted someone who was not negatively impressed by the somewhat dangerous reputation of this particular type of airplane, and you chose the right moment and the right act for ending my little search. You will also teach me to fly that airplane as well as you fly it and you will be at my immediate beck and call at all times. Understood?" And the good colonel looked at George for an answer. All that he got back was a muttered, "Understood, sir."

George did an excellent job during his tour as executive pilot and soon earned the "right" to go in to combat. He was shot down on his fourteenth mission and now rests in a common grave with the rest of his crew in the National Cemetery at San Bruno, California.

Colonel Kelly later led the air armada forces on historic D-day and enjoyed an illustrious career before retiring as a general.

While General Kelly was serving as the Commander of the Military Airlift Command and I was a major under his command, I always thought it unwise to remind him that I was the second party in that long-ago B-26 episode. I slipped by any punishment back in those days, but in the military it's never too late.

THE LONG SHADOWS OF OUR SINS

A whole campus filled with army trainees doesn't sound too glamorous, but when all of those officer trainees are women, it gives a different degree of interest to the place. The campus of a college in Ruston, Louisiana, was just a delight with all of its pretty ladies, but it, like its male counterpart, was strictly military. I was convinced of its sincerity when I asked one of the student officers if the underclothing issued them was the same drab color as that given to us and she replied by giving an impromptu "lingerie show" in the middle of the popular Zephyr Room.

Retreat, the end of the day when the colors are lowered, is a proud and traditional time in the military and these ladies did a marvelous job of this ceremony. On this campus at Ruston, it was truly an inspirational sight to see all of these handsome ladies in their perfectly pressed uniforms and shiny brass as they stood at strict attention and saluted the flag as it was lowered. It was an impressive, solemn, and sacred ceremony—until one evening when things went rather badly.

On this particular evening, one of the Barksdale B-26 crews was returning from a training mission and they decided to make a "low pass" over this formation of dedicated lady soldiers. It was dusk and the sun was on its last rays for the day. The B-26 pilot aimed his airplane at the formation, turned on the blazing landing lights, flattened the props so that they would really scream, went to full power, and made a dive at the parade ground. Orderliness gave way to chaos and what had been a proper military formation now dispersed as though they were trying to avoid an air raid.

No one on the ground saw the large "buzz numbers" that were painted on the fuselage of the airplane and, since there were several airplanes in the immediate area, no one could positively identify the offending airplane. All of the crews that had been airborne at that particular hour professed indignant surprise that anyone would do such a dastardly thing, especially to lady troops. Threats of all kinds failed to produce any volunteers to accept credit or blame for the incident, particularly after the B-26 base commander received a nasty note from the commander of the cadre at Ruston College. To the best of my memory, the note read something like this:

Sir:

Your airplane crew in its low-level performance of this past evening produced marked and tangible results. We lost two potential officers to heart flutters, three others suffered miscarriages, and the campus laundry is seriously overloaded. The offending flight crew must be identified and punished.

XXXXXXXXXXXXXXX

The lady's letter produced no results and the incident was soon forgotten due to the press of more serious wartime matters.

A few years later, after the end of the war, two former military officers were married. One day they were exchanging war stories and the husband told of the time when he as pilot had buzzed the Louisiana training campus at Ruston. The startled new wife remembered the event with a vengeance, for she had been one of those badly frightened students. She vowed to get even, and from what I have seen of their married life, she has successfully done just that— for at least the past 35 years.

Like the old philosopher observed, "Our sins cast long shadows."

THE HISTORIANS

In a B-26 outfit in Sardinia, there were a couple of aerial gunners who seemed to have a bit of an edge on everyone else when it came to enjoying life—no matter what the circumstances. One of them, Jimmy O'Keefe, was a fun-loving Irishman from Corona, New York, who talked just like the actor James Garfield. The other, Bill Largent, was a suave, sweet-talking former radio announcer from Ohio. These guys were on the same crew and shared the same tent.

Through some form of midnight requisition, they acquired a typewriter and kept it going full blast far into every night. It was so unusual to see these guys working hard at anything that this frenzied typing activity aroused the curiosity of almost everyone in the squadron. When questioned about this nighttime project, Jimmy and Bill became very secretive and then let it "slip" that they had been commissioned by a publisher to write a history of the squadron, including detailed profiles of each of the men in it. It was also leaked that Bill still had NBC contacts and that the squadron might be featured on a radio show.

Everyone in the squadron wanted to be well treated in the book, so Jimmy and Bill suddenly became extremely popular. They were the recipients of all sorts of favors and gifts. Troops returning from the rest camp on the Isle of Capri would bring them bottles of exotic booze, the mess hall officer allowed them the best of the food that was available, and they drew only a few of the undesirable squadron extra-duty chores. They were the pets and the darlings of the squadron and they played the part to the hilt.

At the height of their popularity, a pilot who had a rough mission was interviewed by this journalistic duo. After the interview, he became curious about what had been written, so he sneaked a peak at the manuscript while the authors were out of their tent. He found no "manuscript" at all, only several reams of paper with "NOW IS THE TIME FOR ALL

GOOD MEN TO COME TO THE AID OF THEIR COUNTRY'' typed over and over and over again. Nothing else was written, only that elementary typing phrase, repeated hundreds of times.

When the word of this discovery got out, Jimmy and Bill defended themselves to the best of their abilities but they still wound up nearly drowned in a tank of cold water, all of their gifts confiscated, and a career of dirty squadron extra duties to perform. But they were soon forgiven and the whole scam eventually became a squadron joke.

Most everyone likes a good con game, even in a combat zone in wartime—or maybe especially so during those times.

WOMEN'S LIB — CIRCA 1942

We had flown a practice cross-country mission with a full combat load and had stopped at West Palm Beach, Florida, to refuel the airplane and ourselves. There wasn't a formal military base there so we walked to the civilian terminal and took our places at the bar, a position to which we were well accustomed. Next to us was a crew from a B-24 that was being refueled next to our B-26.

"You guys flyin' the B-26?" the B-24 pilot asked.

"You bet," answered our pilot, a little guy who was very proud that he had been selected to fly the B-26.

"Oh," the B-24 guy answered somewhat disdainfully.

"What do you mean by that 'Oh'?" our guy asked.

"Nuthin', just that I'm glad that I drew an *airplane* instead of a Tinker-Toy like that," the B-24 guy taunted.

Then a violent discussion erupted, the B-24 versus the B-26. The merits and shortcomings of each airplane were discussed and the two pilots, agreeing on nothing, had reached the classical Mexican standoff or impasse.

"It takes you and that B-24 the whole state of Texas to make a turn and I could do a pinwheel over Waco," our guy bragged.

"I can turn inside any turn that you can make with that B-26," the B-24 guy argued.

On and on the battle raged until our Bonaparte-like pilot proclaimed, "Well, you can say what you want, but they call the B-26 "The Separator" because it separates the men from the boys and it takes a *man* to fly it."

Before the B-24 guy could respond to this, the attention of everyone was directed toward a couple of tiny, pretty ladies in military flight gear. They spotted the motley gathering of flying kin at the bar and joined us. They wore the insignia of the *wasp's*, lady fliers who were trained to perform ferry flights, maintenance test hops, and other noncombat duties.

"Hi, gals, what are you flyin'?" the B-24 guy asked.

"We're ferrying a couple of B-26's to faraway places," one of the ladies answered.

The waitress chose that inopportune time to ask our pilot what he wanted for lunch. He looked at the smirking B-24 pilot and at the tiny WASP pilot. "Nothing, thank you," he said. "I just lost my appetite."

MY GRANDMOTHER, THE FLIGHT MECHANIC

World War II had come upon us so suddenly that the reservoir of trained people in the aviation industry was extremely low. As a result, we had a lot of very young men doing jobs that had formerly been assigned to highly skilled and experienced men. By virtue of having gone to work for the Glenn L. Martin Company when it was small, my responsibilities grew as the company expanded into a defense plant giant. As a 19-year-old, I was given the duty of teaching young Air Corps people the workings of the B-26 airplane. This involved a lot of in-flight maintenance and the demonstration of emergency procedures.

Quite often I grew a bit overenthusiastic when we had real in-flight emergencies and I had been called on the carpet several times for taking too many personal risks. I was repeatedly warned that my duty was to instruct and not to perform. A short while after receiving one of these lectures, I was at Barksdale Field in Louisiana where crews were being trained as replacement combat crews.

After a flight which involved doing all kinds of training maneuvers, we found that the nosewheel would not lower when we prepared for landing. To mechanically release the lock that held the nosewheel in the retracted position, it was necessary to hang onto a ladder in the wheel well, reach across the top fo the retracted nosewheel, and to actuate a hydraulic valve with a screwdriver. This was sort of a testy experience because the nosewheel fell away from under you when the valve was sprung and there was nothing but open space below. There was not enough room to wear a parachute, so that added to the fun. I volunteered for this particular task and found that the valve would not move as easily as it was supposed to and I got so wrapped up in making it work that I allowed my weight to rest on the retracted nosewheel. When the valve finally worked and the nosewheel fell free, I almost went with it but I managed to grab some hydraulic tubing that ran along the side of the well. The crew chief of the airplane grabbed me by a leg and, after I reluctantly let go of the lines, hauled me back into the airplane.

I had to report the incident to the company and there was a space in which the crew was to be listed and the person to be contacted regarding the reported malfunction. I left that space blank and hoped that it would go unnoticed but it didn't work. Within a few days of submitting the report, I received a telegram from the Martin Company requesting the name of the in-flight mechanic.

I used my grandfather's first name and my grandmother's maiden name, promoted her to technical sergeant, and got away with it.

LATE DATE

A B-26 aerial engineer, a close friend, was injured in a takeoff accident when his aircraft ran off of the runway and burned. His injuries were slight but still serious enough for him to be hospitalized. The accident happened during the early morning hours and it was late in the afternoon before the medics would let me visit him. I found him swathed in bandages and smelling of burn ointment but otherwise quite intact. After the usual greetings, he motioned me to come close to his bed, within whispering distance.

"How about bringing me a uniform?" he asked. "And try to get the kid in the orderly room to issue me a first-class pass because mine burned up in the fire. Another thing, I want to borrow your car," he added.

"You're singed like mess hall bacon," I cautioned. "What are you planning to do with a pass and all that other stuff?"

"Well, you know, Mary O., that little girl at the dairy store, and I are pretty close and I kinda want to see her alone for a little while. Seeing that they brought me in here in a burned-out flying suit and won't give me a pass and that I don't have any transportation, I figured you could provide them for an old flyin' buddy," he explained.

Simple and straightforward, except that he was injured, was restricted to his hospital room, and that he would be a subject of the 10 o'clock bed check. I reminded him of these minor details.

"No sweat," he countered. "I don't plan to leave until after ten."

Being a bit on the outlaw side myself, I did all of these things for him and at 10:30 P.M. he took off to visit Mary O. I went to the hospital early the next morning to see if he had made it back safely. He wasn't there.

While I was waiting in the hall, the errant sergeant ambled in, calmly changed from uniform to hospital garb, and slipped into bed. He looked awful, red-eyed and hung over. He smelled like an empty barroom that hadn't been cleaned but had been sprayed with some sweet-smelling stuff to cover the staleness. He was dead tired, his bandages were a ragged mess, and in seconds he was sound asleep.

Before I could leave the ward with the smuggled uniform, the flight surgeon stopped by the sleeping sergeant's bed and rudely woke him up. The surgeon looked him over, took his temperature, ordered a nurse to change his dressings, and ordered that he be dismissed and returned to active duty. The sarge protested wildly but to no avail.

"You're fine," the doctor said while he suppressed an amused grin. "All that you really needed was a good night's rest."

B-26 REST AND RECUPERATION

Some of the B-26 flying stories got a bit raunchy and did not lend themselves to after-dinner drawing-room conversation. Some were true, some were not, and some a little bit of each. One such story was about a B-26 crew that was enjoying a rest and recuperation (R & R) stay at a Miami Beach luxury hotel. Even in this plush environment, they were often called upon to answer roll calls and to fill out more of the bureaucratic forms. This particular crew had spent their first night with their wives and had gone to attend to the mundane duty calls while the five wives were left to enjoy the luxury of a slow breakfast.

The pilot's wife really looked haggard and drank lots of coffee. "I didn't sleep a wink last night," she volunteered. "George kept pulling on my arms and legs and yelling things about getting the nose up or down or some such nonsense."

The radio operator's wife joined in with her complaint about her husband who had twisted on her breasts all night long yelling for some radio station to answer him.

The gunner's wife was heavily bruised, she said, because her gunner husband had beat on her all night while screaming that he couldn't get the damned gun unjammed.

The navigator's wife then confessed that she had round, dark bruises all over her body and explained that her husband kept punching at her with his finger and insisting that his navigational fix was good and that they were indeed "right there."

During all this, the bombardier's wife, a shy and retiring southern beauty, was quiet and reluctant to discuss her night with her combat-returnee husband. But after being pressed by the others, she revealed that the night had been relatively quiet and that after a suitable reunion she and her bombardier husband had fallen into a satisfied and peaceful sleep. Later during the night, she was startled to near hysteria when her husband probed between her thighs, sat bolt upright, and screamed, "My God, we left the bomb bay doors open!"

Probably not true, but a good barroom story, particularly if you were a pilot who didn't like bombardiers.

A B-26 BLUEPRINT FOR DISASTER

EMERGENCY INSTRUCTIONS, B-26 AIRCRAFT, 11 APRIL 1942
WHEN MAKING A SINGLE-ENGINE LANDING, IT SHOULD BE REMEMBERED THAT THE AIR-PLANE CANNOT MAINTAIN ALTITUDE ON ONE ENGINE WITH THE LANDING GEAR EXTENDED. ON SUCH A LANDING, THE PILOT SHOULD UNDER NO CIRCUMSTANCES PERMIT THE SPEED TO FALL BELOW 135 MPH UNTIL HE IS DEFINITELY SURE OF MAKING THE LANDING.

Note: This story is included to illustrate the youth, inexperience, and lack of maturity of flight crews when they left for aerial combat. It normally took only one combat mission to convert them to mature, competent, and often prematurely old men. It might also be noted that the 135 mph landing speed was pretty swift for 1942.

Walker's Wildcats, a band of happy warriors, headed for the unknowns of Europe and of aerial combat. Our battle steed was the short-winged B-26 Martin Marauder, sometimes called "The Widow Maker" or "The Flying Prostitute," the fastest of all the bombers and, in the minds of our crew, the most magnificent machine in the air.

The six of us, pilot, copilot, navigator-bombardier, radio operator, engineer, and rear gunner crawled aboard, performed our preflight tasks, and taxied out for takeoff. Although it was mid-January, a rather ominous 13th day, the Florida sun was hot and we all sweated in the wool flying suits. The airplane was heavier than usual because of her load of full combat gear. Two "drop-away" fuel tanks filled the bomb bay and they too sweated from a full load of fresh fuel.

At the end of the runway, everything checked out okay and we started the takeoff roll and we rolled, and we rolled, and we rolled. A railroad track ran perpendicular to the far end of the runway we were using and as we were attempting to takeoff, a freight train was rumbling along the tracks. We lifted off at about 130 mph, ran a dead heat with the train on altitude, and beat it to the crossing by a short nose. Gear and flaps came up and the belly of the airplane flirted with the tops of the palm trees while we tried to gather airspeed rather than altitude. Slowly the speed increased and we started a cautious climb. We leveled at 8,000 feet with the shining Atlantic Ocean beneath us and took up a heading toward destiny.

"Pilot, this is Nav. I'm going to put up the dome and get a sun-shot for a good departure fix," the navigator called.

"Rog," the pilot answered.

The pilot cautioned the navigator to make sure the airspeed was within the limits for extending the dome, and after making sure that it was, the navigator lowered the metal hatch and the cold air that flowed into the airplane was a welcome relief from the heat. He then put the glass dome in place and went to work.

"Pilot, this is aft gunner. Do you guys smell gas up there?" he called.   "Sure do," the pilot answered. "Matter of fact, it's getting pretty strong. Everybody put out their smokes and don't actuate any electrical equipment until we find the problem."

"It's the tanks in the bay, sir," the flight engineer advised. "Both of them are leaking at the filler necks. One is real bad and raw fuel is flowing down the longeron channel. I can't tighten the release clamps, so we'll have to start using fuel from the bay as soon as possible."

"Nav, give me a heading for getting back home," the pilot commanded.

"Rog, will do, but it looks like we have another problem,"

the navigator answered. "There's a big tear in the rudder and the loose fabric is flapping all over the place.

"Let's get the fuel transferred and out of those bay tanks," someone called.

"Negative switches on," the engineer cautioned.

"The hydraulic filler door is gone from the top of the fuselage," the navigator added. "Looks like that's what went through the rudder."

"ADF (radio compass) is on West Palm Beach," the radio operator advised.

"There's raw fuel all over the bomb bay, it's blowing all over the place," the gunner called. "Looks like there's a leak some other place than the bay tanks."

"Open the bomb bay doors and let's get some air blowing through there," the pilot ordered.

"It's a triangular tear in the rudder of about 8 inches on the side but it doesn't seem to be getting any bigger," the navigator said.

Chatter filled the interphone. Problems were compounding themselves and solutions were elusive.

Everyone put on parachutes and flotation gear at the pilot's order. Life rafts were checked, ditching procedures were reviewed by all crew members, and preparations were made to ditch the airplane if the problems got any worse.

"Nav, get out of that dome and give me a direct heading back to Drane Field at Lakeland," the pilot ordered.

"Why to Drane? Why not back to West Palm?" the copilot asked.

"Because that's where they can fix our airplane," the pilot explained. "West Palm is just a jumpin'-off place and they can't do much for us. Besides, the runway at Drane is longer, the approach is better, and the emergency guys are geared up for our needs at Drane."

"Radio, call West Palm and advise them that we are heading for Drane," the pilot ordered.

"Keerist! The right engine is on fire!" the copilot suddenly yelled.

"Feather and hit the fire bottle!" the pilot yelled back.

The engine was shut down, the propeller feathered, the

fire extinguished, and now the crippled airplane hung in the air on one engine.

The navigator advised the pilot of the heading and estimated time to Drane and was told that it would be dark when they arrived. There would be no moon and the subdued wartime runway lighting would make for a dimly lit approach. Nevertheless, we headed for Drane, driving past a couple of good airports with adequate runways and still visible in the descending twilight. We called Drane, detailed our problems, and requested advice.

The Squadron Commander and the Engineering Officer came to the Drane tower to talk with us. The bomb wing had experienced heavy airplane losses during training and everyone was a bit spooky about advising us what to do. Finally they advised us to jettison the bay tanks, burn (and we shuddered at that choice of words) down to minimum fuel, and land.

We flew over an isolated area to drop the tanks, but when the bombardier toggled the switches, nothing happened and the tanks hung in place. Several more tries were made but the tanks wouldn't drop.

"Try using the screwdriver emergency release method," the pilot suggested.

"Won't help, they're hung up at the necks," the engineer replied.

We advised Drane tower of the new problem and were told that we could either bail out or try to land without hitting hard enough to jar the tanks loose. "You guys are closer to the problem, it's your decision," the commanders advised us.

The problems and the choices were discussed among the crew. We were low on altitude, it was dark, the parachutes had small canopies, and some of the bigger guys on the crew didn't want to try a bail-out. The pilot had made only one real single-engine landing during training and the copilot had made none. Each one had made many simulated single-engine landings but none under the cover of darkness. We searched for other options rather than bailing out or landing on one engine and found them to be non-existent.

"Let's try to restart the right engine, maybe it'll be okay," the pilot suggested. "If we have another fire on it, we'll shut it down during the roll after touchdown. If it really burns when we start it, the choice will be made and we'll bail out." About that time, anything sounded like a good idea. Without advising the Drane tower, we started the right engine and it ran beautifully. No fire, just a clean blue plume of exhaust flame.

"Drane, we now have two good engines and request a straight-in approach with emergency equipment standing by," the pilot called.

"Roger, you have it, sir. Emergency equipment is at the runway," the tower operator responded.

"We are on a long final, before-landing checklist is complete, and 1085 is ready for landing," the pilot called.

The night was cold and the orange groves that surrounded the landing field were dotted with yellow flames from the burning smudge pots. Inside the airplane we were all sweating bullets.

"Looks like you're coming in short," the copilot cautioned.

"Damn! I was concentrating on that row of smudge pots and not on the approach lights," the agitated pilot answered.

The pilot then eased both throttles forward and the engines responded like obedient children, when suddenly the right engine exploded in a shower of sparks and fire that looked like a Chinese New Year's celebration.

The Marauder yawed violently to the right and started to roll. Chaos took over. The right wing tip hit the ground and we cartwheeled across the threshold of the runway. The landing gear broke away from the fuselage and we hit the concrete of the runway spinning like a well-launched top—fortunately, still right side up. A mild explosion in the bomb bay shook the airplane. Fire seemed to erupt from everywhere at once. Wiring was torn loose in brilliant showers of sparks leaving more fire in its wake. The belly of the airplane grated across the rough concrete of the runway. The ambulances and the fire trucks illuminated the whole scene with their ghostly red lights.

We yelled and maybe we screamed—I don't really remember and don't care because it was surely a time for screaming. I had often wondered about what last thoughts would intrude into my mind when I knew that death was imminent, and as the mortally wounded airplane continued her blazing, noisy path to destruction, I thought that I would soon know the thoughts that would go along with the death rattle. Then it was all over, the airplane stopped, and the only noise was the whooshing of the fire.

"Get the hatch open!" the pilot yelled.

The copilot seemed transfixed. He would alternately release and fasten his seat belt, making no effort to leave his seat or to open the overhead hatch.

I had placed a seat cushion in front of me prior to the impact but still had banged my face and head on a map case and a rack in front of me. Teeth were broken, my jaw didn't want to work right, and blood ran down my neck and soaked into my undershirt. My left thigh was bleeding and my right leg was bent forward at the knee.

The flight engineer put out the fire that was in his hair and sprayed the compartment with the portable extinguisher. He was burned but still seemed to be able to help others.

I looked at the operator beside me and almost got sick. His feet had jammed under some floor-mounted radio equipment and pulled violently free during the convulsive gyrations of the airplane. It appeared that only bloody stumps remained where his shoe-clad feet had been. His nose was smashed and he seemed to be barely conscious.

After what seemed to be an eternity, the hatches were jettisoned and the five of us in the front of the airplane crawled and jumped to safety. We gathered in a cluster in front of the wreckage, unseen by the rescue crews in the darkness. We found the tail gunner, blood-soaked, incoherent and nearly unconscious.

"Get my crew out there!" the squadron commander yelled at the firemen. He stood dangerously close to the burning airplane—a potential bomb, still filled with fuel.

We all lay still and whimpered a bit until an officer spotted us and sent the medics to pick us up. As they loaded us into ambulances, I looked through the maze of smoke and the flickering lights at the remains of the airplane. Its full plexiglass nose was broken and we could have crawled out that way to escape rather than fighting the stubborn hatch and then aggravating our injuries by jumping to the ground. But reason and logic had surrendered to panic.

The good medics put everyone back together with string, wire, plastic, and tape, and by the morning we were all answering the first questions of the accident investigating board.

My God, the mistakes we had made! The fallacy of our logic, the lack of reason, and the dumb decisions. One airplane destroyed and a crew all busted up. It was unbelievable! The interrogators belabored each of our mistakes for the following several weeks. It seemed easy enough to see the bonehead plans and actions without reconfirming them daily, but the board had to have its due.

The patient in the hospital bed next to me had had his feet blown off by a land mine on one of the Pacific Islands. He was a black soldier with magnificent, white, sparkling teeth. With my broken fangs, I envied him, never considering the fact that I still had two good feet. We became close friends. I told him the story of our carelessness and bad judgment, and he told me how, in a moment of neglect, he had stepped on a land mine.

"With all of the unknowns like snipers and booby traps around you, how in the hell were you so careless as to step on a mine?" I asked him one evening.

He raised his eyebrows a bit, looked at my mummy-like bandages, and just smiled. He didn't need to say a word. I got the message loud and clear. It's like that when you're talking to a friend.

AND THE SARGE WAS RIGHT

When we were having so many B-26 training accidents, the main topic of conversation in the barracks was one of survival. Most of the guys felt that it would always be "someone else" involved in the accidents, so they pretended not to be worried. One particular sergeant with a very difficult Polish name, one that I can't remember and couldn't spell if I did remember, was adamant in his claim that the B-26 would not kill him. He stated that belief so many times that it became sort of a barracks joke and some of the guys mimicked him whenever they went out to fly.

We did a lot of foolish things during those days and among those which we enjoyed the most was the low-level, high-speed buzz-job. It was here (and it still is) that you could really feel the sensation of speed and power. Often we chose our buzzing targets at random and with the irresponsibility born of these spontaneous decisions.

The crew on which the Polish sergeant served as tail gunner once buzzed the beaches at St. Petersburg, Florida, so low that they blew over the beach umbrellas and scattered the elderly sun-worshipers. The crew made several passes over the beach and then turned out to sea with the airplane going at full bore. They were so low that the props hit the water and were bent so severely that it set up an unholy vibration throughout the airplane. The pilot pulled up abruptly to gain escape altitude. The back camera doors opened and the Polish sergeant jumped out without parachute or survival floatation gear. The airplane, with the rest of the crew still aboard, crashed into the sea.

Spectators on the beach rushed to the badly injured sergeant and brought him to the beach on a rubber raft. He was so badly beat up and injured that those who saw him were sure that he could not survive.

But several months after this leap for life, I was a witness at the sergeant's wedding. He was in a wheelchair and stitched up like a baseball but he was alive and alert. I watched him in admiration and thought "when it's my turn, I'll do it like you did, Sarge. Yeah, just like you did."

THE SMOKING SECTION, PLEASE

I don't suppose the term "black humor" had been coined yet during World War II, but, in retrospect, we had our share of it during those years. It seems that most of this humor developed during periods of pain or duress and that it was a "pain pill" that seemed to help.

One of our B-26's had broken up on landing and the radio operator's foot had jammed through the skin of the airplane. He was trapped by the jagged metal as though a bear trap had closed on his ankle. The airplane's fuel tanks had ruptured and the entire area was awash in raw high-octane gasoline. The radio operator was also soaked in gasoline. A sheet-metal mechanic was called to cut away the metal around the radio operator's leg, the trapped man was given morphine to sedate him while the cutting operation was going on, and the entire fire department was standing by trying to neutralize the chance of fire. The commanding officer, the engineering officer, the chaplain, and the flight surgeon were also all standing by, reassuring the injured man.

"Is there anything we can do to make you more comfortable?" the chaplain asked.

"Yes, sir," the radio operator answered. "I'd like a cigarette, a Lucky if you have one." And he smiled the laconic smile of someone who enjoys his own jokes better than those to whom he tells them.

ALWAYS THE LANDING GEAR

The B-26 landing gear retraction-extension handle was designed so that it was necessary to make five distinct mistakes in order to confuse it with the adjacent wing flap operation handle. As a precaution against someone making all of these mistakes, there was a safety or "squat" switch located on the main landing gear. This safety switch was supposed to render the gear retraction system inoperative any time that the weight of the airplane was on the gear. With this arrangement, it was theoretically impossible to retract the landing gear while the airplane was on the ground. But as with Bobby Burns's plans of mice and men, so it was with airplanes, and someone was always making mistakes and systems malfunctioning.

Perhaps one of the most interesting of the premature "gear-up" accidents happened after a spectacular flight at McDill Army Airfield in Florida. The pilot of A B-26 called in an emergency after his right engine had failed. He then nursed the airplane at a dangerously low altitude for 400 miles and landed safely at McDill. At the end of the landing roll, he signaled for the copilot to raise the flaps. Predictably, the copilot moved the landing gear handle to the up position, the safety switch didn't work, and the airplane settled gracefully to the ground. Because of the single-engine landing, a lot of emergency equipment was at the airplane and they moved in swiftly to prevent any fire that might start from the now-ruptured fuel tank. The crew crawled from the airplane and the pilot refused a ride in a staff car and elected to walk from the accident site to squadron flight operations about one mile away.

"You guys take care of the airplane," he told the engineering officer. "I've taken care of the copilot."

He had punched the copilot squarely in the nose and left him a bleeding mess in the cockpit.

TEMPER TANTRUM

War and strict discipline did strange things to young men and boys who found themselves in responsible positions in the military. As author James Jones pointed out, they were schooled in frustration so that by the time they arrived in combat they were more than ready to vent their pent-up anger on any target of opportunity.

One of the B-26 crews at Lake Charles, Louisiana, had performed their training duties above and beyond the routine requirements and as a reward were allowed to make a cross-country flight to a place of their own choice. The pilot was from California and, with the agreement of his crew, elected to go there for a visit with his parents and to give the crew a taste of Hollywood nightlife. I was tacked on as an extra crew member as a reward for some extra work that I had done.

We had barely gotten underway when a call came from home base advising us to return because "higher authority" had heard about the "privileged" flight and had it cancelled. We debated about pretending that we hadn't received the message and about using the written orders authorizing the trip to override the verbal message. Reason ruled, however, and we headed back to Lake Charles, disappointed and disillusioned.

The pilot was particularly distraught because visions of sugar plums that had been dancing in his head had now disappeared. No reunion with his family, no dates with back-home girl friends, no hero worship from his buddies, no nothing but the return to the bleak army airfield and a town of strangers. He was mad, and as we neared the field he got even madder.

Just before touchdown, he yielded to his emotions, pulled the airplane up and let it stall into the runway. We hit three-point with a ferocious impact. Bits and pieces of airplane flew in all directions but we stayed intact enough to make it to the parking area. None of the crew was injured but the airplane was a mess.

The pilot, now cooled down enough to realize the results of his actions, started making excuses for the lousy landing and the rest of us testified to support his story. There was no tangible evidence to prove that he had landed in such a manner on purpose and, although he was highly suspect, he was exonerated of any wrongdoing.

An inspection of the airplane revealed that it was structurally damaged beyond reasonable repair, so it was designated as a total washout and used for spare parts.

Sounds like an expensive tantrum, but by today's standards it wasn't too bad—the cost of the entire airplane was about equal to what people now pay for a pure vanilla Mercedes-Benz sedan.

SOUTHERN COMFORT

While conducting final maneuvers with the B-26 prior to going overseas, we were constantly plagued with heavy fog in and round Myrtle Beach, South Carolina. Often it was necessary to divert to other bases at the end of a training flight because of the dense fog at Myrtle, and one or two airplanes had been lost because of it. One flight commander, Major Weir, a West Point graduate, vowed that he would not lose any of his men to this new airplane or to the elements. He was as good as his word.

One time he returned from a practice mission and he found the field completely closed. His flight of B-26's lacked sufficient fuel to get to an open alternate, so he had all of his flight aim their airplanes out to sea and bail out. All crew members landed safely except for one crusty old gunner who didn't show up for several days after the bail-out. When he did show up, he was somewhat the worse for wear, disheveled and hung over. He explained that he had landed near a country saloon and that the family who owned it sort of adopted him. After he was cleaned up a bit, he was ordered to report to the Wing Commander.

"Sarge, you caused us a lot of worry, a lot of work in searching for you, lots of money for civilian help in the search, and a lot of lost training time," the Old Man said. "You're in a bit of trouble for your behavior, but because of your excellent previous record in combat we're going to overlook your little indiscretion. You'll be put back on active flight status with only a notation of your extended stay at the saloon on your record. We all know that you can do better than what you recently did, so what do you have to say to all of this?"

"I sure do appreciate the consideration, colonel," the Old Sarge answered. "Guess that you kind of understand how things really are and I do appreciate your not giving me a bit of AWOL time. Now, about doing better, you're right about that too. During this jump, I saw this little old country beer store and I steered for it but I missed it by about a mile. With a little more 'chute steering practice, I can probably land right in their front yard next time. You are absolutely right, sir, I can do better."

The colonel spread his hands before him, studied them for a moment, and with an unashamed twinkle in his eyes ordered the sarge to steer his ass out of there before he was forcibly steered to the stockade.

A few months later, this same sergeant was shot down over Belgium and hid out with a family in a small village for several weeks. Somehow or another, he evaded the enemy and made it back to his unit, dressed in a borrowed old tweed suit and a visored cap. After establishing his identity, he was allowed to enter the base and he was promptly arrested for being out of uniform.

Some days a fella just can't win.

OF APPLE PIE AND HOME

For some now unremembered reason, I was an escort for a young B-26 gunner who had received a tremendous amount of publicity for the large number of enemy airplanes he had destroyed. The tales were further enhanced by stories of how he would sit up at night and wait for marauding troops who often raided the camp for whatever goodies they could steal. Allegedly, he had mowed them down by the dozens. In the midst of this blizzard of publicity, it was discovered that this hero was only 16 years old and that he had enlisted at the tender age of 14. Now, with a year of combat behind him, a fantastic record, a reputation as a real fighter, and the revelation of his age, he was to be honorably discharged. It was when he arrived in Washington to receive some decorations that I was tied to him as Mother Superior.

We were met by all kinds of newspaper, magazine, and radio reporters who threw a barrage of questions at the baby-faced, innocent-appearing youngster. He fielded all of the questions by referring to a carefully prepared text given to him by the Air Force Information Officer. He covered the whole scene from All-American goodness and purity, through patriotism, to a strong desire to win the war. When he was asked what he was looking forward to the most since coming home, he really did a grandstand act.

"Good food is first," he said. "Some hot apple pie with lots of cinnamon in it and a big chocolate milk shake," was his first preference.

After all of the interviews and picture-taking was over, he and I were left to our own resources. I steered him into one of the better hotel restaurants, naively expecting him to get a big dinner and his pie. Not quite. He wanted straight Scotch and "some dame" to hit the sack with him. The restaurant people refused to serve us any booze because we were both under 21, but after consulting with a policeman and explaining who the young hero was, they served us anything we wanted. He had a private hotel room that night and I have no idea with whom he shared it, but from the adoring crowd that had surrounded him in the restaurant, there were several likely candidates.

The next day after our young hero left for "mother and apple pie," I had to dodge the questions of the reporters as to how he had spent his first night in the States. Several months later, I got a "V" letter from him. He had enlisted in the Navy and was serving aboard a battleship somewhere in the Pacific. Where he went from there I don't know, but I bet that it was not in pursuit of apple pie.

AN EVENING AT THE THEATER

There was a drive-in movie near Barksdale Field, Louisiana, where we were stationed for B-26 crew training. This was an era when we were all young, mostly unmarried, and in pursuit of every romantic diversion we could find. The drive-in movie was an excellent place to hide out from the rest of the guys whenever one had a special date, could borrow a car, or, better still, had a date with a girl who had a car. This particular movie had a big screen with the picture projected from a booth at ground level, shooting the film upward to the screen.

One night during the showing of a popular movie called "Blues in the Night" a B-26 came roaring across the theater, flying so low that it passed through the beam from the projection booth, and then off into the night. Precisely because of some previous low-altitude "work" such as this, our big bosses had planned a bit ahead of time and had big "buzz numbers" painted on both sides of the fuselages of all the airplanes. These numbers had been the undoing of many of us, and such was to be the case on this movie night.

The offending B-26 had come so low that the projection beam had illuminated the buzz numbers and some unsportsmanlike spectator had reported those numbers to concerned and powerful authorities. The fine and noble pilot of this airplane was fined a bunch of dollars, grounded and confined to the base for a month.

The final indignity was that he was not even allowed to go to see the movie "Blues in the Night" after he had tried so hard to see what was playing.

WHAT'S A P-40, GRANDPA?

It was December 1941 and Pearl Harbor had been attacked. We were all emotionally charged with the eloquent rhetorical declaration of war by our president, Franklin D. Roosevelt. We were young, eager, and filled with a desire to enlist in one of the military services. But cooler heads prevailed and we were "nailed" to our airplane jobs at the Glenn L. Martin bomber plan in Middle River, Maryland. My job as flight test crew chief and aerial mechanic on an experimental B-26 was suddenly changed to that of armorer on one of the P-40 airplanes that had been brought in to protect the plant in case of some kind of enemy aerial attack.

The P-40's were flown by young, inexperienced pilots and were maintained by near-raw recruits. Each day, the P-40 pilots flew two patrol missions, each day we loaded ammunition which they test-fired for practice, and it seemed that we lost an airplane each day to an accident. We lived in empty engine crates, were fed from mobile soup kitchens, and were on an around-the-clock duty. The weather was wet and cold, parts for the P-40's were scarce, administration was flexible, pilots were skeptical of their airplanes, and tempers flared whenever there were marked differences that gave us an outlet for our frustrations. But once in a while something happened that gave us another treasure for our storehouse of memories.

One young, handsome, blonde P-40 pilot, not too far removed from a small town in Iowa, was having considerable trouble with his airplane every day. While the other pilots were completing their assigned patrol missions, this young fellow would return shortly after takeoff and complain of the "feel" of his airplane controls. He could not trim it for level flight, it had a tendency to either pitch or roll or to wander off heading. His airplane was physically checked dozens of times and nothing was ever found to be wrong. We could not change pilot or airplanes for there were no spares and each pilot was jealous of his own assigned and proven airplane.

Chuck Hohnickle, a retired Air Corps pilot, was assigned to the Martin Company as an inspector for the government. He was a short, stocky man whose head sported only a few of the hairs left over from what had once been a mop of flaming red hair. Chuck dressed conservatively and usually wore a suit and tie or at least a sportcoat with a tie. He looked the part of a stern, perfection-demanding, no-excuses government inspector.

Chuck watched the mini-drama between the P-40 pilot and his ground crew and was well versed on all of the details of the controversy between them. One day, almost casually, he asked the young lieutenant if he could fly the airplane that he was having so much trouble with and he got an immediate okay. Procedures, approvals, and other aggravating bureaucratic restraints weren't too prevalent at this time, so we got the P-40 ready for Chuck to fly.

A different Chuck came out of the hangar and crawled into the cockpit of the classy little P-40. He wore the "pink" pants of the Air Corps officer and a battered leather A-2 flight jacket with an emblem of Lady Luck as a patch over the right breast. The classic soft helmet with the ear flaps turned up and big "Barney Google" goggles covered the bald head. A white scarf was looped into a neat ascot around his neck and a seat-pack parachute swung from his shoulders. He was a dazzling one-man Clark Gable, Humphrey Bogart, Richard Arlen, and Jimmy Doolittle. He looked a lot like Pappy Boyington, who was to become an ace later on during the war. More than anything, *he looked like a fighter pilot.*

Chuck's preflight, engine start, taxi-out, and takeoff were smooth and professional without being spectacular. He flew out of sight of the field and after a few minutes called in to request permission to do some aerial demonstrations over the field. Permission granted, he started his one-man show that, to this day, I believe could only be equaled and never surpassed. He buzzed at grass-root level, performed rolls, did loops, did the falling leaf, made noisy Immelmans and chandelles, threw in a few split-S's, dove and climbed like a happy bird, and did things that were never intended to be done in a P-40. As a finale, he buzzed the airport, put the P-40 in a loop, lowered the landing gear at the top of the loop, and rolled out on final to make a perfect landing.

During his show, all work at the airport stopped. It was as if everyone was hypnotized, and they were, not by a swaying medallion and soft words but by a master pilot putting an airplane through its seductive and gravity-defying act.

Chuck taxied in, got out of the airplane, and gracefully acknowledged the applause of the group that had assembled to greet him. He sought out the "owner" of the P-40 and laconically told him, "Son, I can't find a thing wrong with your airplane." The lieutenant, his somewhat embarrassed face wreathed in a big country smile, was almost in tears as he embraced Chuck in hero admiration. From that day forward, he flew his airplane to its fullest capacity, put on a little air show of his own when he left for a combat assignment, and later carved himself a niche in aviation history as an excellent combat pilot.

A few months later, after all of the P-40's were gone and we were back in the B-26 business, there was some sort of an investigation regarding Chuck's unauthorized flight demonstration. All of the people who were questioned got an immediate case of "the dumbs" and losses of memory so bad that they couldn't even recall such a flight. When I was questioned by the investigators regarding my part in the show and asked my opinion about what Chuck had done, I do recall my answer. I said simply, "What is a P-40, sir?"

SERGEANT LARGENT

One of the crew members who was involved with me in the B-26 accident described earlier in this book, was Sergeant William Largent. Bill recovered from his injuries and went on to have one of the more fantastic of those experiences encountered by soldiers in any war.

Bill was an admirer of General George Patton and tended to pattern himself after the flamboyant general. He had a couple of chrome-plated .45 automatics which he carried in shoulder holsters, one under each arm. He told of how he would not ever allow himself to be captured if he was shot down over enemy territory. Instead, he would draw his formidible weapons and shoot it out with any would-be captors. I was quite close to Bill and I always felt that he believed his "shoot-out" philosophy completely. However it was not to be.

During a mission over Belgium, Bill's B-26 was shot down and he was forced to bail out into that unfriendly territory. During the bail-out, he struck another airplane in the same formation and suffered two broken legs. After he was on the ground, he crawled behind some heavy bushes, hid his parachute, and drew his trusty .45's. He waited in agony as he listened to the noises of the ground troops who were searching for him. He was in extreme pain, going into shock, and desperately needed help. Realizing his predicament,

Bill gave up on the fatal heroics, hid his guns, and yelled for help. The searchers proved to be underground Maquis, friendly to the Allies, but they had neither medicine nor doctors to work on Bill's critical injuries. The only alternative was to turn Bill over to German troops in the area, a move that would accomplish two things: it would get medical help for Bill and establish the Belgium underground forces as sympathetic to the Germans.

Bill was received badly by the enemy. Disregarding his injuries, they struck him and spit in his face as he lay on the stretcher. They shouted obscenities at him and threatened to hang him. Finally, they moved him to a German hospital commanded by a German admiral. Here, his legs were set and put in casts and he was put in a ward with other prisoners of war, none of whom were American.

The day following his hospitalization, Bill was shown an X-ray that was said to be of his damaged legs. He was told that the work done on his legs was only temporary and that if additional surgery was not performed the legs would heal and he would be a cripple. In exchange for information about his unit, the necessary operation would be done. Bill didn't buy this scam, so they next sent a lovely nurse in during the night to make a more exciting offer. With two legs in casts and suspended by ropes, Bill wasn't too receptive to this offer and his counter offer to take a rain check was refused. One more attempt to gain information was made in the guise of a "defector" who would advise Bill's unit of his condition and whereabouts in exchange for some information. After Bill refused this last offer, he was left alone.

The hospital had a large number of Allied prisoners, a larger number of wounded German troops, and a staff of about 600. The hospital was in a direct line with the now-rampaging French Maquis forces and off the line of the advancing American troops. The hospital staff did not want to play host to the avenging Maquis, had no real defensive strength, and wanted to surrender the entire place to the American troops. Technical Sergeant Bill Largent was the ranking American among the prisoners and, in one of the oddities of war, the German admiral surrendered his sword and his hospital to Bill. The Germans gave Bill an interpreter, a vehicle, and two big white flags and sent him toward the American lines with their offer of surrender.

Once Bill reached the American troops, he found that they could not spare anyone to relieve him as hospital "commander," so they gave him a big American flag and sent him back. He returned, put the American flag on the hospital mast, and "commanded" the hospital for 43 days before he was relieved by a senior officer.

When Bill was evacuated to the U.S., he was received as a hero. He was offered a big sum of money for his story so that it could be recreated on the radio and incorporated into a book. Visions of sugar plums danced in his head and he planned all kinds of luxurious purchases. The government cut these plans short when they made their own production of his story and rewarded Bill with a $25 savings bond.

(Note: It may be that not all of the details of this story are completely accurate. It is written from memory as it was recited by Bill during a crew reunion in a Baltimore bar in 1947, and a lot of stuff has passed through the memory circuit since then. As it is often said though, "It's close enough for government work.")

OLD SOLDIERS AND ALLIGATORS

One of the best B-26 line chiefs in the whole world was a cranky old master sergeant whom we all called "Pop"—not very original, but appropriate in this case. He had been at Pearl Harbor when it was hit, had been in the Air Corps forever, and really knew his business. Whenever we asked him a technical question, he would not only give the answer but he would tell the whole background of the particular question. We all loved the old guy and always worked a little harder for him than for any of the other chiefs. He was the epitome of the old Air Corps Top Kick and he loved the role.

Pop had one little failing and that was that he would always disappear for a couple of days after payday. This was expected of him so no one ever bothered to complain or to make an issue of his couple of AWOL days. One payday, though, the Old Sarge overstayed his normal couple of days and we started a search of all of the local hotels and motels trying to locate him. It was in one of the 1930-1940 classic roadside motels, or tourist courts, called the Kickapoo Plaza Motor Courts that we found him. He was asleep with one of the raunchiest-looking women in the world beside him. He looked awful, the room smelled foul, and several empty booze bottles decorated the nightstand. We got him showered, shaved, dressed and headed back to the air base.

"Sarge," we asked him, "how could you possibly spend all of your money and time with such a horrible-looking woman?"

"Well, fellers," he said, "It's like this. When I went to the motel with that little flower, her skin seemed to me to be like that of a fresh peach and to stroke it was like fingering velvet. But when I sobered up a bit and stroked that same skin, it was like rubbing an alligator the wrong way."

We figured he was right and that Gertrude Stein was wrong—a rose is not always a rose, especially when it's an alligator.

. . . AND THEY SPELL MOTHER

Wartime is always a time of desperation for those involved in it, but some people suffered desperate hours of personal involvement while others shrugged off the terror and took full advantage of all that the situation offered. A most handsome pilot with whom I flew in B-26's was of the latter group and he used his status to every advantage.

There was a bit of magic in the silver wings that were awarded to and worn by air crew members whether they were the winged bullet of the gunner or the shield of the pilot. Perhaps the proudest moment in the lives of many air crew men, certainly in mine, was when the mother, wife, or girlfriend pinned on the wings at the graduation ceremony. Many times these wings were used much as fraternity pins were in more peaceful times. This particular pilot used his silver wings to sway more women than a Rudolph Valentino movie ever did.

The base PX's sold copies of the official wings so that a crew member could have several sets to wear on different uniforms and wouldn't have to be changing wings from one uniform to another. The wings could be bought very easily from the charming young ladies who patriotically staffed the PX counters and they seldom asked for verification from the buyers. As a result, almost any soldier could buy any type of wings that he desired—authorized of not. Because of this freedom-of-purchase plan, this particular pilot often dispatched me to the PX to buy several pairs of pilot's wings for him (he claimed to be embarrassed to be buying so many). This happened most frequently when we were on cross-country trips and staying at transient bases.

Since I was a GI and this man was an officer, our social contacts were different and I would usually see him only during duty hours. But one night in the Zephyr Room in downtown Shreveport, I happened to have a table near this romantic pilot and I overheard his solemn dedication to his charming lady companion. It went more or less like this: "My dear, I had planned to give these silver wings to my mother, never realizing that I would meet someone as lovely as you who would steal away my heart and soul in the wink of an eye. So I give them to you, knowing that you will wear them proudly until I return and we can again revive the magic of this moment. Should the fates be unkind and decree that I not return, please wear them in memory of me and as a memorial to all of the gallant airmen who, like me, will have sacrificed their lives in this pursuit of freedom. I will write my mother and explain to her that I have found a different kind of love, a love that demands that I surrender my all to her and that the treasured wings have been given to her as a token of my love. Mother will understand and will be glad for me. Please wear them for me," he concluded with the saddest of expressions. The girl melted and I feel sure that this noble airman did not spend the night in the Transient Bachelor Officer's Quarters.

The next time he sent me for wings, I told him that it

would be necessary for him to give me a copy of the speech he used when presenting "mother's" wings to the lovely ladies that he met. He did a bit of a soft-shoe on the ramp, tipped his hat over one eye, and did a Jimmy Cagney takeoff with a song that went something like this:

M is for the many things these wings buy me,
O is for the orchids they replace,
T is for the timing when I give them,
H is for the heartstrings that they play,
E is for every airfield where I've landed,
R is for the romance at each one.
Put them all together and they spell MOTHER, who
is proud of her Irish Air Corps son.

I went to the PX and bought his wings for him, and while I was there I got a couple of extra gunner's wings—just in case.

MORE FLIGHT CREW GAMES

One of our B-26 pilots had somehow managed to get into and through the cadet program, although he was considerably short of the minimum height requirement. He was about 5'3" and weighed about 125 pounds. He had a tremendous inferiority complex and went to great lengths to prove that his small stature didn't prevent him from being as "big" as the next guy. This tendency caused him some problems since other flight crew members would go out of their way to set him up for a fall. He never seemed to learn.

We were on temporary duty in Lakeland, Florida, and were housed at the beautiful Lakeland Terrace Hotel where the bartender ran a little business of pointing out the "easy" ladies who frequented the bar. On this particular evening, he showed us a statuesque blonde goddess who was "working" her way back to her home in Amarillo, Texas. An evening with this lovely lady could be bought for $20 and dinner. Several of us got up a pot of money and, unknown to our banty rooster pilot, hired her for the night. The plot was that she was to allow herself to be seduced by the pilot as though she was totally overcome by his charms and not any loot that might be involved. The plan worked beautifully, and while we were having breakfast the following morning, the smug pilot took a table next to us with the shady lady to show off his conquest. Later that day, he discovered the plot and gave us one of the roughest B-26 rides ever known to man. He was furious and never forgave us.

A few months later, this pilot was shot down in Italy but managed to parachute safely and to elude capture. He was evacuated back to the States without returning to his base at Sardinia, so it was necessary for his buddies to bundle up his personal effects for shipment to the States. In the bottom of his footlocker, hidden under his clothing, was a photograph of him and the shady lady of Texas. It had been taken by a roving photographer in the bar of the Lakeland Terrace on the night of his "conquest."

We left it undisturbed and it was sent home intact. We had already damaged this poor guy's ego enough and didn't ever really understand the depth of his problem.

THE SOUNDS OF SILENCE

One of the truly great prewar test pilots was Ellis D. "Sam" Shannon. I was privileged to fly with Mr. Shannon during the B-26 operational test program and, with my usual touch of good intentions gone awry, I managed to turn one flight with him into a memorable event.

We were making a fuel consumption test and had specially calibrated fuel tanks for the initial flight portion of these tests. We were to operate from these tanks until they were at near-empty level and then switch to normal fuel tanks. To make the switch, it was necessary to momentarily turn off the booster pumps in order to prevent an electrical overload, select the next tank, and then turn the boosters back on. I failed to turn off the pumps, selected the next tanks, and the electrical circuit breakers blew, shutting off all electrical power and all fuel to the engines. We were at about 8,000

THE B-26

Douglas "Wrong Way" Corrigan and the Curtiss Robin in which he made the historic flight from New York to Ireland in July 1938. He took off with Los Angeles as his destination.

American Hall of Aviation History, Northrop Univ., Inglewood, CA.

THE B-26

319TH BOMB GROUP — *Veteran Marauders*
June 5, 1943 to Oct. 31, 1944

Fifteen Famous Planes
1716 Total Combat Sorties
12,248:50 Total Flying Hours

146 Sorties | 117 Sorties | 102 Sorties
145 Sorties | 110 Sorties | 101 Sorties
132 Sorties | 106 Sorties | 101 Sorties
125 Sorties | 104 Sorties | 100 Sorties
118 Sorties | 104 Sorties | 105 Sorties

General Dynamics, Fort Worth Division, Edwards Air Force Base

THE B-26

General Dynamics, Fort Worth Division, Edwards Air Force Base

THE B-26

THE B-26

There were accidents as a result of trying to stretch a single-engine landing. Author Tate was in in this B-26 accident.

THE B-26

Author Tate was also in this B-26.

THE B-36

THE B-36

"One of our Props is Missing"

THE B-36

"Whoops!"

feet and by the time that I got things straightened out we had been making like a glider for about 6,000 of those 8,000 feet. After fuel was supplied to the engines and electrical power was restored, we zoomed to level flight, gained a bit of altitude, and went home.

Mr. Shannon did not say a word to me but he put me off the test crew for about two weeks, and then when I flew with him again, he maintained his silence and only glared at me. After a few weeks of this treatment, he gradually started talking to me again and soon the wound was healed. This "silent treatment" was more effective than any lecture could have been and I never made another mistake during flights with Mr. Shannon.

Sam Shannon went on to be the first pilot to ever fly a delta-winged aircraft, the Convair XF-92, and he and I had a few laughs while reminiscing about the olden days and about the primitive test-flying procedures we practiced. He remembered the mistake I had made, but I don't think it made the deep impression on him that it had on me.

EPILOGUE FOR THE MARAUDER

Whether you called her "The Marauder," "The Flying Prostitute," or "The Widow Maker," the B-26 was a grand and successful airplane. She was bred in conflict, rushed to maturity, suffered abusive treatment, and then performed as magnificently as any champion. In the same way that most men always remember the first woman they ever loved, so do crew members and pilots remember the first airplane they loved. With me it is the B-26, an airplane with which I shared both my adolescence and my maturity. Sometimes she treated me a bit rough, but she always performed well whenever I asked her.

The B-26 had her problems and many of these airplanes were lost to accidents during the early stages of training. So many were lost that a special committee headed by Harry S. Truman dictated that the funds allocated for additional B-26's be diverted to the purchase of other types of airplanes. There were 3,000 B-26's and in combat they boasted the lowest combat loss of any of the bombers—less than one-half of one percent! The B-26 was the aerial leader on historic D-day. She carried Lyndon B. Johnson on the mission that earned him a Silver Star. She was flown by some of history's greatest pilots:General Doolittle, Lester Maitland, and John Hilger.

Of all of the B-26's that were manufactured, it is ironic that when the Air Force museum at Wright-Patterson Field wanted one for restoration it was necessary to salvage one old hulk found in France. The remains of that B-26 were flown in a C-124 to the museum, a rather ignominious ending for a classic airplane and war hero. She was restored to perfection and today commands a lot of attention from museum visitors. She is relegated to history, though a proud history in her case, and will always be there to share her past glory with generations to come.

I spent a lot of time admiring the old bird at the museum and listening to the conversations of those who viewed her. One man, with what appeared to be a grandson in tow, announced that the B-26 was the airplane he had flown in combat. His young companion rather snootily corrected him and said, "You mean *aircraft*, don't you?"

"No, I mean airplane," the man said firmly. "Today they make aircraft. Then we made *airplanes.*"

PART II

THE B-36, THE PEACEMAKER

The Convair (now General Dynamics) B-36 was a *big* airplane, conceived during the early years of World War II and brought to reality with its first flight in August 1946—after the war had ended. It then served 10 solid years in the Strategic Air Command, and although it never "fired a shot in anger," it is credited with being one of the weapons that stopped the alleged cold war of that era from becoming a very real war.

The B-36 had a wingspan of 230 feet, a distance longer than that covered by the Wright Brothers in the first airplane flight from Kill Devil Hill. It had six Pratt and Whitney R-4360 engines mounted with "pusher" props, and this power was later augmented with the addition of four J-47 jet engines. The B-36 grew from a 200,000-pound-plus gross weight airplane into one of just over 400,000 pounds during its lifetime. It normally carried a crew of 15 men and was capable of delivering a 10,000-pound bomb over a distance of 10,000 miles—without refueling. One B-36 set a record for time aloft without refueling of 51 hours and 21 minutes. The B-36 was a big friendly bear, a forgiving airplane, one in which to feel comfortable and safe.

Of course, the B-36 had developmental problems like all airplanes, and the use of magnesium castings, aluminum wiring, and imperfect electronic devices contributed heavily to the early woes of the airplane. Things got better after these basic problems were solved. Engine fires were quite common on the B-36, but because of the "pusher" props and a good fire extinguishing system, the fires usually did very little damage.

Because of the frequency of engine fires and engine failures, it was a popular joke for crews calling in for landing permission to recite a verse that was much like a canned record: "B-36 number 1074 on long final. Two engines turnin', two burnin', and two at ease."

The B-36 endured and prevailed until the B-52 took over the heavy-duty bombing chores of the Strategic Air Command. Those of us who flew her remember her with love, and it is a nostalgic journey to visit one of the few remaining B-36's that have been preserved in museums.

Peacemakers often die without the recognition afforded herioic warriors and so it is with the B-36. She fired not a shot, dropped weapons only to display her awesome power, and then retired undefeated.

THE DELICATE TOUCH

The B-36 was such a big and forgiving airplane that it was more like a big aluminum teddy bear than a war machine. We could make all kinds of mistakes mechanically and in judgment and the old girl would usually forgive us and deliver us home unscathed. Of course, it was not always this way, as even a teddy bear has its limitations.

During a practice landing at Carswell Air Force Base in Texas, we were lined up on final approach but the airplane was not descending properly nor responding properly to control input commands. About 100 yards from touchdown, the copilot noticed that the flaps were not down and that we were committed to a rather high-speed, no-flap landing rather than the normal full-flap landing. He reached to lower the flaps, and had he been successful it would surely have dumped us into disaster. The observant flight engineer saw the copilot's intended flap-lowering motion and "tapped" him across the knuckles to stop him from moving the flap handle. The landing was then made without incident.

After the flight, it was determined that the copilot's hand was broken and a board of inquiry was formed to investigate the rumor that the flight engineer was responsible for the broken hand. After learning all of the facts of the incident, the board unanimously agreed that it was better to have one broken copilot hand than to have a broken airplane and flight crew. The board exonerated the engineer and recommended him for a commendation for his quick thinking and action.

However, one of the board members posed one final question to the master sergeant flight engineer before the hearing was closed.

"Sergeant, was it really necessary to hit the copilot's hand so hard and with such a big wrench?" he asked.

"Yes, sir," the engineer answered. "You know how hard it is to get an officer's attention."

CHECKLIST PRAYERS

Checklists are an integral part of a pilot's life and are sometimes actually his lifeline. Other times, when they are authored by committees, they are thick enough to use as seat cushions and are rendered almost useless because of their repetitious nature and volume. Whenever we had to use one of these three-and four-volume B-36 checklists, it was required that someone read the item on the list and that the responsible crew member repeat the item and confirm that it was in the correct configuration. These lists were sometimes so long and so unnecessary that the crew members were simply reciting the answers without really checking the equipment. An example of this procedure often went something like this:

Checklist reader: "Intercoolers open."

"The left-hand scanner responded: "Intercoolers 1, 2 and 3 open."

The right-hand scanner responded: "Intercoolers 4, 5, and 6 open."

Checklist reader: "Air plugs open."

The same responses followed as with the intercoolers, and so on through all of the items on the checklist.

During a flight with pilot Neil Slayton, who I think was one of the best in the business and one whom I really grew to love, I was droning off the lengthy items on the expanded checklist and he was rolling back the answers like a poet reciting in a coffee house.

Toward the end of the list, I decided to ad-lib "Ready for landing. Our Father Who art in heaven," I read.

"Ready for landing. Our Father Who art in heaven," Neil answered.

But before I could get the rest of the prayer incorporated into the checklist, Neil realized what was going on and flared the landing so that we hit so hard that my lightly upholstered butt bottomed on the tin bucket seat in which I was sitting and for a moment I really *needed* a prayer.

THE UNDERSTUDY

This is a hard story to tell.

One afternoon in the Officer's Club at Walker Air Force Base in New Mexico, our B-36 crew was enjoying a post-40-mission celebration and behaving as perfect gentlemen of the post Strategic Air Command. A loudmouthed captain, recently returned from B-50 Korean duty, was at the bar explaining to anyone who would listen how he had almost single-handedly won that little war. A German POW tag from World War II dangled from his dog tag chain and several rows of ribbons over his breast pocket verified that he had indeed paid his dues. He was, however, obnoxious, overbearing, loud, and very drunk. We read his name from his nameplate, wrote him off as a drunk dummy, and went on with our recuperation.

A few days later, we were advised that we were to train a new B-36 pilot and later found that our noisy friend from the bar was that new pilot. After the usual "Why us?" routine, we set up a little game to initiate this new guy into our ranks. We interchanged rank, wings, and nameplates before meeting our new pilot so that he would be confused as to who was who. The pilot wore the navigator's wings, the navigator had the pilot's wings, and the aircraft commander and radar operator exchanged their wings. After we were aboard the aircraft, a prearranged argument erupted between "pilots" and "navigators." The new pilot sat in amazement in the massive cockpit of his new airplane toy and paid little attention to the squabbling crew.

"You can't even make a decent takeoff, the "navigator" (pilot) complained to the "pilot" (navigator).

The engineer and the copilot started the engines, explaining the sequence of events to the new pilot as they went along.

"Screw you Nav," the "pilot" (navigator) responded. "You need seeing-eye dog just to find the bloody airplane and then you have the balls to bitch about my flying."

The engineer called that all checks were completed and that he was now waiting for pilot action and ready for taxi.

"Too bad that we don't have a pilot that knows how to taxi," the "navigator" (pilot) called.

"That's enough!" the "pilot" (navigator) answered. "If you think that it's so easy to handle this big bird, you come do it and I'll do your Magellan act as the world's greatest navigator." He paused for a moment, then added: "And have your radar buddy come monitor the takeoff as aircraft commander and we'll just sit on our butts and criticize for awhile. Is that okay with you, commander?" he asked sarcastically.

"Roger," the "aircraft commander" (radar operator) answered. "Sounds fair enough to me."

The new pilot sat frozen in horror as the crew changes were made and as the "navigator" (pilot) guided the airplane to the takeoff position. The "radar operator" (aircraft commander) in the left seat smiled his approval.

The "navigator" (pilot) then made a very sloppy takeoff.

The "pilot" (navigator) downstairs called, "Big deal, you made an acceptable takeoff, but let's see you land this aluminum freight train. Just let me see you do that."

The new pilot came out of his apoplectic trance. He protested, wanted to bail out, tried to call the tower and the military police, grew livid with indignation, and tried to pull rank. All that he got in response were the sounds of giggling and laughter. He refused to accept our explanation that it was all a joke. He demanded that we land and he watched in stark terror while the pilot with the navigator's wings made a reasonably good landing.

He would not taxi into the flight line with us and insisted that he be let out on the taxiway. He ran from there to the flight operations building screaming for the operations officer. When we got to operations, the new guy was demanding an audience with our wing commander, General Butch Blanchard.

"This crew is insane," our outraged new pilot was screaming at the assembled group of listeners. "They're absolutely crazy. They belong to World War I or II or something from a long time ago. They should all be confined under guard at some maximum security asylum. They don't even know who their aircraft commander is, the pilot has radar wings, the engineer tells them when they're ready to taxi, the navigator or somebody flies the damn thing, they don't have any procedures, and they all laugh like madmen. They dress like zoot-suiters and they don't conform to anything. I don't believe that they even belong to the U.S. Air Force. They're spies or saboteurs. They're from some insane movie. They should be executed as traitors. They can't be real. God help us if these guys are really part of Strategic Air Command or any other command. They're crazy and dangerous!"

The operations officer agreed with the aroused captain thoroughly and acknowledged that, indeed, we were all insane. He told the captain that the flight surgeon flew with us regularly to keep his eye on us and that it might take awhile but that he would get used to the peculiar operations of our crew.

"No way!" the captain yelled. "Used to them, hell! I never want to see any of them again! There is a KB-50 outfit down the ramp apiece and I'm asking for an immediate transfer. You guys in this outfit are *all* crazy!"

Finally, General Blanchard came to operations at the insistence of the aroused captain. We had all changed wings again and by the time the general arrived we had the proper wings on the proper person. The captain blurted out his complaint to the general.

"Who made the takeoff?" General Blanchard asked.

The captain pointed to the pilot and General Blanchard assured him that it was normal for the pilot to make the takeoff. After identifying all of the conspirators and really getting confused about who was really who, the captain appealed for a transfer and it was later granted.

We knew that General Blanchard had seen through our little charade and we waited for the worst. Figuring that a good offense might help, we all worked our butts to the bone to be good enough to be selected as the "Strategic Air Command Crew of the Month." Our crew, all in properly arranged uniforms with bright blue ascots tied neatly at our necks, was featured in a full-color portrait on the cover of *Flying Safety* magazine. Along with that honor, we were given certain special privileges—which General Blanchard took away from us in exchange for forgiveness for our little pilot training hoax.

Secretly, I think that the general enjoyed the game as much as we did. Why? Because it's not often that a general interrupts a disciplinary lecture to a crew with bursts of uncontrolled laughter.

CONFIDENCE

During the checkout of new crews for the B-36, one of the tasks to be demonstrated was the emergency lowering of the huge landing gear. To do this, it was necessary to creep into the wheel well, stand on a two-foot triangle of corrugated metal, and to ratchet the lock pin from the up-lock mechanism of the gear. The first thing that happened as the restraining cable wound up on the ratchet drum was that the huge, barn-door-sized landing gear door dropped away, leaving nothing but thousands of feet of space beneath the occupant and his little triangle of security. It was not safe to wear a parachute during this operation because of the possibility of inadvertently spilling the parachute and being sucked out of the wheel well. This had happened once before and the practice of wearing a parachute had been discontinued.

It was during one of these flights that we experienced a real hydraulic failure and the gear had to be lowered in this emergency manner. The entire wheel well was drenched with hydraulic oil and everything was as slippery as a wet elm tree. I was the instructor on this flight and my student was a West Point graduate who had transferred to the Air Force after his graduation. Among his prized possessions was a gold Rolex wristwatch that had been given to him by his parents as a graduation gift. We stood in the wing entrance-way to the wheel well while I explained the emergency operation to him in detail taking particular pains to accentuate the safety factor of having a firm seat on the little platform while he was doing the manual cranking. He was apprehensive at the least and constantly sought reassurance that the operation was practical and safe.

His concern was well founded because it was a big opening after the door opened, the position on the platform was a bit shaky, the ratchet was difficult to operate, and everything in the well was slippery from the spilled oil. Before entering the wheel well, the student again asked if it was really safe to do the operation as I had instructed and I again assured him that it was indeed a "piece of cake." As he turned to leave for the task at hand, I asked that he give me the prized Rolex for safekeeping—just in case. That did it and he refused to do the job. I dropped the gear for him, said nothing to anyone about the incident, and gave him a re-check during a flight when the area in the well was dry and free of hydraulic oil. He did well, his confidence grew, and he became a proficient and respected flight engineer.

A few years later, this same engineer was presented a beautiful world globe and a plaque in recognition of his having flown 5,000 hours in the B-36.

THE RUNAWAY

Following a long test flight on the #2 B-36, designated the YB-36, the airplane turned from the taxi strip to enter the gates of the Convair plant. Halfway into the turn, the left landing gear failed and the long wing dropped to the ground. Splintered parts flew everywhere and the ruptured fuel tanks flooded the area with raw, highly volatile 145-octane fuel. The flight crew did everything right and, after ensuring that all power was off, they abandoned the injured bird in a relatively orderly manner. The fire trucks and the emergency crews took over while the somewhat shaken flight crew was taken to flight operations for a debriefing and a preliminary report of the accident.

After the crew members were assembled, it was discovered that one primary member was missing and none of the others recalled seeing him after the accident. They rushed to the airplane and started a hurried and thorough search but failed to find him. They checked the locker room, the cafeteria, the dispensary, and all of the other places he might have been—no results. The plant security section was alerted, and in a short while one of the security gatekeepers called to report that the truant crewman had run through his gate immediately following the accident. Because the missing crewman lived only a mile or so from the plant and had no telephone, a guard was sent to his home to look for him. There he found the missing man, snug at his kitchen table, nursing his umteenth bottle of beer. He had become so alarmed and upset at the accident that he had run all the way home, leaving his car behind, and telling no one of his departure.

He was allowed a few days off to get over the traumatic effects of the harrowing experience—and of his embarrass-ment.

COOL HAND LUKE

The movies, writers, and some practitioners have romanticized the role of the test pilot to something just a bit short of a man who walks around daily carrying a hand grenade with the pin pulled. From what I have seen of test flying, there is an element of truth in that stereotype, but the moments of high risk and terror are few compared to the less exciting but longer hours of routine testing. Regardless of the danger or the lack thereof, I always admired and almost worshipped the true test pilot, the guy who actually did the nitty-gritty, ball-busting stuff and not the guy who took the credit for doing it. Perhaps I, like the moviemakers, cranked in a bit of romantic adventure that really wasn't there at all. The guys with whom I did some pretty exotic test flying were mostly low-keyed and not very excitable, although there were some notable exceptions. I recall one pilot who used to sweat through a heavy leather flying jacket anytime that he had to do anything more demanding than a takeof or a landing. At the other extreme, the "coolest" of all of those I knew was a handsome, curly-haired Hungarian named George I. Davis.

George had a courageous and colorful career as a World War II combat pilot, but became the victim of some bureaucratic policy-shuffling that ended his promising military career. He then became a Convair test pilot early during the XB-36 program and did an outstanding job just as he did much later on the supersonic B-58 program.

Other test pilots, who normally are not complimentary regarding their contemporaries, said that George was the best "stick and rudder man" in the business. Most of those making this judgment had never actually flown with George and I never understood how they reached this conclusion regarding his ability, but I spent lots of air hours with George in the B-36, B-58, TF-102, and the T-33 and found that he was indeed all that the other pilots had said.

On the day that George was to fly his initial check-ride in a B-36, the Chief Pilot, Gus Green, was his check-pilot and I was a member of the crew. We made the takeoff, climbed out, and leveled off. Gus, very businesslike, turned to George and said, "Okay, George, it's all yours. Let's see what you can do." There was no answer. George was so impressed with this exotic test operation that he had fallen fast asleep.

SUPER SALESMAN

At some time during the dark ages between World War II and the Korean thing, Convair converted a B-36 bomber aircraft into an XC-99 cargo aircraft. The XC-99 was constructed at the San Diego, California, plant but its test program was flown at the Fort Worth, Texas, facility because of the low-density population of the area over which the aircraft was to be flown.

After all of the company tests were completed, the Air Force crew that had been along on several of the test flights was given the aircraft for their evaluation and acceptance flight. The regular flight engineer who had been assigned to the test program suddenly became unavailable and I drew the duty. Being somewhat overeager and anxious to perform well, I filled my briefcase with all kinds of extra fuses, radio crystals, little spare parts, wiring diagrams, blueprints, etc. I still remember all of the names of the Air Force flight crew but I will spare them the torture of remembering by not mentioning their names. The aircraft commander was a lieutenant colonel and the copilot was a major—a great big, big-footed major. Perhaps the actual details and the proper sequence of things that happened during this flight are not perfectly accurate because of the ravages of time upon a relaxed memory, but this telling is close enough for these rambling memoirs.

The first thing that we did wrong was to burn up the auxiliary power unit, which created a significant delay and a few frazzled nerves among the company hierarchy. After a few more minor delays caused by the inexperience of the crew, we finally made a decent and somewhat normal takeoff. During the initial climb-out, we lost the operation of most of the primary flight instruments because of a blown fuse. I went to change the fuse and found that all onboard spare fuses were of a type that was not used in the XC-99 electrical system. Those in my briefcase were of the same type as the spares and were not usable either. A fuse that was used in the electrical system that supplied power to the coffeepot was of the same amperage as the blown fuse and, since we had no plans to make coffee, I pulled that fuse to use as a replacement for the blown flight instrument fuse. But whenever I removed that fuse, the rest of the flight instruments became inoperative, so I hurriedly replaced it. It was inconceivable, but the instruments were *wired through the coffeepot circuit!* After a bit of experimentation, I found a fuse in another circuit that was not used and it worked okay in the flight instrument spot.

We continued the climb and as we passed through 36,000 feet, the turbo cycle on all engines collapsed and we lost the power that was needed for the climb to the 40,000-foot test altitude. With no other option, we started a descent. During the descent, the pilot decided to do a series of sideslips and other maneuvers involving a bit of rudder use. In recovering from one of these exaggerated maneuvers, he put in a bit too much of rudder too suddenly and "popped" the big airplane like a blacksnake whip. The liferaft and its inflation bottle which were mounted in a cubicle on the fuselage flew from their resting places and tore through the big rudder. The windows along the fuselage, of which there must have been hundreds, all broke and we lost cabin pressurization. The great barn-door-sized wheel well doors were banged open by the pulsating stowed landing gear and they fell away from the aircraft leaving a big space and ruptured hydraulic lines dangling like cut human veins that were bleeding profusely. Structural cracks appeared and there throughout the aircraft and cracks in the composure of the humans aboard created a mild chaos.

One of the Air Force crew members took one side of the

aircraft and I took the other to make all kinds of safety checks prior to trying to land the bleeding whale. Each of us had to go out into the hydraulic-soaked open wheel wells, do a bit of manual cranking, and watch in fascination as the big landing gear dropped and locked into place. This done, we inspected the nose landing gear through a tiny access window and assured ourselves and the world at large that the landing gear was down and locked into place. With the gear thus locked, a bright green light on the pilot's panel should have glowed brilliantly to indicate this safe condition, but, instead, we had a bright red light illuminated to tell us that the gear was *not* safe. The normal cycle of the landing gear operation was for the big main gear doors to open, the gear to drop into place, and the doors to then close around the extended gear. Only after all of this happened did the green "safe light" illuminate, so we reasoned that because we no longer had the big doors (they had blown off earlier), the up-lock switch for the doors was not "made" and, hence, the red "unsafe" light. We had visually inspected all of the gear locks, assured that they were safely locked, and determined that the gear was safe for an attempt at landing. So we made a normal approach to Carswell Air Force Base, which at that time had a privately owned cemetery at the far end of the south runway. All was normal and serene during the approach—but not for long!

We touched down gently on the main wheels, rocked over easy on the nosewheel and then: "*No brakes,* the aircraft commander shouted. "Reverse pitch! Reverse pitch!" he yelled at the flight engineer.

The reverse pitch, used to brake the aircraft, had its selector switches high above the engineer's head and he delayed a bit in actuating the switches. When we finally stopped, we were off the runway, in the mud, and looking the little cemetery in the face.

During the post-flight debriefing, one of the company executives produced a bottle of good Scotch whiskey and, although it was against policy, we all had a post-mission, calm-the-nerves drink. Then we learned that the reason that we didn't have brakes was that the circuitry to the brake system was wired through the landing gear *green safety light* and since we had a *red light* on landing, we had no power to the brakes! Such an arrangement was contrary to all engineering and safety practices, but it had happened.

The lieutenant colonel accepted the aircraft for the Air Force with the provision that all damage would be repaired, the discrepancies in the wiring corrected, and that the aircraft performed properly during its delivery flight. Privately, I always felt that the only reason that the colonel accepted it was so that he wouldn't have to fly it again.

The XC-99 went on to be the first aircraft ever to lift a payload of 100,000 pounds and she set some fantastic cargo-carrying records. She now sits as a permanent monument at Kelly Field, Texas, mute testimony to man's triumph over fear, mistakes, and foibles.

HOLLYWOOD HOOLIGAN AND COLONEL FROG

While the B-36 was the mainstay of the Strategic Air Command, we used to take loads of various types of people, including air traffic controllers, for orientation rides. Sometimes we would have 15 or 20 of these guys aboard and we stayed in constant communication with the gods who govern flying begging that we wouldn't have some sort of emergency while all of these untrained people were aboard. Naturally the inevitable happened and one time a B-36 with 18 of these folks aboard broke a vital piece of its landing gear during the takeoff. The broken piece was designed so that the fore and aft wheels of the main gear would be sequenced during touchdown, allowing the front to touch first and then, after that contact, the rear wheels would complete the contact with the runway. The mechanical connection between the front and aft wheels was called a "walking beam" and it was this part that had broken during takeoff. With this beam broken, it was possible for the wheels to fold upward when they touched and for the vertical landing gear strut to dig into the runway. Should this happen, the aircraft would probably pivot about the dragging strut and do some kind of fancy ground loop. During such an action, the fuel tanks could rupture and a disastrous fire could be started. It was with this possibility in mind that the aircraft commander, a man we'll call Hooligan, radioed an emergency to the tower. As punishment for some past and unidentified sin, I was the officer of the day as this airborne drama unraveled. The day was dark with a light misty rain.

The aircraft commander, who had done a bit part in a movie about the B-36, had picked up the nickname of "Hollywood" and he usually managed to live up to the name, "Hollywood Hooligan." Hollywood called the base and, after a long consultation with senior officers, decided that the basic crew would stay with the aircraft and that all others would bailout. The bailout was safely accomplished and troops were scattered all over the rain-swept plains of west Texas. The B-36 was then flown low over the Carswell Air Force Base tower so that a group of assembled expert observers could get a look at the damaged gear. The commanding officer of the wing to which the aircraft belonged was secretly called "The Frog" because of his deep and guttural voice, and with this deep voice called the commander of the stricken aircraft.

"This is Colonel Propername and I believe that you are in a pretty tight spot, Hollywood. Is there anything that I can do to help your situation?" he asked.

"Roger, Colonel Frog, er uh, uh, Colonel Propername, this is Hooligan, and the only thing that I can think of that you could do to help is to change places with me," came the curt reply.

The landing was made safely, the scattered troops were gathered up, and after the official debriefing, Colonel Frog and Hollywood Hooligan had a private briefing all to themselves.

BOMBS AWRY

One of the requirements of the B-36 flight test program was to haul aloft and then accurately drop a monstrous 43,000-pound concrete bomb. This was to demonstrate the aircraft's capability to carry such a weapon and the accuracy of the current "state of the art" radar system. The proposed target was a surplus navy vessel of some sort (battleship, destroyer, or whatever, I never learned the differences) anchored in the gulf off of Eglin Air Force Base in Florida. The ship was to be used as an offset target—that is, the ship was the primary aiming point but the bomb was to be "offset," a correction that could be cranked into the system so that other aiming points could be used whenever the primary target could not be seen or the bombing aircraft didn't want to sight on the primary. Using this method, the accuracy of the system could be determined without destroying the target ship.

The bombardier for this mission was Air Force Major Morris, a man we called "Bulldog" because of his vague resemblance to a noted boxer nicknamed "The Toy Bulldog." With the B-36 bombing platform at 45,000 feet, the major called the ground controllers and asked where they wanted the bomb delivered. Someone, in the jesting manner that sometimes was commonplace during such tests said, "Down the smokestack, sir." That then is exactly where this huge chunk of aerodynamically sculpted piece of concrete went—right down the smokestack! The target ship sunk, a near tidal wave was created, skippers of lesser boats were nearly capsized, and the mission was completed.

The moral of that day was never to challenge an excellent bombardier, especially if he looks like a toy bulldog.

WELCOME TO ENGLAND

For a simulated combat mission, we deployed a flight of the huge B-36 aircraft to England. At this time, somewhere in 1952, the aircraft was still not perfect and the British landing and navigational aids were not the best. This unhappy combination created situations both tragic and humorous. Fortunately, the fun outweighed the sadness.

During the final landing approach of one of the B-36's to the Boscombe Downs aerodrome, there was some breakdown in communication between the aircraft commander and the British ground controller. The entire countryside was covered with a hoary frost, making it difficult to distinguish one kind of terrain from another. This particular aircraft commander, thinking that he had the landing field in sight, advised that he had the "field in sight" and would make the landing visually. He had, however, made one tiny mistake in his recognition of the airport and landed in a cultivated farm field, a bit short of the runway. The hard, frozen British turf received the aircraft gracefully and, other than some superficial damage caused by running through some barbed wire fencing, the aircraft rolled to a stop undamaged.

The cockpit of the aircraft was about 20 feet above ground level and the aircraft commander opened the side window and looked at the frozen ground beneath him in absolute disgust. An English farmer strolled by about that time, looked up at the distraught pilot, and tried to console him a bit.

"I say, Governor, there is a much more proper airfield about a mile up the road, straight ahead and you can't miss it," he advised.

Before the aircraft commander could react, the farmer escaped.

Now, who says the British don't have a sense of humor?

ANOTHER WELCOME TO ENGLAND

When we arrived in England to begin the first B-36 deployment exercise, the weather was awful—thick fog below, heavy clouds in the sky, and the ground covered by heavy frost and snow. Boscombe Downs was our destination and they had an early model radar (Ground Controlled Approach) to help us with the landings. The radar approach system was a bit new at the time and the operators were equally as new and inexperienced, so we had a few problems in getting safely on the ground. One aircraft commander, after several bad instructions from the ground, decided that the landing effort was not worth the risk and that he was too low on fuel to spend any more time at the landing attempt, so he aimed the aircraft out to sea and had his entire crew bail out.

One of the crew members, the flight engineer, had screwed up his parachute during an en-route stop at Goose Bay and had it replaced with a British type chute equipped with "quick-release" hardware—a device on the harness of the chute by which the wearer could release himself from the harness by turning and pushing a big button on the front of the chute. At the time of the bail-out, this guy failed to do any of the required things such as take along survival equipment and any records that might later be helpful in justifying the abandonment of the aircraft; he just jumped out into the blue. He landed in a tree, suspended upside down but without any serious injury. Not being familiar with the new parachute, he kept fiddling with buttons and straps until he hit the right button and was unceremoniously released. He hit the ground below and broke his shoulder plus a couple of ribs.

The loss of such an expensive aircraft required quite an investigation, and because the wounded engineer had no records of the amount of fuel remaining and other pertinent data, he was hassled and reprimanded by the members of the investigating team. After several hours of this harrassment the engineer made his required statement: "At the time I heard the bail-out alarm bell ring, I was thinking only of the safety and welfare of myself and the other crew members and had no thoughts of any damned aircraft performance records."

The board, unimpressed by the statement, then assigned the engineer the task of reconstructing the complete mission from memory and of creating appropriate records to confirm the report. This involved many, many hours of work and burning the midnight oil, as well as lots of paper.

The engineer was in England working on this report so long that he easily qualified for British citizenship, and perhaps he would have been better off if he had seized upon that opportunity. The B-36 which he showed in his report to be "nearly out of fuel" at the time of bail-out flew for just eight more hours before finally crashing into the sea.

DEPTH PERCEPTION

B-36 flight crews got a lot of verbal flak from fighter pilots and we were the butt of a lot of jokes. Some of those old stories have survived and are often retold on present flight crews, changing only the type of airplane and the names of the crew members. One that I sorely remember was told by an RCAF (Royal Canadian Air Force) crew at their Officer's Club near Goose Bay, Labrador.

They told of a B-36 crew that was making a practice no-flaps landing at a base that had a 15,000-foot-long runway. As they approached the field, the pilot remarked that the field sure looked short to him and that they should use partial flaps. The copilot complied and lowered the flaps a few degrees. A moment later, the pilot asked for more flaps and finally yelled for full flaps before they approached the threshold of the landing. As the aircraft touched down, the pilot applied full brakes, reversed the props at max power, and finally stopped the aircraft on the runway.

"My God but that's a short, short runway," he panted to

the copilot.

The copilot looked out of the side window at the great expanse of concrete runway to his left and right and at the short piece of strip behind them.

"Yeah," he agreed, " it is short, but take a look—it's the *widest* one I've ever seen."

SURVIVAL SHOES

As B-36 Strategic Air Command select crews, we had to be groomed to the teeth at all times in the latest dictates of SAC and General LeMay. This grooming extended to our flight clothing and that too had to be according to regulation and impeccable at all times. Prior to each flight, the aircraft commander inspected all crew members with a ferocity normally seen only at the military academies. Most of the crew members took a great deal of pride in their appearance and did their best to always meet the approved standards; some often went a bit overboard in their eagerness.

One of the officers in our crew had been on an assignment in Brazil and while there had a magnificent pair of glove-soft leather flying boots custom-made. He had these boots polished to a mirror finish and he passed inspections with no problems until one day when our wing commander, General "Butch" Blanchard made a spot inspection. We were doing great with the inspection until the general spotted the flashy Brazilian boots.

"What the hell are those supposed to be?" he demanded.

"Custom-made flight boots, sir," the crewman answered proudly.

"Are they regulation issue?" the boss asked sarcastically.

"No, sir," and the confidence evaporated.

"You are aware that the issue boots are designed for maximum retention during bail-out and for rough use if you are involved in a survival situation?" the boss asked.

"Yes, sir," the crewman answered as he tucked his chin in a bit tighter.

"Those damned fancy thin dancing shoes you are wearing

would only allow you to walk in a survival situation if you landed on a well-tended golf course. You delay this flight until you have changed into proper flight footwear," the general ordered.

The commander turned away and then glanced back at the offending officer who was still standing at rigid attention and added an additional opinion. "Yes, lieutenant, only on a golf course could you survive in those shoes—and then it would have to be on a par 3 hole."

OF FIRES AND PEANUT BUTTER

The relatively untested R-4360 engines on the B-36 air-craft and a notoriously weak exhaust system caused a lot of in-flight fires. It was not at all unusual for an after-takeoff scanner report to read something like, "Fire on number 2, fire on number 3, and number 1 and number 6 are smoking so heavily that we can't tell whether they are on fire or not!"

Our chief pilot decided that the very word "fire" put fear in our souls and terror in our hearts and caused us to react excitedly. It was his philosophy that if another word were substituted that we would not tend to be so alarmed, so we were directed to use only the word "flame" In using "flame," it was to be reported in degrees of severity, such as "light flame," "moderate flame," and so on. One scanner used his own rating system and at the top of the scale he substituted "God-awful flame" for a severe fire. His rating system was not approved by the chief pilot.

Several of us argued that the semantics made no difference in our reactions since we knew what the condition was regardless of the words used to describe it. For emphasis, we insisted that a fire could be reported in any terms chosen, a ridiculous example being "peanut butter on number 4," and that we would damn well know that an engine was on fire and would react the same as if the report had been "fire." Our objections were overruled and a departmental memo was issued directing the use of the word "flame" in its various degrees.

The chief pilot liked to ride in the various crew positions every now and then so that he could better evaluate crew requirements and performance. During his first flight after the "flame" order, he elected to ride in the rear scanner position. At the critical time of takeoff on this particular flight, the number 4 engine exploded in a shower of sparks and started to burn with a serious intent to do harm to aircraft and crew.

"Fire on number 4!" the chief reported.

"You mean that we have *flame* on number 4, don't you, sir?" the pilot-in-command answered.

"No! I mean *fire!* The damned thing is on *fire!*" the chief called.

The fire was extinguished, the flight was completed, and the "flame" order was rescinded immediately after the landing.

THE CANNIBAL

Survival School was always one of the "fun" parts of being in the flying business with the Strategic Air Command. This school was designed to teach and then to test the student's ability to survive in all types of terrain or at sea with little or no provisions. For some students, the school was fun and they enjoyed the challenging games; for others, it was pure hell.

We had a boy from Boston in our crew who hated and feared all of the survival courses. Whenever a school or exercise was planned, he wouldn't sleep for worrying about the horrors of the exercise ahead. He bitched and complained before, during, and after all such schools or exercises.

"On one such exercise, after we had been wandering in the wilds of Nevada for 14 days and surviving from what we could scrounge from the land, we were picked up and taken to Reno. We had completed the test and, after getting cleaned up, we headed for a night of good food and fun.

During dinner and while bending an elbow at the bar, our

Boston boy complained to anyone who would listen to him. He raved about the hardships, the lack of food, the insects, the cold ground, the stupid crew, the ridiculousness of the whole exercise, and about why God was punishing him with such a pestilence as Survival School. One of his listeners was from another SAC crew who had also just returned from the bush and he would frequently interrupt the Boston boy to tell him that he had such a rough time because he didn't have a good aircraft commander.

"I don't know what that has to do with it," our boy argued. "It was just plain cold and miserable and there was no food."

"You just didn't have a good aircraft commander," the listener countered.

"What the hell did you do—*eat* your aircraft commander?" the Boston boy demanded.

We broke up the fight before the military police arrived.

THE GRADUATE

While conducting a training flight for a new Texas A & M graduate who had also just completed Aerial Performance Engineer's School, we were demonstrating the fantastic capabilities of the B-36 bomber. The aircraft at that time had only the six reciprocating engines, and when the load was light and conditions right, it could fly with only one of those six engines operating. This unusual performance always impressed new crew members and gave them confidence in the B-36.

"Feather engines number 1 and 6 and I'll trim to demonstrate four-engine flight," the instructor ordered.

I shut down 1 and 6 and feathered the props.

"Now shut down 2 and 5," he instructed and I complied. We were now flying on only two engines, the inboards, number 3 and 4.

"Shut down 3 and we'll demonstrate single-engine performance," the instructor drawled.

"Wait just a damned minute!" the new student called

out. "Do you want to do that before or after?"

"What do you mean, before or after?" the instructor growled.

"Before or after I bail out of this airplane," answered the shaken engineer-student, "because I'm not staying in here while you clowns go down to a single engine. I know the performance figures on this airplane and I *know* that it will not fly on a single engine."

He was so serious that we cancelled the planned demonstration. We didn't know that the B-36 wouldn't fly on a single engine because we had been doing it for such a long time.

ONE OF OUR PROPS IS MISSING. . .

The B-36 was a monstrous aircraft, its gross weight nearing 400,000 pounds, powered by six reciprocating engines and four auxiliary power plants. Under normal circumstances, the B-36 flew quite well with only the reciprocating engines; the jets were used for high-gross-weight takeoffs and for speed runs over the targets. The airplane could be flown and landed successfully with only three of its engines operating, so the loss of a single engine usually wasn't much of a cause for alarm.

On takeoff from Roswell, New Mexico, we had "lost" an engine on takeoff but elected to continue on to our destination where we planned to have the malfunctioning engine repaired or replaced. Our decision to continue was heavily influenced by the fact that a movie, *Shane*, was playing at a theater where we were destined to land and we were all eager to see it. We arrived at our destination, Fort Worth, Texas, okay, left the airplane for the maintenance troops, and took off to see the movie and to spend the night at government expense at a nice hotel.

The next day, we learned that the malfunctioning engine could not be repaired on the aircraft and that it would have to be replaced. Unfortunately, there was no replacement engine available. We then off-loaded some fuel to lighten the weight, had the propeller from the sick engine removed, disassembled, and put in a long wooden crate. The crated prop was stored in the bomb bay of the aircraft and with this nifty little arrangement we made a five-engine plus jets takeoff and headed home for Roswell.

En route to home base, we called our tower and informed them that we had only five operating engines and that the sixth engine was missing its propeller.

"Where is your propeller?" the tower guy asked.

"In the bomb bay," we answered, knowing full well that the guy in the tower would assume that the propeller had come off in flight and sliced its way into the bomb bay. We were right in the assumption because the tower operator did indeed interpret it this way and he alerted all of the emergency equipment on the entire base, the base commander, the mayor of the town, and anyone else who would listen to him.

As we neared touchdown, I counted 17 pieces of fire and rescue equipment, ambulances of all colors, dozens of staff cars with flashing red lights, and the emblazoned vehicle of the base commander, all standing by for our "emergency" landing.

We landed gracefully, rolled to a rather undramatic stop, and disappointed all of the emergency crews so much that they gathered their toys and went home in pouting disgust. General Blanchard sensed that we had subtly arranged for the misunderstanding and that we were enjoying our little bit of aerial nonsense. He didn't say much to any of us, but there was a rather wicked look in his eye when he left the scene, a look promising of things to come.

The next morning at crew briefing, we learned that General Blanchard did indeed have a sense of humor himself. He assigned our crew to a couple of months of duty as the "test" crew for the newly activated base at remote Thule, Greenland. Among the delights of our assignment at Thule was that we got to spend Christmas in that delightful vacation spot, and we heard by the grapevine that General Blanchard drank a toast to our health and happiness on that memorable day.

OUR FIRST FORMAL

As Air Force officers in the Strategic Air Command under the command of General Curtis LeMay, we were required to dress and act like real textbook military officers. Our wardrobes had to be complete, including very formal dress uniforms. We had to wear the big black bow ties with our formal dress uniforms and it was required that we never be out of proper uniform in any respect. Our only salvation was that there was a regulation that allowed us to dress for sporting events in the proper uniform for that sport. I guess that it was okay to bathe and to sleep in the nude since I never found a LeMay order dictating otherwise.

The requirements for our dress were spelled out in the normal Air Force regulations, the edicts of the general, and periodic special bulletins. Now and then we were required to show that we had all of the uniforms in our possession and we were subjected to frequent personal inspections. The *Air Force Times* newspaper printed a story of the special requirements for SAC personnel (us) and for some reason made a special emphasis of the black-tie formal bit.

Several days after the publication of the story in the *Times,* we were tooling along at a moderate altitude in our luxury B-36 when the radio blared, "This is F-86 number 5434, in trail on your left wing. Request clearance to pull in together and to fly a bit of close-formation escort."

"Rog, glad to have you," our aircraft commander answered. "Join up at your pleasure."

The F-86 did a rain dance all around us and the pilot waved at our crew members as they stared out of the windows of the B-36. After a few minutes of fooling around, he pulled away and our aircraft commander asked why he had cut his escort flight so short.

"Oh, I was just checking to see if you bomber weenies were really wearing black bow ties," he answered as he did a couple of rolls in front of us.

He was out of sight before we could a get a gun charged and get a single shot at him.

RANK HAS ITS PRIVILEGES (RHIP)

After returning from a 40-hour mission in a B-36, we were a mess. We were tired, three of our six engines were inoperative, a fourth engine was showing signs of terminal illness, and we were down to a minimum supply of fuel. Our home base of Roswell, New Mexico, advised that the runway there was covered with blowing snow and that the base was closed to all traffic. They further advised that because of continuing deteriorating weather the base would probably be closed for at least 24 more hours. Regardless of our request for an emergency landing because of our sick and malfunctioning airplane, we were directed to go to Biggs Field in El Paso, Texas, for the landing. We then advised the tower that we probably couldn't make it to El Paso and asked them to please dispatch some trucks along the way as we would probably be bailing out en route. As it developed, we made El Paso okay, landed without incident, and beat a hasty path to the Officer's Club for food and drink. There, we were met by the chief pilot of Convair Aircraft Company, the manufacturer of the B-36, who informed us that our landing was the worst that he had ever seen, our aircraft was the most decripit that he had ever seen, and that as a crew we all looked like escapees from a prisoner-of-war camp. We thanked him for the nice compliments and went about the planning for a night in Juarez, Mexico, just across the border from El Paso.

The only clothing we had was our dirty, ragged flying suits, and only one among us had any money. I called an old friend from cadet days and he brought us enough money for each of us to buy a checkered shirt, a pair of blue jeans, and a pair of moccasins. Next, I contacted an old boxing friend in Juarez and he hosted us to an evening of food and drink at his Juarez restaurant. Fulfilled, we returned to the base and called it a complete day.

We learned the next day that the troops at Biggs did not have the capability to fix our airplane but that they had found and repaired the trouble on one of the malfunctioning engines. That gave us four reasonably good reciprocating engines, and with the aid of the four auxiliary wing jets, a light load of fuel, and a boost from God we could make a safe takeoff. Strategic Air Command headquarters in Omaha, Nebraska, got into the act and agreed that we could make a takeoff in that weakened condition *only* if one of the *colonel*-type instructor pilots from their headquarters flew as aircraft commander for the takeoff. Our highest rank was captain, so we had no choice but to agree. What the hell—one more guy, colonel or not, wouldn't make any difference, and our egoes weren't big enough to be offended by having a senior instructor aboard.

Later that evening, the designated colonel arrived, showed little or no interest in our problem, and invited us to Juarez for dinner. After a great dinner, the colonel advised us that all of the border strip shows were for "orphans, old women, homosexuals, and blue-nosed politicians" and that he would take us to a place where there was a "real" show. The "place" was a notorious house of ill repute way out of town where one could wrestle with a greased nude girl, watch the antics of others through one-way mirrors, or indulge in any fantasies one might harbor. Here, the colonel found a delightful little companion and he settled in like a homesteader. There was a military curfew in Juarez at that time and we literally had to drag the colonel out of the place in order to beat the curfew.

Back in El Paso, we all went to bed and asked for an early crew call so that we could make a cool morning takeoff to assist us over the hills around El Paso. Everyone answered the call except the colonel, and when we checked his room it was empty and his bed undisturbed. I was elected to go to Juarez to look for him and there I found him, back at the brothel, comfortable in the arms of Morpheus and of his Mexican maid. With him in disgruntled humor and dragging along behind me, we returned to the base. By now it was mid-morning, the runway temperature was up, and it was too hot to try our less than ideal takeoff, so we cancelled and rescheduled for the following morning.

I asked to be called an hour earlier than the rest of the crew so that I would have time to go after the colonel if he had again flown the coop—and he had. Once more to Juarez, once more to be physically inspected before I was allowed in the working quarters of the whorehouse, and once more to drag the smelly, hung-over colonel back to the base. This time we got the colonel aboard and prepared for the takeoff.

Our strategy was to plan for a three-engine and jet takeoff just in case the one suspicious engine decided to quit, and it did exactly that shortly after we had become airborne. The colonel, completely unaware of what was going on, was firmly secured to a crew bunk and was fast asleep. Without his profound advice and help, we still made the takeoff safely and he didn't awaken until we were on final approach for the landing at Roswell.

General Blanchard was there to witness our landing and to congratulate us on our performance under unusual circumstances. He shook hands with the colonel, apologized for having made him fly with a renegade crew such as ours, and assured him that without his help we would never have made it. We all shook our heads in agreement, looked for a flicker of a smile on the colonel's lips, but his expression was simply that of a very self-pleased and deserving officer.

As they say, "Rank has its privileges."

CAPTAIN BASINGER AND B-36 NUMBER 1074

One of the best crew assignments that I ever had was on B-36 number 1074 with Captain I. C. Basinger as aircraft commander. As a crew, we knew our jobs well and had a good time doing those things assigned to us. We enjoyed flying and could do our jobs with ease, so we often gave the impression to others that we were too casual. We were an excellent and a compatible crew but we suffered from a subtle sense of humor that sometimes only we understood. We were so involved as a crew that we even enjoyed going through the rigors of Survival School together. The flight engineer on this crew was Captain Nelson Ensor, a friend with whom I had attended elementary school in a small town in Maryland many years before. We were a crew the members of which were predominantly from the south of the United States, and yet we gracefully accepted those who had not been afforded that privilege.

After one rather elegant-type flight surgeon had flown with us, it was his opinion that we were not real, that all crews like us had been killed during World War II, that we were juveniles who had been sent to war too soon, and that we were ghosts from the past who should all be put out to pasture on a funny farm. It's true we were not the ordinary, but we were tolerated because we always put our bombs right on target and right on time. After his first flight with us, this flight surgeon always flew his mandatory missions with us, claiming that we were so unreal that he needed to periodically confirm that we actually existed.

When the Korean war ended, I had the option of staying on active duty or returning to the active reserve forces and civilian life. I was really torn between these choices because I loved that crew position and that crew, but I had been promised a crew position on the futuristic B-58 test program if I returned to my civilian job. I chose the latter, and for the first few weeks as a civilian, I shed many tears over that choice.

It was September when I separated from the Air Force and it was only a few months later that I found myself assigned to a C-54 modification program in Fort Worth, Texas. I had gone to work very early one morning with a strange feeling of dread and impending disaster although I could identify no reason for such feelings. While taking a coffee break, a friend in upper management took me aside to tell me that there had been a B-36 crash and that it was believed to be Captain Basinger and his crew. The Air Force had called the company and requested that I go to the crash site near Sterling City, Texas, to help with the crew identification. It *was* Captain Basinger and his crew and, except for the man who had replaced me and the one who had replaced

Captain Don Tuttle (who had gone to fighters), the crew members were the same ones with whom I had flown for almost 1,000 hours.

While my wife went to the home base in Roswell to be with some of the newly widowed wives, I spent three days at the crash site aiding in the retrieval and identification of the remains of the crew. We gathered many of the charred bones in small cardboard boxes that were normally used for flight lunches. The smell of death from burning was no stranger to me, but the combined loss of friends, the pitiful remains in the boxes, and the prevailing odor of burned flesh conspired to keep me sick for several days. After the retrieval was completed, I was ruled out of being any part of the accident investigation group because I was "too deeply involved emotionally."

The facts of the accident appeared to be that the crew had encountered a squall line with severe winds and that the aircraft was battered about until it was no longer flyable. It had apparently gone into a flat spin in a manner which prevented the crew from attempting to escape by parachute. The airacraft had impacted flat and, while that part of the aircraft forward of the trailing edge of the wing was totally consumed by fire, the papers in the aft section of the fuselage were not even scorched. The wing jets were found a mile or so away from the main wreckage and it was assumed that they had been torn away in the destructive turbulence. All aboard were killed, and I died a little bit with each one of them.

None of the foregoing is really strange nor is it unusual, but while this aircraft was entering the area of deep trouble another airborne B-36 had successfully skirted the killer weather. The flight engineer of this other aircraft had a vision of Captain Basinger as he fought to keep his battered aircraft flying. He had a vision of the ill-fated aircraft as it was torn apart, as it went into the fatal spin, and of its fiery impact with the ground. He sobbed and screamed his story to the rest of his crew while they, believing that he was suffering some kind of nervous breakdown, consoled and comforted him until they made a "medical emergency" landing back at home base. There, the medics determined that the flight engineer had suffered a mild heart attack while experiencing a vision of something that was happening many miles away. Captain Basinger had made no radio calls before or while he was in trouble, and there had been no radio announcements of his accident—but this engineer had described it all perfectly. Other than the fact that the engineer had a heart attack, there was no explanation of his strange recitation and knowledge of the accident. What happened to this flight engineer after that day I don't know, but I certainly sympathize with him and vicariously share his nightmare of tragedy. I had the same "gut" feeling before knowing anything about the accident, but mine was only on the same channel as his and not as finely tuned as was his.

I will always feel some kind of guilt for not having been with "my crew" on that day and will always wonder if I could have done something to prevent the accident had I been along on the mission. I can still hear Captain Basinger calling, in his heavy North Carolina drawl, "Nav, you ready for takeoff?"

"Yes, sir," I'd reply, in a slightly less Carolina drawl. "Nav is ready!"

And I still am.

WHOOPS!

Once upon a time we had a B-36 program with the code name of FICON. This bit of new idea consisted of having an F-84 fighter aircraft hook up to a trapeze that was extended from the bomb bay of a "mother" B-36 and then be drawn into the belly of the big bird. Once there, the pilot of the F-84 could get out of his aircraft, snooze on the bunks in the B-36 while on the way to the target area, and his aircraft could be refueled from the internal tanks of the B-36. Just before entering the combat zone, the F-84, with refreshed pilot in place and a full load of fuel, would be released and then provide fighter coverage while the bomber was on the bomb run. After the mission was completed, the F-84 would again be hauled into the B-36 for the trip back home. It was a magnificent idea.

As with many good ideas, of course, the doing was not as easy as the thought. There was the matter of powering the trapeze, setting up the refueling system inside the aircraft, getting everyone in the right position at the right time, making the dry run hookups, and finally the actual hookup and retraction of the F-84 inside the bomb bay of the B-36. Everything had to work like a finely tuned precision instrument and all of the people involved in the test had to be experts at their tasks.

After all of the problems were worked out, the big day came when the F-84 made a real hook up, the trapeze drew it up inside the B-36, and the rest of the act was performed flawlessly, exactly as advertised. The extension and release of the F-84 went equally as well and the whole thing was thoroughly documented by tons of aerial photographs taken from a flight of chase and photo aircraft. Triumphantly, the successful air armada headed home. The F-84, the star of the show, was the first to land. He continued his starring role to the bitter end as he skidded among a shower of sparks on his belly. After all of his precision work, he had forgotten one of the most simple of his tasks—*to lower his landing gear !*

One more score for Bobby Burns and his plans of mice and men.

INFRACTIONS AND FRACTURES

The B-36 aircraft had a wingspan of 230 feet and the interior of the wing was high enough that a man could walk through the root of it and crawl through to the outboard engines. This created a lot of unused space and every now and then it was used as storage space—which was totally against regulations or handbook instructions, of course. The flooring of the interior of the wings was made of a waffled magnesium bonded to the exterior skin of the wing for strength and for the conservation of weight. This arrangement worked fine while the aircraft were operated in the United States, but each time that they were deployed to far away places with strange-sounding names, the waffles were found to be cracked and the bonds separated. This posed a serious structural problem, so a massive engineering investigation was launched to determine the cause of the structural failures. The investigation revealed nothing; the design was good, the materials were okay, the bonds were secure and properly made, and the vibration during flight was well within the design limits. Repairs to the damaged airacraft were made but the phenomenon continued to plague the engineers and maintenance people.

After one of the overseas deployments, an engineer was shocked to see case after case of booze, motorcycles, hibachi pots, and furniture being unloaded from the aircraft. He watched each aircraft as it was unloaded and found all of the aircraft were similarly loaded. A little investigation then revealed that all of this extra equipment that had been gathered along the way had been carried in the wings. During flight, this heavy load bounced around a bit, put an unusual load on the flooring, and it failed. A simple matter of cause and effect.

The official report on one particular aircraft read: ''32 cases of Scotch bounced on the flooring for 31 hours, leading to material failure.'' The Scotch was impounded, the floors of the aircraft were repaired, and the practice was summarily stopped.

The commanders were horrified at what they had seen and we were all disciplined. It was a good thing that they didn't see the MG automobile that I unloaded from my particular aircraft or they might have really been upset.

"ME AND LINDY"

A young B-36 flight engineer had a rather brash aura about him which he further aggravated by continually telling stories of his wartime duty on the B-29 range program with Colonel Charles Lindberg. We all accepted the guy's claim and his bragging with a grain of salt and only got mildly agitated with his constant "That ain't the way me and Lindy did it."

It then came to pass that Colonel Lindberg was going to visit the Convair plant to make an evaluation flight in the B-36 and we all silently thought that the day of reckoning had arrived for the braggart engineer. When Colonel Lindberg was driven to the flight operations office, most of the company and resident military dignitaries were lined up in the proper pecking order to welcome him. The "me and Lindy" engineer was lounging against a nearby fireplug when Colonel Lindberg got out of the car and started the obligatory handshaking routine. As he scanned the group gathered there, he suddenly saw our braggart and broke off all other greetings to rush to him and embrace him as an old friend. After a bit of the "old-home" routine, the reunion ended and Colonel Lindberg turned his attention to the task at hand. We were all really impressed and now more than ready to accept the "me and Lindy" routine.

After this meeting with Colonel Lindberg, the flight engineer never again mentioned him. He had made his point.

LATE ARRIVAL

We had terminated our training mission and had arrived over home base at 40,000 feet to fulfill a training requirement. After calling traffic control for descent and landing instructions, we were told that there was a lot of heavy traffic and that we had to hold. A few minutes later, the controller called and advised that he had a break in traffic and could get us down.

"Can you get down to 2,500 feet in a minute?" he asked.

"Roger, sure can," answered our aircraft commander.

"Good. You are cleared for an immediate descent to 2,500 and to hold there," were the next instructions.

"Rog, I understand," the aircraft commander replied. Then he added, teasingly, "Like I said, I can get to 2,500 in a minute, but it will take a bit longer for the aircraft to get there. Is that okay?''

Negative! Control understands your message. Stand by and hold,'' the embarrassed controller answered.

''And hold we did, until were almost out of fuel and nearly starved.

Controllers never were noted for their sense of humor.

AIRBORNE SEMANTICS

The faithful old B-36 with its pusher props and many engines survived lots of in-flight fires that a tractor (puller)-prop-equipped aircraft would have found fatal. In addition to the frequent fires, we also experienced an unusual number of internally failed engines in flight. In aviation jargon, when an engine had failed and had to be shut down, it was said to be ''lost''—for example, ''We just lost number 4.'' The incidence of these failures became something of a joke among crew members and the wags around the airbase said that a standard call for landing was ''B-36 number so-and-so on final—two turning, two burning, and two at ease.'' This translated into ''two engines operating, two on fire, and two with the engine shut down and the props feathered.'' It really wasn't quite that bad but it made a good story and excellent conversations at the club.

With a philosophy such as this, it wasn't thought to be unusual when one Captain Green from Carswell Air Force Base called in to report that, ''We have lost number 3 engine and request an immediate emergency landing.''

''Feather it and come on home,'' a rather blase tower operator called.

''Can't. We have *lost* it!''

''Big deal,'' came the reply, ''guys lose engines every day. What do you want us to do, have a ceremonial parade or something?''

''No,'' Green answered, ''just get the emergency equipment standing by, give me immediate landing clearance, and send some guys up around Denton, Texas, to look for our number 3 engine. It caught on fire, burned through the mounts, fell off and, like I said, we *lost* it."

With engine number 3 lost, it meant that numbers 1 and 2 would not be able to get fuel because the common fuel manifold had to be closed to keep all of the fuel from escaping through the ruptured number 3 line. Captain Green had a B-36 with only three of its six engines operating and all of those on one side of the aircraft. Like the skilled pro that he was, he landed the aircraft without incident or damage.

For a while after that, we didn't use the term "lost" for a failed engine, but after the excitement died down we all fell back into the same old semantic pattern and kept the tower operators a wee bit nervous.

THAR SHE BLOWS!

The gigantic B-36 aircraft had an excellent pressurization system that provided the proper environment for the forward and aft crew compartments. A 90-foot tunnel connected the two compartments and it too was fully pressurized. Whenever a glass or structural failure occurred at high altitude with the aircraft pressurized, the loss of the interior high-pressure air created a real blow as it exhausted through the failed portion of the aircraft. Whenever these failures, called rapid decompressions, happened, the fast flow of air and the loss of oxygen created mild chaos in the aircraft. We had several incidents where crew membrers who had not observed the proper safety precautions were actually sucked out of the aircraft. Unfortunately, we didn't have automatic oxygen systems like the modern airliners and had to rely on our own actions to get on oxygen, get on some warm clothing, and to get the aircraft to a livable altitude as soon as possible. Some of these incidents were truly tragic, while others had their humorous moments.

We had taken off from Goose Bay, Labrador, on the second leg of a deployment to England. We were part of the first massive exercise of this nature that had been attempted and we had our problems. We had experienced a lot of trouble with the ice and snow at Goose and were happy to leave the place, but it was a happiness of short duration. As we leveled out at 45,000 feet, I was operating the engineer's panel and had just relaxed to enjoy a cigarette. A triangular glass panel directly above my head suddenly failed, a cyclone of air rushed through the opening, the interior of the aircraft fogged over, the interior temperature dropped to about minus 50 degrees, and everything that was not tied down was sucked from the aircraft. After the first few moments of panic, we all got on oxygen, got into some heavy clothes, and organized things inside the aircraft, including giving resusitation and forced oxygen to one crewman who had a clogged oxygen mask. Our aircraft commander then called our flight leader.

"Sir, this is Aircraft 1085. We have experienced a glass failure and a resulting explosive decompression. All crew members are okay, the aircraft is performing okay, but we have neither pressurization nor heat. We are presently descending and returning to Goose Bay with a declared emergency."

"Negative," the good colonel flight leader answered. "Put the flight engineer's butt in the window to stop the air flow and continue the mission."

"Can't do that, sir," the aircraft commander countered. "One engineer (me) is too small and the other one is scared half to death."

"Knock off the chatter and we'll see you in England—or at least we *better* see you in England." the leader commanded.

We froze and breathed oxygen from the old-fashioned bag masks all the way to England, but we did make it.

For the return trip to Fort Worth, Texas, I made a "minor error" in computing the fuel required, an error in our favor, and we were the only crew to make the return trip without a refueling stop en route. We made the required air miles, made the estimated time of completion, and landed with the required reserve of fuel. For that little feat, we got all kinds of commendations from several sources and were the belles of the ball for a couple of days.

Old B-36 Flew Range of B-52

BY MARSHALL LYNAM.
Star-Telegram Aviation Writer.

A veteran Convair test pilot said Thursday it's nice to know the Air Force's latest Boeing B-52 can fly as far as Convair's B-36 did 11 years ago.

The remark came from B. A. Erickson, former chief test pilot and now assistant manager of operations at the Convair plant here.

* * *

ERICKSON WAS asked by a reporter what he thought of the Air Force announcement Wednesday that a B-52G had set a world's record of 10,000 miles without refueling.

"We all view this flight of 10,000 miles as very admirable and very revealing," he replied.

It demonstrates, he said, the B-52G is capable of flying as far over a closed-circuit course without refueling as did the B-36 on several occasions beginning in 1949.

It's an admirable achievement, he said, even though the B-52 carried neither a bomb load nor missiles, while the old B-36 was somewhat handicapped by 10,000 pounds of dummy bombs which it dropped midway in its missions.

* * *

continued
next page

"Down Memory Lane"

THE B-36 continued from previous page

B. A. ERICKSON
... it's (ho hum) admirable.

THE B-36, AN aerial dreadnaught powered by six piston and four jet engines, was retired from Air Force duty early in 1959.

The B-52G is the latest version of an eight-jet bomber built by Boeing. It currently is the mainstay of the Strategic Air Command's manned bomber force.

"We recall rather fondly that the B-36's designed mission was to fly 10,000 miles with a 10,000-pound bomb load to be dropped at the midway point," Erickson said.

The B-36 proved on several occasions it was capable of doing just that, Erickson added. On two such flights he was at the controls.

"The first time was in July of 1949," he said. "That mission was a closed course between East Coast and West Coast cities."

The flight lasted approximately 40 hours, and covered 10,117 miles, he said.

"We did better than that later on," he added.

* * *

THE STRATOFORTRESS for which the Air Force claimed a record Wednesday took off at 7:07 a. m. Tuesday from Edwards Air Force Base, Cal. It flew a closed-circuit course to El Paso; Andrews AFB, Md.; Harmon AFB, Newfoundland; Fairbanks, Alaska; Philip, S. D., and back to Edwards.

Erickson made clear he wasn't challenging the Air Force claim that the flight set a world's record. He noted that an Air Force crew was at the controls, while the B-36 flights were made by Convair crews.

Erickson conceded the B-52's average speed of 500 m.p.h. was considerably faster—probably twice as fast—as that of the B-36.

He noted, however, that the B-58 which Convair now is building for the Air Force has flown 1,324 m.p.h.—plus.

* * *

AND THAT, he pointed out, is twice as fast as the 650 m.p.h. speed of which the B-52 is capable.

"Speed is a major factor in war," Erickson said. "If you try to penetrate enemy territory with bombers, he may not like it."

Erickson noted the B-58 has demonstrated its ability to fly long missions at altitudes of less than 500 feet. This technique would allow it to sneak in under radar coverage, he said.

THE B-58

Convair Jet Ripped By Mid-Air Blast; Two Test Pilots Die

By JACK MOSELEY
Press Aviation Editor

One of Convair's ace test flyers was killed instantly at 5:02 p.m. yesterday and another was reported missing when their supersonic B-58, carrying "secret" devices developed here, mysteriously exploded at 35,000 feet near Lawton, Okla.

The body of Donald A. Siedhof, 25, of 3824 Winfield, was discovered minutes after the shattering air blast. An unopened parachute was found a few feet away.

Convair spokesmen said they had not found pilot Raymond Fitzgerald, 35, of 4429 Tamworth.

Top security was enforced at the scene of the crash. Military officials moved in from Fort Sill and quickly removed the body of Mr. Siedhof, who is the father of a small daughter. Duncan police told THE PRESS they had been warned to give out no information.

continued
next page

Donald A. Siedhof

Raymond Fitzgerald

THE B-58

THE SUDDEN BLAST was preceded by radio failure, a Convair spokesman here admitted. Toni Page, publisher of Cross Country News at Meacham field, told THE PRESS that "many people here saw two puffs of black smoke followed by flaming streaks of red on the horizon." Meacham Field employes averified that the fire in the western sky appeared at exactly 5:02 p.m.

At the disaster scene, witnesses described the crash of the fifth B-58 produced here as appearing "like a skyrocket." They said pieces of the ship drifted to the ground still burning.

A Convair spokesman stressed the fact that no atomic warhead is ever carried on a test plane.

He said later that special telemetering equipment in the ship did not go out at the same time the radio failed. "We have hopes that remote control graphs made here as the Hustler flew over Oklahoma will reveal the cause of this awful accident."

(Telemetering is a system of relaying facts on altitude, speed, mechanical systems, and other functioning systems in the Hustler to earth by means of sensitive graphs. Experts will be able to tell exactly what was happening inside the ill-fated plane prior to the mid-air explosion.)

AS TO THE TOP SECRET systems being tested, the spokesman admitted that he himself had not been told.

Witnesses said a sonic boom sounded from Hustler No. 5 seconds before the jolting explosion. They said the ship made a speed run, they heard the boom, then the blast, which shook windows for miles in every direction.

It appeared neither man managed to get out of the plane prior to the explosion. Mr. Seidhof may have been in the process of ejecting when the plane burst into a million pieces. His body was found on the farm of Roy Wilkins. F. A. Lindsey discovered part of the engineer's body still strapped to the ejection seat several miles from the main wreckage.

MR. LINDSEY USED his pocket knife to free the torso from the tangled straps of the seat .The body was removed to Brooks Funeral Home in Duncan but later claimed by the Air Force.

Both bodies were believed to have been horribly mutilated by the explosion.

Here at the Convair plant, security officers were checking all cars entering the main gate and holding all persons without special passes until they could be cleared for entrance into the mile-long plant.

The plane was already overdue here. Convair confirmed that the plane was on a "one-hour test run." No explanation was offered as to why it was supposed to be landing here.

Last night's crash was the fifth disaster for a twice-the-speed-of-sound Hustler. One exploded in flight in New Mexico last spring, killing two crewmen. A second burst into flames on the Convair ramp here May 14. A third crashed on takeoff from Carswell Air Force Base here in September, claiming two of the three crewmen. Last Tuesday, another test flyer for Convair, Harry N. Blosser, was killed in a similar mid-air crash near Hattiesburg, Miss. Two Air Force flyers were killed here in early September when their B-58 crashed in flames on takeoff.

continued
next page

WHILE FRANK W. DAVIS, Convair division manager here, and other top officials attempted to piece together the facts of last night's crash behind closed doors, the family of the last victim of last May's blast here prepared for his funeral. Dead of burns received in the raging fire that followed the plant blast was Sidney A. Cauthen, 32, of 7421 Llano. He was the last of three injured to be killed by the ramp explosion. He died yesterday in a hospital.

Early today, Convair prepared to examine the telemeter graphs in hopes of finding some clue to the cause of the mysterious blast.

Podless TB-58 starts takeoff run.

L. Wilson gets TB-58 first flight "stamps."

Test Phase Done, B-58 to Become Bed For New Jet

Airplane number three this month was the first B-58 Hustler supersonic bomber to complete its phase of the flight test program at Convair Fort Worth.

Final flight in the program was completed when B. A. Erickson touched down with crew members Grover C. Tate, project flight engineer, and Rex R. Smith, flight test engineer. Erickson, manager of flight, was pilot.

Awaiting the Hustler's landing were engineers and crewmen who had worked on the project since the aircraft went into its initial testing months ago.

According to W. G. Griswold, team captain, final B-58 test program phases included development testing and primary nav-bomb system component testing. The development testing, he said, involved the automatic pilot.

"The ship eventually will be flown to Edwards Air Force Base in California," Griswold added. "There it'll go into modification."

He said the Hustler will be modified to serve as a flying test bed for a new General Electric jet engine.

This B-58 has been in advanced phases of the B-58 test program for the past eight months.

Other Hustlers are expected to finish the program and go into modification in the near future.

FINAL PHASE—Left to right, W. G. Griswold, team captain, goes over report on final phase of flight test with B. A. Erickson, Grover C. Tate and Rex R. Smith.

THE B-58

After first flight, B. G. Reed, Convair FW assistant manager-operations, discusses flight with crewmen, from left: Earl Guthrie, second station; author Grover Tate, third station; Val Prahl, first station.

TB-58 in full dress carrying pod aloft for first time. Note distinctive paint job.

Ernie Lain, FW

Sometimes things sort of balance out, especially if you know just how big of an error to make when computing the required fuel.

AND JUSTICE SHALL PREVAIL — SOMETIMES

While making a preflight inspection on a B-36 airplane, I found a safety wire that had been installed backward and I called for a mechanic to correct it. The mechanic who came to fix it was a silver-haired, short and muscular veteran of the aviation business whom everyone called "Pop," and he was known to have a terrible temper. I showed him that bad safety and he growled at me in real anger.

"Who the hell are you to to say that it's backward?" he demanded.

"I'm the first flight engineer and I know when something is wired backward," I countered.

"You a mechanic too?" he grumbled.

"Matter of fact I am, and I have all of the mechanic licenses, if that will help," I said.

"What's the number of your license?" he asked.

I reeled off the six-digit number and he snickered as he showed me his single-digit license.

"It's still safetied backward," I insisted.

"Yeah, guess it is," he conceded, and then he resafetied it correctly.

Later, I asked someone who this "Pop" guy was and learned that he was an old-timer who had been the personal mechanic for a very famous and successful lady aviator. The story was that he had been badly treated by the lady and he finally chose to extract a measure of revenge. While her airplane was being prepared for a long-distance flight, a special relief tube had been designed and installed in the airplane. It was much the same as those tubes designed for men except that it had a special fitting that more closely matched the needs of the female anatomy. Otherwise, it was just a tube with an outside venturi, a funnel-like device designed to create a suction through the relief tube that would draw out the waste that had been put into the other end of the tube. As "Pop" was pulling the wheel chocks prior to the lady's departure, he reversed the venturi tube, creating a blowing wind into the cockpit instead of a suction. With this arrangement, whenever the lady opened the valve to use the relief tube, air would be blown into the cockpit, spraying any waste that had been put into the tube all over the airplane interior.

After this happened, the lady fired "Pop" and tried to ban him from aviation for life, but he kept a low profile, especially after the lady's husband bought the company that he worked for, and he continued on in the business until he retired in dignity.

I later asked him about the incident and he denied it emphatically. He would say only that "Some people just don't have a sense of humor, and others can't appreciate or forgive a simple mistake by a mechanic who doesn't understand physics."

EPILOGUE FOR THE B-36

The B-36 lived and retired without ever "firing a shot in anger," but she is credited with being one of the reasons why the cold war of the fifties and the Korean "police action" didn't explode into a full-bore war. She performed nobly, was most forgiving of our flying mistakes, and was retired with the dignity becoming her queenlike bearing.

It was not uncommon for crew members to have accumulated 5,000 or more accident-free flying hours in the B-36 since she was a safe and a loyal machine. Many times she was abused but she always responded gracefully. We once wondered if she would fly with all of her six reciprocating engines shut down and their props feathered, using only the thrust of the tiny J-47 jet engines on her wing tips for power. Wonder developed into reality and when we did a low-level fly-by in this configuration, the plane performed like a thoroughbred. When the geniuses of engineering dictated that the engine cut off position of the fuel mixture controls be reversed, we didn't learn of the change quickly enough and once in a while we made a mistake and shut down all of the engines in flight. Whenever this happened at night, it was one of the loneliest and most helpless of feelings, but the good old lady B-36 always hung in that black sky until we got everything organized again.

The B-36 could carry a tremendous weapon load for long distance and her potential combat targets were deep within enemy territory. She had a very special mission and would have performed it well had she ever been called upon. For an annual display of our military might, we used to train more than a hundred 500-pound iron bombs spaced a few yards apart so that the result on the ground looked like a gigantic automatic punch press had been at work. Unlike the lady gambler who carried a small-caliber Derringer in the dark recesses of her bosom, the B-36 carried a cannon. She was always literally and figuratively loaded for bear, particularly the big bear that was threatening us during those days. Fortunately, no one ever called her hand, and when she had served her years and given way to the next generation of aircraft, she retired to enjoy the peace which she had been so influential in maintaining.

PART III

THE B-58 HUSTLER

In most romantic stories the leading characters have a rather simple true love and an overwhelmingly exciting sort of latter-day affair with a more exotic love. This same "two-loves-have-I" was somewhat true with me and my airplanes. The B-26 was the first love, the walk in the park holding hands, the shy kiss when no one was looking, the pressed flowers, the souvenir movie tickets and the white dress while we walked down the aisle. It was the soft and tender love affair that could never be anything less than it was in my memory. The B-58 was the more mature love, the backstreet mistress who wore the sexy red dress and did the enticing things. She seduced me with violence and left her marks upon me. In memory, there is a hallowed place for each of these airplanes and each of them was a tremendous influence upon my life.

The Korean War had ended and I planned to make a career of the Air Force until I was shown a mock-up of the B-58 Hustler. It was incredible; it was from another world, something beyond even the movie-maker's imagination. Sitting as majestically as any king or queen ever sat upon a throne, the B-58 looked like it was going 1000 miles an hour when it was just sitting still. I was promised a position on the test crew of this magnificent aircraft it it was given a production go-ahead and if I would get out of the Air Force. I got out as quickly as possible, worked at mundane tasks for awhile, flew as a crew member on modified B-36's and waited for the B-58. The contract was finally approved for a test program and the promise of a production run. From that day forward, and for many years, I spent most of my waking hours learning as much about the B-58 as was possible.

The B-58 was a delta-winged bomber with no horizontal tail. The ailerons and elevators were combined on the trailing edge of the wing and were called elevons. The B-58 accommodated three crewmen in tandem—pilot, navigator, and defensive systems operator. The tail of the aircraft was equipped with a 20 millimeter Emerson automatic cannon that operated much the same as the legendary Gattling gun. The aircraft sat on spindly legs, eight wheels on each main leg and two on the nose leg. It had big open ejection seats that were made wide enough to be comfortable for the broadening butts of the Strategic Air Command crew members.

There was no internal bomb bay. Instead, a giant weapon pod that was almost as long as the airplane, was carried beneath the B-58's belly. One version of this external "bomb" consisted of one big unit with a smaller unit nestled within it, somewhat like a hot dog in a bun. The object of this external bomb arrangement was that the B-58 could use fuel from a tank that was designed into the bomb and then drop the bomb on a target without being penalized with a big empty bomb bay on the return trip. The hot dog arrangement allowed the fuel to be used from the "bun" part of the bomb and then dropped away before entering the target area. The hot dog part of the unit contained the explosives and it then could be dropped on the target, again leaving a "clean" airplane for the return trip home.

The B-58 was put together with a new method of bonding and screws rather than the conventional riveting. It was as aerodynamically smooth as a newborn baby's butt and looked like a gentle cocker spaniel with its ears laid back. It was a bomber but it had a control stick like a fighter. The flight control system was a nightmare of electrical, electronic, hydraulic and mechanical mystique. The system was one of electrical selection, hydraulic powered and mechanically operated through a package that looked like "the remains of two motorcycles after they had-experienced a high-speed collision." It used special things such as a special hydraulic fluid, special fuses, and special everything else for it in itself was a very special aircraft. It would go faster than twice the speed of sound and operate at altitudes above 65,000 feet. Sometimes it would take a 200-knot groundspeed to get her off of the ground and damned near that much of an approach speed to get her back on the ground.

Only 116 of these birds were built. More than 20 percent of those were lost in accidents, and the remainder now rest in ignominious disarray at the Davis-Monthan Air Force Base in Arizona. A couple have been preserved in museums.

We, as initial test crews, lost four of the B-58's during the test program, the exact number that a prominent pilot in the program had predicted that we would lose. I was one of the fortunates who survived the program, a program in which I flew tests for stability and control, autopilot, weapon drops, multiple weapon drops, sudden engine failure, flutter, performance, environmental, quick crew reaction, trainer development, refueling, aerial gun firing, and everything in between. I flew first flights with 13 new pilots, with dignitaries, and with generals. Some of these flights were dramatic, some hilarious, some tragic and some a mixture of all three. The B-58 was the true backstreet romance—she was exciting and unforgiving.

Just as it must be with an exotic mistress, I loved the B-58 but I didn't want just anybody to know it.

FIRST FLIGHT

The first flight of any new airplane is always an experience for all concerned, and with the B-58 it was a super-special experience. Here was a new aircraft with all kinds of new concepts, an aircraft capable of flying at speeds in excess of Mach 2, an unheard of takeoff and landing speed for a bomber, and unbelievable performance. State-of-the-art computers and simulators said that the beast would fly, but all of this had to be proved with an actual flight—the real moment of truth.

B.A. Erickson, J.D. McEachern, and Charlie Harrison

made up the crew for this first flight, and Doc Witchell, and Bob D'Abadie, and I were the backup crew. The big day of this historic first flight arrived on what was then called Armistice Day, November 11, 1956. It was late in the day when the aircraft lined up for the takeoff from the Carswell Air Force Base runway in Fort Worth, Texas. Thousands of people lined the ramps and roadways leading to the base to observe this first flight and the news media were present en masse.

I was the ground controller for this flight and was saddled with the responsibility for making a last-minute inspection of the exterior of the aircraft before it started its takeoff roll. A peculiarity of the B-58 was that it used a special type of hydraulic fluid and with this fluid absolutely no leaks could be tolerated. While all engines idled, I carefully inspected the lower surface of the aircraft and was dismayed to find a slow trickle of the golden hydraulic oil seeping from the area of the flight control package—the very heart of the aircraft. Dutifully, I called Mr. Erickson and reported the tiny stream of precious fluid.

"What do you think?" he asked in his usual low tone.

"Well, it's only a seep but I can't really see where it's coming from," I answered.

"It's up to you," Mr. Erickson advised.

"Stand by, sir," I requested.

I went to the mobile unit parked nearby and had one of the engineers in it join me in evaluating the leak. His opinion was that he felt that it was okay but that he didn't want to be the final authority. I reported this to Mr. Erickson.

"We'll go on your opinion," Mr. Erickson told me.

If ever I did any soul-searching, it was at this moment. It was as if my whole life and world was at stake. Had I been on the aircraft crew, it would have been somewhat different, but this was making decisions that involved the lives of others. I looked and I thought. I visualized the mechanism that was under the cover from which the fluid was leaking and I tried to decide where it was coming from but this gave no satisfactory solution. The idling engines were using fuel at a monstrous rate, the crew was on pins and needles, and the watching natives, mainly the corporation executives, were getting restless. I closed my eyes and actually prayed for guidance, and then, without it seeming to be really me, I called the crew.

"I feel that it's safe to go, Mr. Erickson," I said with as much confidence in my voice as I could muster.

"Rog, disconnect your interphone, give me an all clear, and we'll be on our way," the great man responded.

I did as directed, stood by the aircraft, gave the "thumbs up," and then the B-58, the "Hustler," the world's first supersonic bomber, roared down the runway for a spectacular takeoff. Although the crew couldn't hear it, the crowd of spectators gave out a resounding cheer and a burst of applause. Thirty-six minutes later, the B-58 landed safely, having completed a most successful first flight.

After all of the post-flight ceremonies were over, I took a long drive in my T-Bird with the top down before going home. It was cold and refreshing and I needed a bit of calming down before going home to the family. I was supremely happy and relieved. The drive was good medicine for the post-flight happiness and I needed to be alone for just a short while. I was so pleased that the flight had gone so well and that my decision had worked out okay.

I guess the real reason that I drove around a while before going home was that I didn't want them to see a grown man cry.

DOWN MEMORY LANE

At Convair (now General Dynamics), we had transitioned from the big lumbering B-36 to the sleek, doubly supersonic B-58, and we felt a bit smug about our new lofty position. We also felt a bit superior to our Air Force friends across the runway at Carswell Air Force Base who were flying the new and mighty B-52. As a gesture of friendship and for an exchange of information and flight techniques, the commander of the B-52's invited our manager of flight, Mr. B. A. Erickson, to be guest pilot during a B-52 training flight. I was also invited to go along as a sort of lackey or groom for Mr. Erickson.

We were accorded every courtesy, our personal flight equipment was modified to fit the B-52, and we were provided with excellent in-flight lunches. Regardless of the niceties, it was obvious that there was an undercurrent of "we'll show this hot-shot test pilot how it's really done," and Mr. Erickson sensed this little bit of human jealousy. We flew a 14-hour mission during which we refueled a couple of times, did both high-altitude and low-level bombing, and then threw a couple of visual "bombsight of last resort" bombs for practice. Mr. Erickson was allowed to actively participate in each of these activities and he acquitted himself magnificently at each one of them. In reality, he outperformed the regulars in all operations.

After the mission, we were met by a bunch of newspeople who wanted Mr. Erickson's opinion of the big, new, all-jet, transcontinental and operational bomber. I won't risk trying to remember his exact words but he told them that he enjoyed the flight and sincerely appreciated all of the courtesies that had been extended to him. He then equated the flight to a step back in time, back to the days of the recently retired B-36 where a large crew was required, where each crew member had a couple of bags full of flight equipment, where the aircraft had to be stocked with lots of food for the long slow flights, and of the demands in flight upon crew members. He noted that the B-52 was the B-36 in all respects except that it was a bit faster. For him, it wasn't an advance of any particular significance but a pleasant trip down memory lane to the B-36 which we had been flying for the past 10 years or more. "Now," by contrast," he added, "take the new Mach 2 B-58. . ."

We weren't invited back.

AUTOMATIC LANDING SYSTEM

One of the new and exotic features of the B-58 was the automatic landing system. With this system working, the pilot could aim the aircraft at an electronic beam from the airport and the little electronic goodies would then take over the landing task. Automatically, the aircraft would be turned to the proper landing path, the throttles would be adjusted for the correct power for the required approach speed, and the flight controls would be controlled as required. A great idea, but in 1957 just a bit ahead of the so-called "state of the art."

For the first real test of this electronic miracle-maker, we intersected the proper glide path at 1,500 feet and at a 45-degree angle and flipped on the automatic switch. The system suddenly turned from a helpful big brother into a vengeful monster that flipped the airplane on its back and pointed its nose straight at the oh-so-close ground below. I disengaged everything automatic that I could find, the pilot wrestled the aircraft to some degree of level flight, lighted the after burners, and pushed the throttles through the wall. We did a tree-top high-speed run that blew concrete roads away, upset several parked light airplanes, and caused general chaos on the ground—not to mention a similar chaos in the B-58.

For public consumption, it was revealed that there was a slight electronic malfunction that had caused the aircraft to behave a bit erratically but that it could be easily corrected and a more successful demonstration would be performed in the near future.

Not with me on the switches, Charlie!

NIGHT FLIGHT (WITH APOLOGIES TO ST. EXUPERY)

Early during the B-58 test program, it became necessary that we demonstrate the capability of the onboard "star tracker" to lock itself to a low-order star and to stay locked up to, and including, Mach 2, twice the speed of sound. The "star-tracker" was a relatively new device that would tie into the navigation system and permit the navigator to do automatic celestial navigation. For this test, I flew with our manager of flight and premier test pilot, Mr. Beryl A. Erickson.

We took off at about 10 p.m. and, after some preliminary work over the wilds of west Texas, the equipment started malfunctioning, so we headed back to the Fort Worth area. I did a bit of trouble-shooting and found that an electrical connection at the floor level had broken and that by physically holding the electrical plugs together the star-tracker worked okay. To do this, I had to loosen all personal equipment restraints—shoulder harness, safety belt, etc.—and get down on the floor where the troublesome connection was located. This was not the ideal place to be during a high-speed flight in a somewhat unexplored flight regime, but it seemed like a good idea at the time so I did it.

We accelerated to Mach 2, the star-tracker held okay, and I peeped out of the window to be surprised to see that we were lined up to pass directly over the centers of Fort Worth and Dallas. With the cannon-like sonic boom dragging behind us and rocketing all over the terrain beneath us, we split the two sleeping cities just a few minutes before midnight. Sonic booms were not well known then, and the booming crack of the big firecracker awakened almost everyone in both of the cities. The test completed, we slowed and prepared for landing. The scene beneath us was like a gigantic Christmas display that was just being lit. Lights were everywhere as if every household had turned on all of their lights at once. We had startled and awakened thousands of sleeping families with our booming bomber.

After landing, we were met by representatives of just about every official branch of all governments known to man: civil defense, national defense, State Police, City Police, sheriff, newspaper people, TV people, and, worst of all, our highest company executives.

We denied all allegations and claimed that it must have been someone else, but there was no "someone else" who had a four-engined Mach 2 bomber. There were only four such aircraft in existence—three were safely hangared and the fourth was ours. Regardless of the overpowering evidence against us, we stuck to our story and were finally released to go home.

After all of the visitors and investigators had left, I asked Mr. Erickson, "Why?" It took a long time for his slow, easy smile to develop before he answered. "To let everyone hear the new sound of freedom," he said.

It was an answer that I didn't really understand until a few years later. I had checked into a room in a fancy new hotel in Fort Worth near the air base and on the table in a room was a sign that stated, "Please do not be disturbed by the noises of the aircraft operating nearby and overhead. The noises you are hearing are *the new sound of freedom*."

Mr. Erickson, as a prophet, was seldom wrong.

JUST A ROUTINE TEST, GENERAL

Lots of high-ranking military officers, senators, dignitaries and cabinet members flew with us on the B-58 program. Some of them had a genuine interest in the aircraft and its potential while others just went along for the prestige and the goodies—a golden Mach 2 lapel pin, a wallet card, and a gold-embossed certificate. To keep from wasting the cost of the flight, we always tried to make these flights as productive as possible without compromising the safety of our gilded passengers. During one such flight, we needed some autopilot data in the high supersonic speed range, so we planned our flight around that requirement. Our passenger for that day was a two-star general.

We made it to Mach 1.6 without undue incident, but when the autopilot was re-engaged with some new settings at that speed, it was as if some angry dog had taken hold of the aircraft and was shaking us all over an unfriendly sky. The aircraft pitched, rolled, shuddered, and sliced through the air almost sideways. Frantically, I turned every switch in sight to the off position and yelled that information to the pilot.

Pieces tore from the aircraft as she shuddered about the sky and she protested violently about an irregular center of gravity as we slowed to subsonic speed. As suddenly as the gyrations had started it was over and the aircraft became a serene, well-behaved lady once again.

"All part of the routine test," I advised our general passenger. There was no response over the interphone.

The whole world was waiting for us when we landed and the photographers took a thousand pictures of the general. The company photographers took another thousand or two pictures of the damage that had been inflicted upon the B-58.

No one took any pictures of the pilot or of me. They said that they were using color film and that our green faces wouldn't reproduce too well.

A PRIVATE FOURTH OF JULY

The test was the first night takeoff for the B-58 and, as was usual, I was in the seat in back of the excellent test pilot, A.S. "Doc" Witchell, Jr. No real big deal to this test except that the aircraft had been giving us enough trouble in broad daylight and now we were going to let her operate under the cover of darkness.

We started the takeoff roll and just before we hit refusal speed (in this case about 150 knots), all hell broke loose inside the aircraft. Sparks flew from almost everywhere and everything electrical stopped working.

"*Abort!* I yelled.

"Doc" pulled back on the power, popped the deceleration chute, and stood on the brakes. We came to a screeching, brake-smoking "whoa" very close to the end of the runway. We were in pitch darkness and the rotating lights of the fire trucks and ambulances were like ghosts coming to claim us after our brush with the unknowns of the world of electronics.

It can be said that in times of stress that we do strange things and that heroics are often born of those things that created the stressful situation. This little matter demanded that I relieve my bladder before it did it involuntarily. I opened my hatch, threw the escape rope over the side, slid down the rope, and responded eloquently to nature's demand. When the fire trucks arrived, I was in the final act of zipping up the flight suit so I immediately turned my attention to directing the fire fighters to the onboard source of the fire.

We did everything properly, went through the post-crash procedures and returned to the flight office for debriefing. When we arrived at the flight office, the project engineer congratulated me on my expertise during the emergency.

"The firemen said that you were out of the aircraft before it had stopped rolling and were right down there to direct them to the source of the problem the minute that they arrived. Good work!" the important man said.

I accepted the good words and was basking in the admiration of the welcoming group until I noticed "Doc" mouthing invectives in my direction. By the time I had finished the debriefing and made it to the locker room, someone in the know had hung a sign on my locker door:

"HEROES ARE SELF-MADE, NOT BORN!"

SNOOPY

One of the B-58 aircraft was modified for a special flight test program for the Hughes Aircraft Company and the long nose added to the aircraft made it look a bit like the comic page hero, Snoopy. After getting special permission from Snoopy's creator, Mr. Charles Schultz, we had a portrait of the little dog as a fighter pilot painted on the nose and we christened her "Snoopy." Great fun so far.

The takeoff for the first flight of Snoopy was great and we climbed to about 36,000 feet, where we leveled off to do some routine tests. One of the required tests was to shut down each engine, one at a time, and to determine that the engine could be restarted at this altitude. The process was to be repeated until we had demonstrated that each of the four engines would restart satisfactorily. After the first engine was shut down, we found that it would not restart, so we headed back home on the three remaining operating engines. During the descent, we discovered that one of the three remaining engines could not be advanced above idle power and then it unceremoniously just quit running. We made it to home base on the remaining two engines, but on the final approach to landing one of those two quit. After landing, the fourth and only remaining engine quit and we had to be towed to the parking ramp.

The project engineer for Hughes gave us each a framed picture of Snoopy, the photographers took our picture, another first flight was successfully done—and we drove home very carefully because we figured that we didn't have any luck left to call upon.

IN THE BACK OF THE BUS

The crew of the B-58 sat in isolated seclusion in tiny compartments three in a row, in tandem. The pilot had reasonably good visibility through his windshield and side windows but the other two captive crew members had only postage-stamp-size windows on each side of their compartments through which they could glance out to assure that there was indeed a world outside. The installation of some 98¢ mirrors from an auto supply store helped a bit to see what was behind us, but at Mach 2 there wasn't anything there except empty sky.

Each time that a new crew member or guest was given his first ride in one of these backseat positions, the human-factors psychologists would question them about their reactions to the dark and near-windowless compartments. Usually, the occupant would go through some long-winded dissertation in the language of the human-factor inquisitor and few of the other people who were present knew what he was talking about. Now and then someone would have a more colorful explanation, such as riding in the closed compartment of a Jaguar or in a vacuum cleaner bag or in the restroom of an out-of-control airliner. Nothing much was ever said that was worthwhile quoting until a long, raw-boned Air Force officer was put to the test after his first flight.

"What is your impression of riding in the backseat of the B-58, lieutenant?" he was asked.

"Well," he answered, "the best that I can figure, it's like playing the piano in a whorehouse and never knowing what's going on upstairs." He was then excused from any further formal questioning.

AIRBORNE MAFIA

For the B-58 flight test program, we had special custom-fitted helmets made; attached to the helmets were clear plexiglas visors that could be raised out of the way or pulled down to cover the entire face. Some of the guys wore this plastic visor over their faces for the entire flight while others wore it only as required by regulations—at supersonic speeds. To protect this visor when it was not in use, a soft cloth cover was snapped over it, making it necessary to remove this cover before lowering the visor when it was to be used for facial protection.

A common practice among flight crews to ease the tensions and to make our tasks a bit more pleasant was to play games, argue, tease, berate, criticize, and to question the heritage of each other during idle periods. One of our navigators, a Sicilian with the unlikely name of Vince Kane, was a close friend and we always had a friendly word-battle of some sort in progress. My usual attack was to accuse him of being an active member of the Mafia who was just waiting for the right moment to hijack the damned airplane. He, in turn, accused me of being mad at the world because I was so short and said I was planning to fly the airplane into the tallest building in the world just to get even with things that were tall. Most of the time we ran pretty even in our contests.

After a routine takeoff in a B-58, we were preparing to accelerate to Mach 2 and, being an obedient crew member, I removed the cover from my visor and lowered it over my face. Suddenly I realized Vince had scored a point, for painted on the visor and staring me in the face was a big black hand and the caption "Gotcha!"

PROTOCOL

In the military, it is usually best to let your superiors answer a stated question before you put your foot in your mouth and your rank in jeopardy with your opinion. This truism was usually evident during flight test programs, and if you were a captain flying with a general who thought that the in-flight lunch was a gourmet delight, you surely didn't want to volunteer that it was so bad that food poisoning was in the offing. So it was in the B-58 test program, especially with the visibility situation, in which it was fine up front but almost non-existent in the back.

After a flight in the B-58, General Al Boyd, the epitome of all airplane drivers, the best general officer in the corps, and one of the world's outstanding gentlemen, was asked his opinion of the visibility from the cockpit.

"With the addition of the rearview mirrors, I found it to be very satisfactory and acceptable," the general answered.

The second station observer during the flight, a full colonel, was asked the same question and he parroted General Boyd's answer.

At this point, Captain Fitzhugh Fulton, who had flown in the airplane in each of the compartments, interrupted the proceedings with his own evaluation. "General and gentlemen, I don't want to contest the opinion of the colonel," he said, "but just for the record I feel that what he really means is that if one looks closely through the aft crew compartment windows, he can tell only if it is daytime or nighttime."

The colonel's statement stood, and while he soon faded into obscurity, Captain Fulton went on to become a valuable test pilot of the B-70, the SR-71, and the 747 that carried the space shuttle piggyback.

Class will tell.

TO THE REAR, MARCH!

It seems that everything involved in the test program of a new aircraft is always of the utmost urgency and if it is not done on time then the whole world will immediately fall apart. Hardly anything could ever wait for tomorrow and even then it was always a day late. Such was the case when we were supposed to drop a small weapon pod from the B-58 on a target at Salina, Kansas, at a speed of 610 knots and from an altitude of 500 feet. Our takeoff was from Kirtland Air Force Base in Albuquerque, New Mexico.

We had a "special" weather observer who was supposed to give us an up-to-date weather report from Salina and we were then to make the go-no-go decision. The weather report that we received was vague and tempered with corporate urgency but we accepted the marginal weather and we went. We were to be directed to the exact drop-point by a ground radar operator at Salina, but we had our doubts, so we hedged the bet by painting a series of parallel lines on the windshield to be used as a visual "last resort" bombsight. The lines were so arranged that as soon as the pilot saw the target under the first line he was to announce "Ready." This was to be repeated with the next two lines and the bomb was to be released whenever the target appeared on the fourth line, at which time the pilot was to announce, "Release."

The scenario then became, "Ready, ready, ready, *release!*" It all seemed simple enough and not of sufficient complexity to require a talented Shakespearean actor, but simple it was not to be this day.

We approached Salina in a snowstorm and as we neared the target the snowfall became so heavy that we could barely see the ground. As was expected, ground radar could not pick us up, so we decided to make the run with our makeshift visual bombsight. Before we started the run, we rehearsed the procedure and the pilot had his lines memorized to perfection. Things happen rather quickly at that speed and altitude so we were all a bit on edge. The moment of truth arrived in a hurry and the target was aligned with the first painted line when the pilot yelled over interphone, "*Release*, ready, ready, ready!" The shock of the goofed-up signal was so great that I delayed the release of the bomb until the last "ready" and, incredibly, we hit the target right on the nose.

The pilot tried to buy up all of the tapes and other recordings upon which this blooper was recorded, but no one was selling.

LOUDMOUTH MAVERICK

Test pilot Jack Baldridge and I were on a late in the day B-58 test gun-firing mission that had taken us from Fort Worth, Texas, to Eglin Air Force Base, Florida. During the firing run, the onboard test navigation system developed a fire and created a bit of havoc. We did all of the right things, got the fire extinguished, and headed home. A heavy squall line stood majestically between us and home but we felt that we could skirt around it with no problem. Then, to add to our woes, the aircraft started an erratic pitch oscillation that could only be stopped by adjusting engine power and speed within a narrow band of selection. If we went faster than this speed, the oscillation started, and if we went slower, it did the same thing, so we were limited to that one speed. While all of this was going on, Jack lost his radio and all communication with ground stations. Buried in the compartment behind him, I could not see Jack, but I could talk to him by interphone except for the minor flaw that he could not answer back. By experimenting a bit, we found that he was receiving me okay and that by depressing his mike switch he could make a clicking sound. I then set up verbal control with the ground and would relay all of this stuff to Jack who would answer with one click for affirmative yes or two clicks for a negative no.

I then called the emergency ground angels called STARGAZER, poured out our tale of woe, and got a directional steer for Fort Worth. I also asked them to relay to Fort Worth center that we were coming home without the proverbial wing and a prayer—only the prayer. After all of this chitchat, I relayed the information to Jack and he click-clicked that he understood.

The before-landing checklist was a virtual dictionary-thick book of things to check before landing, and as I read off each item Jack would do his clicking number. This system worked fine until the clicking stopped working and we had not yet confirmed that the gear was down and locked. We were so low on fuel that we didn't have time to do any additional checking so we aimed in for a landing, gear or no gear. Fortunately, we did have a safe landing gear so we landed without incident.

When I walked into the flight office, someone asked, "How'd your flight go?"

"It was only through the sheer excellence, intelligence, magnificence, and superiority of this particular crew that we got this miserable dog and ourselves back in one piece," I answered flippantly.

"That is very interesting," someone remarked, and I looked up into the face of the corporate president who had come to witness the landing after he was advised of our emergency. "You did indeed do a very good job," he smiled.

I was home free, both physically and politically—at least for the moment.

OF CABBAGES AND KINGS AND AIRPLANES AND SOUR GRAPES

Mr. Beryl A. Erickson, the longtime Chief Pilot and Manager of Flight for Convair/General Dynamics, is my selection for the dean of all modern-era test pilots. I held him in such high regard that when he told me to stop calling him Mr. Erickson and to just use "Eric," I declined because for me to address him in such a familiar manner would be like taking the Lord's name in vain. As with most people, Mr. Erickson's reputation was checkered and opinions of him varied, but I was always proud and pleased to be associated with him and especially to fly with him. Once in a while, I accompanied him to high-level company and government meetings—not for my expertise but mostly to carry his well-filled briefcase.

At one point in the B-58 development program, the aircraft was in deep, serious, operation and political trouble. The life of the aircraft as well as the entire contract was being threatened. The aircraft suffered the usual operational problems of a new engineering concept; there had been several disastrous crashes with loss of lives and some corrections had to be made. A meeting of the highest ranking executives who were responsible for the project, for the individual troublesome problems, and for the test program was convened in an effort to solve the problems and to get the program back on the right track. Mr. Erickson, as Manager of Flight, was called upon to recite the flight operation difficulties and to evaluate the proposed corrective actions suggested by the assembled leaders. At his invitation, I went with him and kept his notes and paperwork in order.

The meeting was held in one of those paneled rooms with a long, highly polished conference table and we were served coffee and pastries throughout the meeting that endured for two days. At the conclusion of these meetings, the chairman asked Mr. Erickson for an evaluation of the proposed corrective actions. He arose with a wry smile and a subtle sigh, told me to pack away all of our papers (for a fast getaway), and stood tall and poised.

"Gentlemen," he said. "If we were all aboard an ocean-going vessel and that vessel had just been rammed by another vessel to the degree that it was taking on water enough to sink it unless something was done immediately to repair the damage and you gentlemen were in charge of those necessary repairs. I would have but one suggestion. If that repair decision was of the same caliber as those you have just proposed for the B-58, I would have the same advice for each of those situations. Simply stated, *Man the lifeboats!''*

We weathered the shock of indignation and escaped unscathed, but I had one more nail in my corporate coffin— just by association.

GREAT BALLS OF FIRE

Somewhat like rabbits, malfunctions in airplanes seem to have a way of multiplying in intensity and in number. For that reason, I always hated to start a mission with a single thing not working properly because I instinctively felt that something else would probably happen along the way to make matters worse—and it usually did.

"Doc" Witchell and I took off in a heavyweight B-58 from Carswell Air Force Base knowing that the first 3,000 feet of the 12,000-foot runway was closed for "mud-jacking" repairs. Immediately after takeoff, one of the aircraft's two hydraulic systems failed and the other one started losing fluid. Without hydraulic power, the aircraft could not be flown and there was no backup or emergency system, so we became a bit desperate and called for an immediate emergency landing. We initiated a fuel dump and the dumping was still in progress while we were on final making a ticklish center of gravity and fire hazard problem. We touched down over the closed 3,000-foot marker at about 180 knots, pulled power off to idle, and deployed the deceleration chute— except that it failed and we roared down the runway riding the brakes at a maximum. Toward the end of the runway, all of the tires started blowing out and pieces of wheels and tires, of which there were 18, peppered the airplane like flak. The wing fuel tank was punctured by the flailing shrapnel and the spilled fuel ignited when it hit the blazing hot brakes. The aircraft stopped off the runway with the 16 maingear tires blown and both main landing gear assemblies on fire.

A cockpit-level fire truck, one of the many deployed, pulled alongside and a fireman extended a hand to help me from the cockpit since my movements were somewhat inhibited by the corset-tight pressure suit in which I was encased. I had some recorded data to retrieve, some switches to turn off, and some numbers to record so I asked the fireman to wait for just a minute. He asked a couple of more times and when I delayed again he shouted, "Son, this sunuvabitch is on fire on both sides and if you want to hang in here for a ringside view of the fireworks, that's up to you, but I'm getting out of here!" When he put his offer that way, I took it and we scrambled from the cockpit hole.

The following day, Doc was given an engraved certificate for being the first pilot to successfully blow 16 tires simultaneously, and I was given an honorary fireman's hat— except that it was pointed and more closely resembled a foolscap.

"SHUTTING DOWN NUMBER 4 . . ."

"There are within each of us many emotional experiences during a flying career and usually there is one such experience that stands out above all the others. This particular experience remains etched in our memory and it is not faded nor changed with time so that the memory remains shot full of details. Sometimes it is a subjective view of the incident and it might be contested as to its validity by others who were involved. This, then, is such a story, the story of an event that will forever remain a scar on my memory and upon my soul.

The flight test program of a new aircraft involves many tests, one of which is to prove the structural strength and integrity of the aircraft. Another test program that goes hand in hand with the structural test is that of the stability and control of the aircraft. These tests are performed to ensure that the aircraft is structurally sound beyond those loads normally imposed upon it and that there are adequate flight control forces to fly the aircraft normally and under certain emergency conditions. Normally, these tests push both the test crew and the aircraft to their limits, and although not spectacular in the performance, they are among the most serious and dangerous of all of the tests.

In the B-58 test program, it was necessary to demonstrate that the aircraft could suffer an outboard engine failure at Mach 2 speed and still be recovered safely. Tests of this sort are normally accomplished incrementally, first at lower speeds and then on an increasing speed program until the maximum required speed is reached. The B-58 tests were to be accomplished at subsonic speeds, then at Mach 1, 1.2, 1.4, 1.6, and then in lesser increments until the maximum Mach of 2.0 was reached.

To set up for these tests on the B-58, a special fuel shutoff valve was installed in the engine so that when it was closed the engine would stop immediately and suddenly. This arrangement was to ensure that the engine stoppage would be as sudden as it might be in the case of a massive real-life engine failure. With normal engine shutdown, the fuel in the long line between tank and engine allowed a slow decay in the power output of the engine, so it was necessary that this special shutdown valve be utilized for the test program.

One of the first errors compounded into this test program was when the ground test data for the flight was obtained from a test stand where the fuel line was like that of the aircraft and did not represent the shutdown time that was programmed with the special shutoff valve of the actual aircraft. This difference in physical configuration created erroneous data in computing the suddenness of the engine shutdown, the time and degree of the corresponding yawing motion of the aircraft, and the amount of control required to control it.

The B-58 had a rudder-aileron interconnect that provided rudder inputs under certain conditions, and the amount of rudder for the given movement of the ailerons was automatically programmed into the system. The data for this input was in error too because of the faulty time data, and so a second, and compounding, error was introduced into the test flight.

The third, and perhaps fatal, error was to brief the test pilot to accomplish the test without using any manual rudder input, leaving this function to the automatic aileron-rudder interconnect. I shared an office with the pilot who was scheduled to perform this test and listened daily as the engineers cautioned him to do the test with "feet on the floor," emphasizing that he was not to use the rudder pedals.

Then there entered an economic and political element that aggravated these already erroneous conditions. After the successful completion of tests at Mach 1.6, it was decided that the incremental slow crawl to Mach 2 could be leapfrogged and that interpolated data from the previous lower speed tests could be used as a base for the Mach 2 test. That is, the idea was to skip the in-betweens and go directly to the ultimate. This procedure would hurry the program along, save money, and improve the stature and opinion of the aircraft. There was much opposition to this approach, the more conservative people advocating that the incremental approach continue to be followed; some even recommended that the steps be in lesser increments than those originally proposed. However, the lure of success and program survival prevailed and the plan for the test at Mach 2 was cast in concrete.

In addition, a planned refueling operation for the flight was abandoned prior to the flight, and a chase, or observer, aircraft was not provided. I never knew or understood why there was no chase aircraft, since it was a procedure usually followed during tests of this nature.

Thus, the stage was set for the test.

The day of the test was a bit cold but it was bright with a sky so blue that the visibility extended to forever and back. Many people were taking advantage of this beautiful November day to play golf, picnic, ride horseback, and do other outdoor things. The flight test engineer assigned to the B-58 test flight was a near-neighbor, and he and I raced our cars to flight operations that morning, betting coffee and donuts on the outcome. With my "hopped-up" T-Bird, I beat him hands down and he later chided me for driving so fast and recklessly. After arriving at flight ops, the pilot and I joked about the "tremendous" bonus of $1000 to be paid to each of the two crew members for the successful completion of the test. This would be the last time we would talk, and the bonus money became an ugly factor in the chaos that was to follow.

The crystal-clear of the sky over Oklahoma was a perfect frame for the cotton-white contrails of the B-58 as it accelerated toward test speed, and it attracted the attention of thousands of the people on the ground who were enjoying the beautiful day. As the aircraft passed over the flat country below, the sonic boom that followed it alerted other observers to the machine plowing through the skies above. A single disturbing fact was that there was a cross jet stream wind of about 100 knots blowing across the flight path of the test aircraft. All factors were weighed by both the flight crew and the test people on the ground, all agreeing that things were okay and that the test could be done. The crew then announced that they were on speed, at the correct altitude, and that the weight and balance were properly set. Then there was a countdown, alerting everyone that the test was being started, the traditional diminishing count of 10 down to 1 and then the zero point of beginning.

"Shutting down number 4—now," the pilot announced.

The number 4 engine was shut down using the special valve and the thrust of the engine was suddenly reduced to zero. The aircraft yawed violently to the right, skidded across the sky, and broke into pieces. What went on inside the doomed machine only the flight crew and God knows, but the thousands who were watching on the ground and the engineers who were monitoring the flight knew that it was all suddenly and tragically ended. There were no more transmissions from the crew and the pieces of the aircraft fell violently to earth while others floated like pieces of torn paper until settling on the Oklahoma farmland. Some pieces would drift as far to the east as Davis, Oklahoma, some 75 miles away.

Another flight crew member and I were dispatched from Fort Worth, Texas, to the crash scene and directed to use our own car to get there. We left with only casual clothes and light flight jackets, not anticipating the extreme cold that the night would bring. Using bad logic and injecting a bit of flair for the dramatic, I drove my T-Bird over the icy roads at a foolish speed and we averaged 75 mph getting to the crash site. Others from the company and from the Air Force joined us some time after we arrived.

The main section of the fuselage of the aircraft was located immediately and the body of the test engineer was still strapped in the seat. The pilot could not be found and the report of a parachute sighting caused us to request that the commander of Fort Sill Army Base call out some ground troops to search the surrounding area. I prayed that through some miracle the pilot had survived and was somewhere out there in the cold, black night, trying desperately to survive. The commander of the base refused the request, basing his opinion on his subjective conclusion that there was no way in which the pilot could have survived. I objected bitterly to his decision and he and I exchanged some loud and harsh words. Our confrontation took place in a building named McNair Hall, named after an army general who was killed in a misdirected B-26 bombing attack in Europe during World War II. The commander, apparently still smarting from war-time service differences, ventured the guess that I was part of the Air Force, yes, that I *had* to be Air Force to have such an irresponsible attitude as to disturb sleeping soldiers to go on such a "fool's errand search." I assured him that I was a member of the Air Force and that I had once been a member of the squadron that had done the bombing in Europe. We departed under circumstances a great deal less than pleasant. As it developed, the commander—the parachute that had been sighted was the aircraft deceleration chute that had been deployed when the aircraft came apart.

The next day, we found the pilot's body, hidden under a piece of wreckage. He was still strapped in the ejection seat with his head horribly mangled. The army commander whom I had confronted the previous evening asked that I disarm the ejection seat of its ballistic devices before his medical people recovered the body. At this time, I was totally destroyed emotionally and was unable to even look at the remains of my friend, much less work close to his body

131

while removing the ballistic devices, so I refused. The army colonel berated me extensively for not cooperating in this effort and I was never sure whether the salty tears on my face were from sadness at the deaths of two friends or for a dumb army colonel who seemed to lack even the most basic element of human compassion.

An accident investigating team was immediately organized and crews started searching for pieces of wreckage and, more specifically, for the onboard recording tape that could give the investigators some hard data as to what happened at the precise moment of failure. Because the accident had been witnessed by so many and been so widely covered by the news media, it was easy to get the people of Oklahoma to help in the search for wreckage and tape. The helicopters, off-road vehicles, and walking people were joined by several old-fashioned "posses" on horseback, all looking for anything that could be helpful. A public relations representative from the parent company was sent to Oklahoma to help in the tast of hunting, but one day of Oklahoma backroads and roadside cafe food caused him to flee back to the comfort of his office. The PR gentleman had been most intimidated by a cafe waitress when he had ordered breakfast with super-specific requirements such as blocked-bacon, toast just turning a golden brown, and tea made from only black tea from Tibet. When he then asked the waitress if the "chef" could cook three-minute eggs, the lady leaned toward him, hissed that the cook could tell time so he could damn well cook a three-minute egg. The PR weenie recoiled at this cruel and inhuman treatment and went home.

The search for the recording tape produced many interesting sidelights, all of no consequence regarding the recovery of the tape but of a nature that caused them to be remembered. Perhaps the one with the most impact was a front-page news article that I wrote to advise people of the importance of locating the tape. Bitter over the loss of friends, I wrote, "I don't know why anyone does test flying anyway—the pay is less than that of a third-rate New Orleans stripper and the risks a great deal more severe."

When the paper hit the streets, I was summoned to the home office and ordered to justify my claim of pay differential between test pilot and stripper. Fortunately, I was able to retrieve an article that told of the pay of strippers and I was exonerated to some degree, but it surely put another scar on my "illustrious" career.

We used the Lawton police station as headquarters for coordinating the search and the police there extended us every courtesy and convenience. When the police chief learned that I had been searching in a bootlegging community where he "wouldn't allow any police officer to go alone," he issued me a gun permit and a .38 revolver. He would have been much more disturbed had he known that I had paid one of the people in the community for some tape they had found. We were paying 10¢ a foot for tape containing no data and $1 a foot for tape with data. I had paid the "outlaw" bootlegger $90 for tape while his alleged renegade neighbors watched me peel the money from a large amount I carried.

One gentleman who lived in somewhat austere circumstances had some tape but refused payment when I offered it. I thought that he could use the money and became very insistent about paying him. He then led me outside his house and pointed to the far horizons while telling me that he owned all of the land that we could see plus a lot more. I thanked him and on the way back to home base stopped at a home bearing this gentleman's name to learn that he virtually owned the town including the bank. He was one of Oklahoma's wealthiest citizens and lived as he did by choice.

A lot of the aircraft wreckage had fallen on a ranch owned by a marvelous Indian lady. She allowed the recovery crews to cut her fences and to use vehicles to recover the wreckage provided that they would repair the fences and not allow any of her livestock to escape. Her house was usually the first stop on my itinerary and I sometimes enjoyed a friendly cup of morning coffee with her. One late night she called me, angry as a chased tomcat, and demanded that I get out to her ranch immediately. Some of the recovery crews had cut fences and allowed several head of cattle to escape. When she asked "a smart-assed New Yorker" about getting the cows back into the pasture, he had answered, "Hell, lady, don't you watch 'Gunsmoke' on TV? Get a horse like they do." I had to hire a bunch of local cowboys to round up the cows and the Air Force had to pay for it. Hello, taxpayer.

This same Indian lady wore a sweat shirt with a small L-shaped tear in the bosom area and, as she moved about, it sometimes revealed a bit of her that was normally covered. A visiting accident investigation expert visited this lady with me and became fascinated with the revelation through the torn sweat shirt, to the point that he stared at it intently. Without ceremony, the lady suddenly arose, pulled the sweat shirt over her head, and removed it. She wore nothing beneath it and as she sat there in her exposed glory, she asked the visitor if now he would be more comfortable not having to worry about what was under the shirt. The expert fled to the car and refused to ever go with me on my daily visits again.

During a run to Fort Worth, the Oklahoma police stopped me once for driving at speeds in excess of 100 mph. They accepted the explained urgency of my accident-investigating role and gave me a long warning ticket, but from that point on every highway patrolman in Oklahoma knew me and my vehicle by sight.

During the month following the accident, we recovered most of the wreckage but never found the critical pieces of recording tape. The accident board made its findings, other aircraft were then modified to correct the design discrepancy, and the flight tests were assigned to other aircraft and other test crews. This time, the incremental Mach increase steps were reinstated and the more conservative approach produced a successful program.

So the tragedy ended for those who had given their lives, but the shallowness of human nature that often rears its ugly head continued. There was a reluctance to pay the crew's survivors the flimsy $1000 extra risk bonus because the test had not been "successfully completed." After realizing that if the payment was not made it would be very difficult to get other crew members to fly the next tests, the payment was finally made.

And I thought of how much easier life might have been for me if I had the equipment and talent to be a New Orleans stripper.

A FAREWELL SALUTE

When General Clarence Irvine completed his spectacular career in the Air Force, test pilot George I. Davis and I were selected to give him a farewell flight in the B-58. Prior to the flight, I discovered that the canopy in my station would not lock properly and that the unlock warning light was illuminated. I could visually inspect the lock and monitor it during the flight so we decided to go with it that way. We took off from Carswell Air Force Base in Fort Worth, Texas, and accelerated to Mach 2 on the way to Randolph Field for a fly-by and a landing at Kelly Field in San Antonio, Texas.

We got to Mach 2 okay, arrived at Randolph in record time, and my arm was numb from hanging onto the canopy latch, a sort of contortionist feat which required reaching backward with the right hand and pushing the lock-bar in place. At Randolph, George put on an airshow worthy of any Thunderbird or Blue Angel air circus. We rolled, buzzed the field, lighted the afterburners, made high-speed passes over the field, and performed some spectacular zoom climbs. During this Snoopy and the Red Baron display, I was white-knuckled and paralyzed in position hanging onto the canopy latch-bar.

The tower operator at Randolph called us and offered to trade two of every aircraft on the base for just one of those like we were flying. I told him that I'd trade the damned thing for a used bicycle if we ever got back on the ground, but George and General Irvine overruled me.

LOOK AT THE CAMERA, SIR!

Test programs for new aircraft usually attract a lot of media attention, particularly if the aircraft involved is a new and sophisticated machine. Some of the guys that I knew were so impressed by the news coverage that they would wear their decorated flight helmets as they buzzed down the highways in their convertibles. They claimed that it was not for show but for protection in case of a rollover. Others were not receptive to publicity and made serious efforts to avoid the public-relations-inspired scenarios. General James McMullen, then Captain McMullen, was one of those who dodged the cameras and the "May I quote you" guys.

Jim was one of the first military pilots to fly the B-58, and that, coupled with the fact that his father was an Air Force general, made him interesting copy for the news media and for Convair. When Jim taxied in after his flight he was met by a horde of newsmen, photographers, and TV cameramen. Jim rolled to a stop on the apron, a big stand was pushed up to the cockpit, and Jim opened his canopy to greet the newsmen who waited on the platform of the stand. Somewhat dramatically, he removed his flight helmet and smiled into the lenses of the waiting cameras. He was wearing a brilliant orange "Orphan Annie" wig and had every other tooth blackened out.

The evening's five o'clock news left Jim to his own pursuits and replaced his scheduled story and pictures with a story about a man who was having a fight with the City Hall about raising pigs within the city limits.

ADULT AERIAL MISCHIEF

He had a head to contrive, a tongue to persuade, and a hand to execute mischief. — Edward Hyde

136

Perhaps the honorable Mr. Hyde, way back in the seventeenth century, had flight crews in mind when he penned the literary jewel quoted above. It was the mischief that we could get away with that made the difference between flying being work or fun. Sometimes it worked to our advantage and sometimes it backfired.

During a flight of the B-58 that involved some high "G" and crazy maneuvers, we were given little plastic bottles in which to collect samples of our urine during the flight. The aero med lab wanted the samples for some reason that we didn't question, so we dutifully filled the little bottles during the flight. The flight terminated late at night so we left the bottles on a designated desk for pickup the next morning. I eyed the tiny inoffensive-looking bottles and it seemed to me that it would be a good idea to add a tad of red ink to the contents of one of them—to add a bit of color to the program, as it were. I did that and went home for some needed sleep. But sleep was not for long, because as soon as the lab guys saw the red-dyed bottle of urine, they called me back to the office and were ready to send me to the experts at Lovelace Clinic for a complete urinary tract analysis. It took a lot of backpedaling to convince them that it was all a joke, a gag, a bit of fun, foolishness, and a harmless departure from the routine of logic and routine.

The chief pilot didn't seem too amused, and he somewhat angrily suggested that I get the hell out of his sight as quickly as possible. I think that he was just sore that he didn't think of the idea himself.

TRY, TRY AGAIN

Problems were the norm in flight test programs, particularly in those days when things were not predicted by computers prior to flight. As a result of these early in-flight problems, we always kept in close touch with ground control where experts in all phases of the aircraft were available for consultation. Doc Witchell and I had a problem with a fuse blowing and each time that I would replace it the thing would blow again. It was in a circuit that was critical to the test being performed, so we called the experts and advised them that the 20-amp fuse kept blowing. They told us to replace it with a 30-amp fuse and assured us that the 10-amp overload wouldn't create a safety hazard. The 30-amp fuse blew as easily as the 20-amp and test control then suggested that we try a 40-amp fuse. As most folks know, flight test crews aren't too smart or else they would be making a living at something else like real estate or selling insurance. However, in this case, we were smart enough to know that if a malfunction was present, which obviously it was, that a bigger fuse could possibly create an electrical fire. We even remembered the dangers of putting pennies or pieces of tinfoil in simple household circuits whenever the normal fuse blew. We felt that by putting the 40-amp fuse in the 20-amp circuit that we might be extending an invitation to disaster and we really didn't need that.

"I have an idea, Doc," I called. "Let's tell ground control that we're putting in the 40-amp as instructed. Then we won't answer any of their radio calls for a few minutes, turn off all telemetry and tracking equipment, and let them sweat a bit for giving us such dumb and dangerous advice."

"Naw, we can't do that," Doc reasoned. "They'll think that the fuse created some kind of overloaded circuit and that the damned airplane blew up or something."

"But that's the idea," I insisted.

"Okay, but just for a second or two, just to give them a slight taste of alarm," Doc agreed.

"Ground Control, this is 663. We are putting in the 40-amp fuse *now.*" Then we turned off all communications equipment.

After a few minutes, we called in to announce that it was only a game and that we were not going to change fuses because we thought that it was a stupid and dangerous idea—"Just a game to show you guys the seriousness of such irresponsible advice." But it was too late. We were silent too long and all emergency and search units had been alerted. We tried to reverse the field and pleaded that it was accidental—we had changed the wrong fuses, the systems went out by themselves and then mysteriously came back on, gremlins were at work, peculiarities in the atmosphere, any excuse we could think of to hang it on. All of our denials were to no avail and the air was filled with search aircraft, the Civil Air Patrol had their guys in the air, the Civil Defense units had set their wheels in motion, and the local sheriff's department had stopped chasing bad guys to look for us.

When we got back on the ground, the troops couldn't find any physical evidence to nail us to the cross and they suffered a bit of guilt because they had given us such poor advice, so they made all of the necessary apologies to the search-and-rescue troops and let the matter drop.

A few days later I found a neatly wrapped gift in my mail box. It was a child's book entitled *The Boy Who Cried Wolf.*

GOD TAKES CARE

Sometimes things happen that no one can explain the whys and hows of in the aftermath. So it was with the first refueling tests of the B-58. The receptacle of the B-58 was on the nose of the aircraft, immediately in front of the super-expensive windshield and the expendable pilot. For the boomer in the tanker and the B-58 pilot to make a connection at relatively high airspeeds was a bit precarious and required a certain gentle skill. For the very first refueling test, I flew with a pilot who had never, ever made an actual in-flight refueling—in any kind of aircraft. One of those happenings.

When we made our first call to the tanker, I suggested to the pilot of the B-58 that he advise the tanker that it was his first refueling experience and that he would appreciate their help in this first effort. He called the refueling boom operator.

"Boomer, this is 663. Just wanted to tell you that this is my first try at this airborne filling station business and that I'll need all of the help I can get from you," he advised.

"Roger 663, this is KC boomer, understand your message

and the little problem. Can't promise much help though because this is my first time to operate as a boom operator. Welcome to the 'First Timer's Club' and good luck, sir,'' was the reply.

Things went well and, as with most things, there were side benefits—my rosary beads were much shinier when we landed.

SPACEMAN

While flight testing the B-58, we often stayed at the Western Skies Hotel in Albuquerque, New Mexico, since the aircraft was based at nearby Kirtland Air Force Base. A test day usually started with a crew alert at 3:30 a.m. for an on-base show at 5:30 and a takeoff at 7:30. For this series of flights, we had to wear partial pressure suits that had been tailored to us individually. For some unknown security reasons, each of us was charged with having the suits in our possession or locked in a secuirty vault at all times. For this particular flight, we had our suits with us in the hotel room.

A movie company making a picture called "Lonely Are the Brave," starring Kirk Douglas, had most of the other rooms in the hotel rented and it seemed that their main goal in life was to raise hell all night long. The movie people in the room next to mine had the TV blasting away, they were singing and arguing and making so much noise that sleep was impossible. A complaint to the manager of the hotel resulted in a big zero because the manager didn't want to offend the movie people who were paying him a bundle. I then called these next-door guys, told them of the early flight, and asked that they quiet down a bit. They promptly told me to go to hell.

The pressure suit consisted of a tightly fitted suit with a series of capstan tubes wrapped around it, a big white helmet with a hinged faceplate in front, and a bright Indian orange suit that was worn over the inner suit. A pocket of the orange suit contained a big switchblade knife for use in emergencies. I put on the helmet and the bright orange suit and palmed the survival knife.

Thus attired, I banged on the door of the offensive room next door and when it was opened by a bleary eyed bald guy, I sprung the switchblade open with a snap, opened the faceplate of the helmet, and screamed at the terrified guy: "If you don't turn that TV off and go to sleep, I'll cut your damned heart out and take it back to my planet!"

The guy turned white, slammed his door shut, and turned off the TV. His room became as silent as a funeral parlor, I went to sleep, made the flight schedule, and had a good flight.

A few days later while dining in the Albuquerque airport, I heard one of the movie guys telling about a couple of their bosses who had been so stoned or drunk that they imagined that someone from outer space or some other spooky place had made them turn off their TV and go to bed.

They probably hired someone with a better imagination than me to write a movie script about it and made a fortune.

GAMES THAT TEST CREWS PLAY

In the test flying business, there are all kinds of people and all kinds of motives involved. Perhaps the most prevalent motive is the prestige or status. As a great pilot once told me we fly in these crazy programs because of our heavy egos; it makes us feel apart, above, and a tad bit better than our earthbound fellowmen. Sometimes this was not the only reason, though, and some people did test flying for the money involved—although the money was never that great. We had one such guy in the B-58 program and we took great delight in antagonizing him during flight.

This particular guy sweated a lot, partly from normal physical necessity and partly from the huge quantities of booze he drank. Whenever we upset him during flight, he really sweated, and although the aircraft was air-conditioned, he got wringing wet. Other crew members alighted from the air-conditioned Rolls Royce of bombers cool and collected while this guy came out a sweaty, nervous wreck.

He was good at his business, liked the status, needed the money, and hung in there regardless of his fright.

A favorite game that we played with this guy was to get all lined up for a takeoff and then over the interphone utter a teasing, "uh oh."

"Uh oh *what?*" he would inquire.

"Oh nothing, it looks like it'll be okay so we'll go ahead and fly with it," would be a typical answer. No amount of questioning on this guy's part would result in any kind of elaboration regarding the "uh oh" problem.

Among the peculiarities of the B-58 was that during the first flight to Mach 2 speeds the big navigation package would settle into place with a resounding thud. Each time that this happened our concerned crew member would suddenly become a basket case although he knew what was happening and that it posed no threat to our safety. To assure his decay to a quivering hulk, we would drop things on the floor of the aircraft and then categorically deny that we had heard a noise or a thump. Why we were so often so sadistically cruel I'll never know, unless it was that we envied his expertise and resented his unusual fright during flight.

This guy had a lot of hobbies, each of which he pursued relentlessly. After flying with us for a while, he took up an intensive study of the Bible. Perhaps he found within his Bible a way to even the score with us when we got on that last and final approach down the road of life a piece.

AN OLD MAN AT 36

One of the somewhat hairy aspects of the B-58 test program ws the dropping of the huge bomb pods that were slung beneath the aircraft. I dropped a couple of dozen of these little jewels and not once did the drop go really smoothly. A story could be told about each of the drops, but maybe they went better than I thought and I just had an affinity for melodrama. Whatever the case, I think that this particular story is worth the telling.

We were scheduled to drop an "aircraft-length" simulated nuclear warhead pod on White Sands Missile Range from 45,000 feet at a speed of Mach 2. It was a compulsory requirement that we have a photo and safety chase aircraft in position at the moment of the release or drop. For this particular mission, we had two Lockheed F-104 Starfighters, one flown by an Air Force colonel and the other by one of our company test pilots. Our B-58 had old engines on it and accelerated so slowly that we had to start our run at Pueblo, Colorado, in order to have the maximum speed over the target. The F-104 aircraft were to depart Kirtland in Albuquerque and to rendezvous with us as we approached the target. All went as planned until the F-104 that was flown by the company pilot developed an overheat condition and started vibrating a bit. The mission was cancelled and we all went home.

The company F-104 pilot and I were sharing a hotel room, and after the aborted flight we were discussing the problem that he had encountered in flight. While we talked, the mechanics at the base called to say that they couldn't find any trouble with the aircraft and that they could not make the overheat warning light illuminate to indicate the reported overheating condition. They requested that the pilot come to the base and run the engine to see for himself. Over my shouted objections, he agreed.

When he returned after running the engine, he reported that he had operated the "sick" engine throughout its power range many times and that it ran perfectly. He then had agreed to fly the aircraft on its mission without any additional work being done.

"That's dumb," I said. "You should refuse to fly it until the trouble is found and corrected or a new engine is installed."

"I don't think it's so dumb," he countered. "If I keep mickey-mousing around with this thing, they'll send one of the other pilots in to fly it and I'll wind up with egg all over my face. Not only that, but I'm the newest and youngest of the company pilots and I have a lot of catching up to do."

"You're the one who'll be caught up with if you don't

knock off this foolishness about flying an aircraft with something wrong with it that hasn't been identified," I said. "You, my friend, are fixin' to bust your young and ambitious ass. Suppose that you lose the engine in flight—what'll you do then?"

"The book says that if I have 10,000 feet of altitude, an operating ram air turbine, and the airfield in sight, that it's okay to 'dead-stick' it on the runway and that's exactly what I plan to do if I have trouble," he recited.

"Now you're crazy on two counts," I yelled back. "First, you plan to fly a sick airplane, and then if it really breaks you're going to 'dead-stick' it. That 104 is an old one with a downward ejection system that has already killed a few people and the whole thing isn't worth a dime—much less the risk of your life!

"You're just getting too old for this kind of business," the pilot taunted. "You ought to retire and write poetry or something and let us younger guys fly this new generation of aircraft."

"What do you mean, too old? I'm barely 36 years old and I got there by not doing foolhardy things whenever it could be avoided," I replied angrily.

A few more words were exchanged, tempers flared, and the bitterness grew so great that we abandoned the argument, him convinced that he had made the right decision and me thinking that he was full of crap.

Prior to this argument, we had also had a slight disagreement about poetry and to settle it had checked out a book of poems from the library. From some unknown source there was also a tube of bright red lipstick in the room, so I used the lipstick to write a quotation from the poetry book on the huge mirror above the dressing table: "The paths of glory lead but to the grave." When my ambitious young roommate awoke for the crew call and saw the message on the mirror, he was furious. During breakfast and the ride to the base, I muttered that he could still change his mind but I got only growls and dirty looks for my efforts.

The mission went fine, we all met as planned, I dropped the pod somewhere near the target, and we all headed home. En route, the Air Force pilot in the other F-104 called our 104 guy and told him that his (our guy's) engine had apparently suffered a hemorrhage and was spitting all of its parts out of the tailpipe. The warning was acknowledged and our guy called for an emergency 'dead-stick' landing at Kirtland Air Force Base in Albuquerque. He had the field beside him, had almost 8,000 feet of altitude, and was on the way to landing when he suddenly changed his mind, veered from the traffic pattern, aimed the aircraft toward the Sandia mountains, and ejected. As he went sailing downward, he barely missed hitting a B-52 that was flying beneath him. He landed safely and suffered only a slight headache. When I arrived at the hospital to visit him, he cautioned me not to say one damned "I told you so" and I observed that caution. We both smiled and understood.

In subsequent years, I flew many test flights with this same guy and his attitude never really changed. He always regarded me as an "old man" although I was still enjoying my thirties. He survived many tests, several accidents, performed a few heroics, and then retired to a lucrative business of his own.

He now operates from the confines of a luxurious office that never overheats.

AN AIRCRAFT OF A DIFFERENT COLOR

Tooling along with Mr. B. A. Erickson at the controls, we had just reached Mach 2 at 48,000 feet and were stabilizing for a test on the new B-58 aircraft. Without any prior indication, the number 4 engine, a J-79 jet, exploded into a million pieces. The aircraft was showered with sparks, coated in black smoke, and peppered with bits of flying metal. It looked like the fireworks of all of the Chinese New Years exploding simultaneously. The aircraft yawed violently to the right, then to the left, and then started a horizontal seesawing like it was suffering from some convulsive spasm. The sky around us turned black as a chow dog's nose and the smell of raw jet fuel intruded into the interior of the pressurized aircraft. Mr. Erickson, the premier test pilot, soothed the rampaging beast and nursed it to subsonic behavior. With the limited view from inside the aircraft, we surveyed the damage.

Big, heavy pieces of cowling from the number 4 engine were torn away, the entire tail section and afterburner of number 4 engine were missing, and ruptured tubing had sprayed everything with engine oil, hydraulic oil, and fuel. The aft fuel tank was ruptured by the flying flak and we were losing fuel rapidly. Black smoke curled all around us and raw fuel sprayed around the other engines. We didn't know whether there was an external fire or not and we didn't have a chase aircraft to look us over. Mr. Erickson shut off everything to number 4 and I pulled all of the applicable fuses and circuit breakers. We were riding the dangerous edge of the center of gravity of the aircraft and couldn't do much about it because of the imbalance created by the loss of fuel from a ruptured tank. With raw fuel running over the trailing edge of the wing like a waterfall, the cabin pressurization system contaminated with fuel and the unknown condition of the exterior, I knew that we would have to eject and leave the wounded bird to its own fate. I also felt that the loose fuel would surely ignite from the hot engines whenever we got down to where there was enough oxygen to support combustion.

We sort of voted on what to do and Mr. Erickson won with an overwhelming majority of one—the decision was to try to land. I resigned myself. I figured that I had been privileged to enjoy a full and interesting life, there was lots of insurance for my family, it would only hurt for a little while, and, besides, there wasn't a damn thing I could do about it but go along with Mr. Erickson's decision. I read the checklist, did my little chores, fingered my beads, and we went on to land without further incident. Dozens of fire trucks and a couple of ambulances escorted us to an isolated parking area.

After we got out of the aircraft and inspected the exterior, I was ready to swoon but I settled for a quick trip to the bathroom. The side and belly of the aircraft looked like they had flown through the flak of a dozen anti-aircraft guns. The heavy, machined center section of the nacelle of number 4 engine was driven through the lower surface of the wing and fuel still flowed from the wound. A compressor wheel for number 4 had whirled across the belly of the aircraft, leaving cruel cuts and slashes in its path. The compressor wheel had hit the steel armor plate that covered the heart of the flight control system but had failed to penetrate it. All in all, the aircraft was a mess. And so was I.

"There was a slight bang, the aircraft yawed a bit, there was some light flame and some smoke. I followed normal emergency procedures and returned to land with no difficulty nor further incident," was Mr. Erickson's dry account of the incident during a high-level post-flight debriefing.

When it was my turn to testify before the assembled group, I declined any comment other than "I cannot add anything to that, as it is perfectly obvious that Mr. Erickson and I were not in the same aircraft today."

BLIND LANDING

Every now and again some of us like to play judge, jury, and executioner to those people who rub us the wrong way or who are in outspoken disagreement with our opinions. If such people are also extremely arrogant, then we really enjoy driving a few nails into them. We had just such a guy in the B-58 test program, and when it came time for him to actually take a first ride in the aircraft, we had our opportunity for revenge and played it to the hilt.

Colonel Joe Thompson was flying the machine, I was the navigator, and our "know-it-all" passenger stuffed into the third cockpit behind me. Before takeoff, Joe and I rigged the whole deal. A control handle for the radar at my station had some limited authority to move the aircraft about during bomb runs, to make some rather small and minute corrections in the aircraft's heading. It was never intended to be used as a control for landing the aircraft and the guy in the third station was fully aware of this limitation.

After tooling around a bit and taking this guy to Mach 2 so that he could get one of the cherished golden Mach 2 Club lapel pins (a period in which he had maintained a deathly silence until we were subsonic), we started home and Joe and I discussed the landing.

"Do you suppose that you could land blind from the second seat if I gave you a bit of visual help for aligning the runway?" Joe asked.

"Don't know, but it's worth a try," I answered.

The third-seat guy then spoke up and spouted all of his engineering know-how about how there was not enough control to land with the radar control handle, that it was very dangerous to even consider such a thing, suppose we were committed to the landing and a problem arose and we couldn't get control back to the pilot fast enough, and on and on with a list of reasons that were perfectly logical and which Joe and I already knew.

"Never know without trying," Joe drawled in response. "For example, remember an old gal back in Tennessee, pure Victorian I thought, and then I took her to a barn dance one night and . . ."

"I don't care about your girls in Tennessee or anywhere else, Colonel Thompson," the guy pleaded. "Just land this aircraft normally and let me out! Land it according to normal procedures and don't pursue that radar handle idea."

We ignored the guy, got our landing clearance, and started on a long final approach. The approach speed was about 185 knots so we were moving along at a pretty good clip while Joe was giving me verbal instructions for the "blind" landing. Joe, of course, was really flying the airplane manually and our chatter was strictly on interphone. All that I was doing was reading our airspeed to Joe and making believe on all of the other stuff.

"You're off to the left a bit," he said.

"Rog, how's that?"

"Better. Now bring the nose up just a bit and hold what you have."

"Rog."

"You're drifting left again and letting the nose get too

high,'' he warned.

"Rog. How's this?"

"Okay, but watch the airspeed."

We kept up the charade until we had safely touched down on the runway. We dropped a hint that it would probably be best if our passenger didn't mention our landing experiment, but it did no good. This guy was a bloody fountain of words when he told his story. He embellished the story with all of the horrors that went through his mind during the "navigator's landing." Everyone told him that it was absolutely impossible for such a landing to be made but he vociferously insisted that it happened just as he told it. We never did tell him any differently.

I bet that whenever this guy gets with other airplane types or anyone else that will listen that he still recites his horror story about the two "hillbillies" who were allowed to fly exotic aircraft and didn't have sense enough to know or observe the limitations of the aircraft and its systems.

LAURA

On the evening before a scheduled B-58 high altitude test flight, one of our pilots and his wife had just taken possession of an adopted baby daughter. They had gone through a thousand names and had not decided on one for their new jewel.

The test aircraft was equipped for three crew members in tandem: a pilot, navigator, and weapons systems operator. Radio equipment was a primary set and an emergency standby. Each of the crew members could select one radio or the other but only the pilot had control of the frequency selection on either of the radios. We made the takeoff with the primary radio on control tower frequency and the standby radio on "company" or private test frequency. We took off and climbed to 50,000 feet to start the tests.

"That's what we'll call our baby girl," the pilot suddenly announced.

"What are you talking about?" I asked.

"Can't you guys hear them playing 'Laura' on the radio?" he said. "It's clear and beautiful." He then started humming the song.

The other guy and I were getting nothing but the pilot's transmissions and a lot of static on the radio, so we switched from one radio to the other and still couldn't hear 'Laura' or any other music for that matter. We called ground control to see if they had some radio that might be playing and bleeding into the test circuit. Negative. We told the pilot that we knew that we were flying pretty high but not quite high enough to be hearing heavenly music. He didn't even acknowledge our sarcasm and continued to hum 'Laura.'

After we completed the flight, we played all of the onboard and ground recording tapes and there was nothing about 'Laura' except the off-key humming of the pilot. We never solved the mystery. The pilot stood by his story and grew somewhat belligerent whenever he was questioned about it.

Somewhere in this big world there is a young lady named Laura, a name that was mysteriously received by heavenly endowment while her pilot dad was flying at 50,000 feet. I wonder if he ever told her the story?

OF AIRPLANES AND MULES

The B-58 aircraft acquired a reputation for being a very difficult plane to fly, and it was said that only a few pilots, those with lots of specialized jet experience, could fly it. It was also said that an extensive training program was required before those pilots with the experience could tame this new, supersonic beast. To disprove this reputation and gossip, the manufacturer invited the Strategic Air Command to send them a pilot with bomber and jet flight experience and promised that they would have him flying the B-58 at Mach 2 speeds within two weeks.

The man selected for this task was Colonel Guy Townsend, a charming gentleman with an equally charming southern drawl. His drawl was so unique that it was said that he could call an aircraft control tower almost anywhere in the world and, after giving only the aircraft number, the tower operator would answer the call by name. It had also been his ignominious experience to have the landing gear on the first test B-52 delivered to Edwards Air Force Base collapse on landing in front of all of the dignitaries who were assembled to meet the new aircraft. Colonel Townsend was a sharp and capable pilot and I was happy that he was, for I was assigned to go with him on his "learning" and "graduation" flight.

After a heavy schedule of ground school, a delay created when all B-58's were grounded after one blew up on the ramp, and a lot of taxiing around the airport, we finally made a routine takeoff with a designated instructor pilot flying chase in an F-104. We did all of the routine preparatory things and then started for the magic speed of Mach 2. Our acceleration was stopped when we found (actually, I found, because I was beginning to sit lopsided in my seat) that we were out of trim and starting to go a bit sideways. In the B-58, this sideways condition was not conducive to health, longlife, or the continued use of the aircraft. We slowed down, retrimmed the aircraft, readjusted the fuel load, and even though our remaining amount of fuel was marginal, the colonel wanted to go for the Mach 2 run, so we did. I calculated the fuel remaining versus that needed for acceleration and we agreed that anytime we got above the computed consumption level we would quit and try again another day. At Mach 1.96 we were above the fuel curve and I called for the colonel to knock off the run and slow down. He responded by sticking the nose down and hitting the Mach 2 speed. *Bingo!*

As we headed back home with precious little fuel remaining, Colonel Townsend called in for landing clearance and instructions. Some clown in another airplane but on the same radio frequency answered and said, "Sounds like a southern Alabama farmer driving that mule."

Colonel Townsend answered, "Son, this is a Mississippi colonel driving this mule and we call folks from Alabama damn yankees. Over?" There was no reply so we went on home to a normal landing.

After landing, there was much celebrating, much picture-taking, and much shaking of hands. A big party was held in Colonel Townsend's honor later that night at a posh country club. When Colonel Townsend was introduced to my wife, he told her that I was either the bravest or the stupidest man he had ever met for going along with him on such an unusual flight. Opinion among my family, friends, peers, cohorts, and employers regarding the colonel's statement was somewhat divided—about 90 percent for the stupidity and 10 percent for the bravery. For once in my life, I voted with the majority.

AND WE DIDN'T EVEN BELONG TO THE CLUB

As with most endeavors, showmanship is used to sell airplanes, whether they are for peaceful fun, commercial use, or deadly war. The B-58, being so new in concept and in performance, needed a lot of selling, so we tried very hard. One of the efforts was a grandiose "Press Day" during which dignitaries from everywhere and everything were invited to join the press corps for an aerial demonstration of the B-58's capabilities. The stage for this play was at Convair, in Fort Worth, Texas, just across the runway from Carswell Air Force Base.

Several candy-striped circus tents were set up on the perimeter of the taxiways and ramps, lemonade and other refreshments were served carnival style, music was piped in, and all of the performing aircraft radio transmissions were relayed into the tents for spectator listening. A party attitude prevailed.

George Davis and I were to fly the aircraft through its paces, announcing things over the radio as they happened— "We are lighting the afterburners now," etc. Unfortunately, we discovered that the aircraft was broken when we pre-flighted it and there was no standby aircraft. The delay was considerable and it was late in the morning when we finally got airborne. The spectators were becoming hot and uncomfortable under the hot midday Texas sun, so an enterprising public relations gentleman moved the whole entourage to the terrace of a nearby posh country club. We did our little aerial dance and were then quite surprised when we were directed to do a fly-by past the country club terrace so that the spectators could get a "feel" for the speed of the aircraft. I knew that the request was a super mistake in bad judgment and that daredevil George would take advantage of such an opportunity to pull out all the stops.

We dropped low on the approach, lit the afterburners, made sure that the pins were out of the golf course holes at the club, and started the run. Before reaching the edge of the club grounds, George asked what the maximum speed allowed for this altitude was and I gave him a figure of .87 Mach. "We just established a new point," George called. "We're at .94!" We passed the terrace at awning level; people scattered, glasses fell and shattered, and we were advised that the show was over.

We really impressed everyone and were quite surprised when we were notified by the country club's board of governors that we were not to be allowed in, near, or around the club ever again. That didn't bother us too much because the initiation fee was too high for any of us anyway.

ENCAPSULATION

Aircraft during the early phases of the B-58 program were equipped with large, open ejection seats dubbed "SAC seats." The name came about because the width of the seat was designed to accommodate the expanding width of the aging Strategic Air Command pilots who would be flying the aircraft operationally. The seat was particularly complicated in that it had "handcuffs" for the wrists, "leg irons" for the legs, "headbands" for the head, and a confusing array of straps to keep the body restrained and the limbs from flailing during an ejection. All of this combined with mechanical hookups to ensure automatic operation of oxygen, seat separation, and parachute actuation to make it a very complicated bit of lifesaving gear. But even with all of these provisions, it was still not a satisfactory system for safe escape from the aircraft at supersonic speeds. In one case, one of our crews who tried to escape from their disabled aircraft at supersonic speed had all of their equipment work just exactly as it was supposed to but they were killed from the speed and the elements as they ejected from the aircraft. To create a safe escape system, a "capsule" or "cocoon" was designed and the B-58's were retrofitted with this equipment.

The capsule was a little cockpit of its own and the crew member sat within it as in a dog house with rounded corners. In the event of the loss of cabin pressure, the capsule would close and provide sufficient pressurization for a descent to a safe altitude. In the event of an ejection, the lids of the capsule, much like the covers on a caterpillar ride at an amusement park, would enclose the crew member, actuate special oxygen and pressurization, a rocket would fire and drive the capsule from the aircraft, and a large parachute attached to the capsule would lower the whole thing to the ground. The capsule would float if it landed in the water and had provisions for extended survival in cold, hot, or sea conditions. It was an engineering marvel and it worked!

Fred Voorhies, Fred Hewes, and I were chosen for the first flight test of this new device and we had excellent results with it. Our flight was made after a thorough test program where monkeys, bears, and one human test had been conducted. Our test was to check for the operational feasibility of the system, to close it around us during flight at various speeds, to fly around a bit with it closed, and to evaluate all aspects of it in general.

The capsule closed around the crew member with a force of about 1,500 pounds of hydraulic pressure driving it and it really made a resounding whack when it closed, sort of like closing an overhead metal garage door when the counter-weights failed. Other than that, it was nothing unusual in flight and we branded the in-flight operational test a total success.

We had taken off rather late, and by the time we had

landed and untangled ourselves from the new contraption, it was nightfall. Everyone except the necessary operations people had gone home and we were a bit disappointed that no one was there to shower us with confetti or something. Our worries about the apparent lack of concern were short-lived, however, for there in the locker room was an ice bucket with a cold bottle of good champagne nestled within. A note tacked to it seemed to make the whole effort worthwhile:

"ENCAPSULATED SPIRITS FOR THE FIRST ENCAPSULATED FLIGHT CREW. *CONGRATULATIONS!*"

GENERAL HAULING

A popular thing among the Air Force hierarchy during the mid-and late-fifties was to ride in the doubly supersonic B-58 and to accumulate the credentials that were presented after such a ride. The "goodies" included a golden Mach 2 tiepin or lapel pin, a numbered membership card in the Mach 2 Club, and a very impressive certificate complete with a golden seal of authenticity. To have flown at the top speed of the B-58 was indeed impressive and deserving of such credentials. The B-58 speed increase over that of the prevailing B-52 was more than the increase that the B-52 had accomplished over the original Wright Flyer—a giant step in speed increase in the relative wink of an eye. Quite often I flew with these dignitaries, among them several generals, and served as lackey or in-flight advisor. Most of these VIP's flew only as passengers or observers, with the exception of General Albert Boyd, who *always* did his own driving.

A scheduled flight with one ranking general ended before it started when a landing gear "walking beam" connector between the aft and forward sets of wheels broke while the aircraft was parked. The broken gear penetrated the wing fuel tank and all B-58's were grounded until the cause was determined. The cause in this case was an improperly heat-treated link—improperly treated because the machine operator allowed his attention to wander as the office girls passed his work station on their way to the refreshment machines.

With another general aboard, we were flying at about 600 knots down the Brazos River in Texas when I remarked that it was strange to see some farmers still using mules to pull their plows. When the general asked what prompted such an "out of context" remark, I told him to look out his window and up about 30 degrees and that he could see the farmland and farmers as we flew past. When he looked and discovered that we were below the banks of the river, he issued a real "general" order that we get the hell out of there and get some altitude.

With still another general aboard, we did a bit of buzz-job at a local country club and whenever the general saw one of the hole-marking pins pass by his window, he also requested some additional airspace in the vertical direction.

We flew so many generals that I had an artist paint a neat logo on each side of my airplane that read "GENERAL HAULING." Fortunately, it was done in watercolors because the first company executive who saw it became apoplectic and made me have it removed immediately. No sense of humor, I guess.

THE BLACK SUIT

Having neither the proper physique for, nor the desire to wear, fancy or expensively tailored clothes, it was a rather rare departure from the norm when I had a special suit tailored in Japan. It was a sort of textured black silk suit with a crimson silk lining and was tailored to my skinny frame. It provided a perfect background for the golden Mach 2 pin that shone in the lapel and the silver B-58 worn as a tiepin. It was ideal for wearing to those frequent semiformal dinners and meetings which we were "directed" to attend.

It wasn't long after getting the suit that I found that it served a more tragic and somber role as the ideal suit for wearing to funerals—and in the B-58 test program we had an inordinate number to attend. Perhaps I was more sensitive to crew losses than the average person, for each of these deaths seemed to take a little piece of me with them. I brooded, not for concern for my own life, but in searching for reasons for the untimely death of my friends. I sought out priests and ministers but they, like me, were only mortal and had no definitive answers. While sitting in a funeral chapel one day, I fingered the coat of the black suit and it suddenly became the symbol of my despair, a thing upon which I could affix some blame. Over a short period of time, I had worn it to six funerals for close friends who were the victims of the B-58. It was the jinx, the cause of it all, and it had to be destroyed.

After this particular memorial, I took off the black suit when I got home, soaked it with fire-starter, and burned it in the outdoor barbecue fireplace. As it was consumed in the flames, I thought of the stupidity of the act, but I was so filled with anger at the way that things were going that it was necessary to provide some sort of an escape route. The burning of the suit was symbolic and made sense to a somewhat tortured mind.

Symbolism may serve a purpose, but it didn't change the accident rate, and we lost several more good men before the test program was completed.

NUNNERY NONSENSE

One of my favorite test pilots whom you will find mentioned frequently in this storytelling epic was Fred Voorhies, a Cajun pilot from Lafayette, Louisiana. Fred had some interesting experiences in Korea as a fighter pilot, including one lower-than-normal fly-by where he wiped out the canopy and part of the tail of his F-80 fighter when he hit a bridge supporting cable. His military escapades were only a prelude for those to come later as a test pilot.

Fred had a sense of humor that was about equal to his skill as a pilot, and part of the fun of flying with him was due to his somewhat laconic treatment of the whole affair. Throughout many risky flights, some close calls, and an accident or two, it seemed that it was his sense of humor that sustained him.

For a test flight of a B-58, it was normal procedure for an F-104 to take off ahead of the B-58, to fly to a position of a long final approach, and to then join with the B-58 during its takeoff roll. Fred often flew this F-104 role, identified as a "chase" pilot. Pilots flying the chase aircraft wore cameras mounted on their helmets and photographed the B-58 throughout its takeoff and subsequent tests. It was a tough rendezvous during the takeoff and the B-58 sometimes reached speeds of 200 knots before lifting off. This put the F-104 at about 10 feet off the ground at the same speed with the pilot jockeying to stay next to the accelerating B-58. During one of these takeoff ballets, Fred zoomed past us in his F-104 and calmly announced, "Flameout." This meant that the fire in his engine had died and that he had no power left in the engine; he was about 10 feet above the ground and in an aircraft that had a downward ejection system.

Fred went out of sight beyond the horizon and made no more transmission on the radio. A search for him and his aircraft was initiated immediately. There was no sign of smoke from a crashed aircraft, no word from Fred, and no witnesses reported seeing or hearing a crash. It was as if the Bermuda Triangle had suddenly extended itself to the plains of west Texas.

After what seemed like hours but was in reality only 10 or 15 minutes, Fred called the tower and advised that he was still flying the aircraft and that everything was okay. After the flameout, he had "settled a bit" at the low altitude, traded a bit of airspeed for altitude, and removed his helmet to get ready for a last-ditch attempt at ejection. The heavy camera mounted on his helmet would have created a "crack-the-whip" (or "crack-the-neck" in this case effect) during the ejection, so it was advisable to get rid of helmet and camera. The oxygen mask which contained the microphone for radio transmissions went along with the helmet so all contact with tower or test control was lost. Prior to pulling the ejection handles, Fred "jabbed" the engine one last frantic time and it suddenly flamed to life. With the engine now operating, Fred eased the nose up and clawed for a bit more altitude, sure that the running of the engine was only temporary and that he would have to eject, wanting as much altitude as possible with the downward ejection system. However, the engine kept running and smoothed out to perfection, so Fred groped around the floor, retrieved his helmet and oxygen mask, put everything in place, and headed for home base. By this time, he was more than 300 miles from the base, and once his radio began to work he called in to explain where he was, his situation, and his intention to return for a hoped-for normal landing.

One of the top management people who had rushed to test control when he heard of the "accident" answered the call: "You okay, Fred? Guess that you were a little excited, huh?" he ad-libbed.

Fred, ever the good Catholic, replied, "Not particularly excited, sir. At least no more excited than the Mother Superior was when she discovered the toilet seats in the convent bathrooms raised to accommodate a man."

The management type said no more and just let the whole thing go at that.

COFFEE, TEA, OR ME—AIR FORCE STYLE

Captain Victor Grubbs and I were to deliver a supersecret model of the B-58 aircraft from Fort Worth, Texas, to Langley Field, Virginia, and our delivery van for this supersonic jet model delivery was an ancient but loved C-47, the Gooney Bird.

We got off from Fort Worth a bit later than planned and were diverted to Langhorne, Ohio, for the first leg of the trip. There, we got very little sleep because a B-47 crew came in shortly after midnight and had a knock-down-and-drag-out battle. They had missed their planned rendezvous with a tanker, had almost run out of fuel, and had to land at Lockbourn under marginal weather conditions. The pilot blamed the navigator and the navigator blamed the pilot so a fierce argument arose that developed into physical combat. The military police were called, there was a lot of activity in the barracks, and soon the offending crew (and the night) were gone.

The weather report the next morning showed marginal weather at Langley but the forecast was for it to improve so we gambled a bit and tookoff. The winds aloft grew more severe than those forecast and fuel consumption ran a bit above the desired usage curve but we thought that we had enough to reach Langley with no sweat. This presumption has been the basis for many famous last words stories. We eventually arrived at Langley and were informed that their radar was out, the field was closed due to heavy fog, and would we please go away and leave them alone. Our fuel gauges were bouncing on empty and there was no alternate field in the area with landing aids to help us to get on the ground in an acceptable fashion. A bail-out didn't seem desirable and we had the secret box with its model in it to think about, so we headed for Richmond where they were reporting about a 600-foot ceiling and no operative radar. We tooled around in the blind for a while while the fuel gauges stood at attention on zero. Without any other visible option, Captain Grubbs pointed the aircraft down through the fog and said, "This looks about right for a landing approach." I thought that he was really out to lunch since we were in dense fog and there was nothing to be seen upon which to base a landing, but we went through the landing checklist and all of the motions as if we knew what we were doing. At about 700 feet and halfway through the checklist and halfway through my rosary beads, the lights of Richmond blazed up at us and we were truly in an approach position to the airfield. We landed without incident and because of our "funny" cargo were directed to taxi to a remote part of the airfield for parking. There was no "Follow Me" truck or any such luxuries so we wandered about until we found the area to which we had been directed. Captain Grubbs shut down the engines, slid back in his seat, and acted as if everything had been perfectly normal. With the

aid of a flashlight, I measured the fuel we had remaining—
with a little imagination, the tiny wet spot on the bottom of
the dipstick could be interpreted as showing less than 10
gallons of total fuel remaining.

No one came to aid us and we couldn't leave the aircraft
alone with its secret cargo, so when Vic Grubbs made it
known that he could certainly use a cup of coffee, I was more
than happy to walk to the flight line restaurant to get it—or
to get anything else for him. In fact, I tried to find a cup of
ambrosia for him because any man who could see through
the black fog of that night as he had surely was some kind of
god.

Many years after this incident, Captain Victor Grubbs was
the captain of the Pan American airliner that was hit by a
KLM aircraft during a takeoff in the Canary Islands. Captain
Grubbs was exonerated of any blame in the accident after a
long and detailed investigation. Hell, I could have told them
that without the elaborate investigation.

YOU CAN FOOL SOME OF THE PEOPLE, ETC.

We experienced many problems on the B-58 with the
small tires that were always overheating after the heavy
braking of a landing. These tires were designed small so that
they could fit into the thin wheelwell of the aircraft; after
developing the heat of landing, they would often blow out.
Normally, the heat buildup required about 20 minutes after
landing to reach its peak but sometimes the tires started
blowing during the landing roll.

To mask this deficiency from the press and other
concerned people, we tried to keep observers away from the
aircraft after landing but it didn't always work out to our
advantage. After a flight we had made for the press and
several congressman, Mr. Erickson and I devised a plan to
shield the aircraft from their sight while the tires blew. After
landing, Mr. Erickson would leave the aircraft and lead the
assembled people away from the aircraft and to the more
pleasant surroundings of a nearby air-conditioned building. I

would stay behind and attend to the post-flight chores such as installing safety pins in the ballistic ejection equipment.

As I was installing the first safety pin, the first tire blew, way ahead of schedule, and I got out of the aircraft to join Mr. Erickson and his group who had made it only a short distance from the aircraft. As we stood at a safe distance and watched, all 16 tires blew for the benefit of the reporters—slowly, one at a time, just to add insult to injury.

A lot of public criticism had been generated because of the sonic boom that was created by supersonic aircraft, and the boom was blamed for many of the problems of mankind. The most prevalent criticism was that the boom cracked the glass in the buildings on the ground and damaged structures. In an attempt to demonstrate that the glass-breaking idea was a fallacy, the Air Force set up a display and demonstration at Edwards Air Force Base. Plate glass of many kinds and thicknesses was set up on the ramp at Edwards under various conditions—framed, restrained, vertical, horizontal, etc. Several aircraft then "buzzed" the ramp dragging their sonic boom shock wave with them to show that the glass was not affected by the boom. The demonstration went well and not a single pane of glass was cracked.

As the demonstration drew to a successful close, Colonel Chuck Yeager, in a Test Pilot School F-104, asked for permission to make one last pass over the field and the glass. He came in like a tiger and broke everything—including the hearts of those who had planned the demonstration.

SURVIVAL OF THE FITTEST

Another B-58 crew member and I were on a survival evaluation exercise in the Palo Pinto hills of west Texas. We had taken the equipment from a typical B-58 survival pack and were trying to survive for five days, augmenting the contents of the kit with what we could scrounge from the land, excluding the cows that wandered by frequently.

Regardless of our military survival training, we had made

some serious basic mistakes, and by the third day we were dirty, cold, raunchy, ill-tempered, hungry, and ready to give up and go home. We had killed one armadillo and that had been our supper for the past two days. We had made camp by a big pond and tried to catch a turtle but were unsuccessful. The weather was cold, wet, and windy so we kept a fire going to keep from freezing. The "training" exercise had become a bit too real for creature comfort.

As we sat by the fire and commiserated, an Aero Commander airplane buzzed low over the pond and dropped a big package that landed smack in the middle of the partially frozen water. We felt that our compadres back at home base had realized our uncomfortable situation and were going to allow us to cheat a bit by dropping us a package of goodies. Using rocks, fishing lines, poles, and prayer, we finally worked the floating package to the edge of the pond and hungrily retrieved it. Its watertight wrappings made it difficult to open and our numb-with-cold hands didn't make the task any easier. Finally the wrappings gave way and we found only a big and almost empty box, empty except for a neatly rolled scroll. We unrolled the scroll in bitter disappointment. The wags back home had added their black humor to our already failing mission by signing all of their names to an elaborately scripted message that said simply: "Smile, you're on Candid Camera."

SHE FLEW BEAUTIFULLY, SIR!

After the first flight of an aircraft, or the flight to demonstrate some new system or concept, the pilot and crew were often interviewed by the news media and they had sort of a prepared script that went something like this: "It was a great flight. The machine did all that the engineers said she would do—and a lot more. There was nothing unexpected or spectacular. It was the best machine that I've ever flown. This is the aircraft of the future, a real pilot's dream."

Usually, in reality, what the pilot would have liked to say was more like this: "What a horrible damned experience. It

was only through a supreme faith in God and our own expertise that we ever got this dog back on earth in one piece. If I
ever catch the guy who designed this beast crossing the
street, he'll be one of those mysterious traffic fatalities. God,
what a dog! Wartime combat was a party compared to this
flight. It'll take 10 years of redesign and rework before
they'll ever get this goat off the ground again. Pilot's dream
my ass! Pilot's nightmare is more like it!''

As a working crew member, I experienced some of these
flights and still awaken in a cold sweat thinking of them. I
could never talk about these flights publicly because it would
create a bad image (and another unemployed crew member),
so I just kept notes. Now that most of these aircraft are dead
and buried, I can relate some of these remembered
incidents.

"SAY IT AGAIN, PLEASE..."

While preparing to taxi out for a B-58 test flight early
during the program, we experienced radio failure and
opened the canopies so that a technician could have a go at
correcting the trouble.

A redheaded, tobacco-chewing Louisiana Cajun technician
leaned over the cockpit sill and immediately discovered a
bad connection that he had made during the installation of
the radio. With his radio headset and mike in place, he reset
the wire and in self-disgust remarked, ''Well, I'll be a dumb
SOB, how could I possibly f--k up like that?''

The flight was being monitored by most of the top executives of the company and among them was the company
president. The president called from his monitoring point
and asked, ''Will the person making the last radio transmission please identify himself and then report to Test Control?
This is your president speaking.''

A Cajun drawl was heard over the radio. ''Like I said, I'm
dumb, Mr. President, but I ain't that dumb.'' And the radio
went dead.

SUPERSONIC PUSSYCAT

The B-58, with the unromantic and unimaginative name of "The Hustler," died a rather ignominious death at the hands of the wrecking crews at Davis-Monthan Air Force Base in the desert of Arizona. Only 116 of these magnificent birds were made and 24 of those ended in tragedy. She met most of her prenatal commitments but, like Leonardo da Vinci, she was way too far ahead of her time. She contributed in many ways, was often deprived of credits due her, and because of the ways of history and so-called "security," she will never reap acclaim for her feats.

The B-58 set 19 world's records, and for one of them she was awarded the coveted Bleriot Trophy for achieving a speed that was believed to be impossible when the trophy was established in 1936. For her crews, she also won the Thompson, Collier, Harmon, Bendix, and McKay aviation trophies. She beat the sun across the country when she flew from the east coast to the west coast in 2 hours and 16 minutes. She flew at 600 knots at 500 feet of altitude from Fort Worth, Texas, to Vandenberg, California, and then climbed to 40,000 feet for a Mach 2 return trip—fooling all intercept devices on each run. She duplicated the New York to Paris flight of Charles Lindberg but it took her only 3 hours and 20 minutes. She carried a deadly bomb load of the most destructive proportions. She was an expensive lady but she contributed enough to the knowledge of aviation and the security of her country to earn her keep. She was exciting to fly and exciting to watch. She was the big stepping-stone from then to now.

I was on the first crew to accumulate more than 500 hours in the B-58 and I loved every hour. I had a custom-fitted flight helmet and one of the Convair artists had painted a Sylvester cartoon-type pussycat with a lighted firecracker on its head on the back of the helmet. Emblazoned across the front of the helmet was my name and the words "SUPER-

SONIC PUSSYCAT.'' Perhaps that should be the epitaph for the B-58—forget ''The Hustler'' name, for she was deserving of better. She was the epitome of the results of the curiosity of the aeronautical engineers and of the curious cat. She really probed the unknown, sacrificed too many of her nine lives, and provided many of the answers for the accomplishments in space still to come.

Truly, the B-58 was a ''supersonic pussycat.''

PART IV

THE F-111 (NEE THE TFX)

The F-111 fighter-bomber was the end result of a contractual battle between the Boeing Aircraft Company and General Dynamics. The aircraft was dubbed the TFX— Tactical Fighter Experimental. There was a lot of political jockeying and playing of procurement games by both of these giants of the aviation industry and among the selection committees. The military board had selected the Boeing version but the then-Secretary of Defense, Robert McNamara, and his civilian board overrode that decision and selected General Dynamics.

The F-111 was unique because of her variable-geometry wing, a wing that could be positioned at 16 degrees forward sweep for slow flight and then swept to 72 degrees for doubly supersonic speed. She was designed to be capable of Mach 2.5 and had a landing speed of about 90 knots. She was made of titanium, aluminum, steel, fibreglass, and boron fibers. The F-111 looked more like a docile pet than a formidable fighting machine, although she could carry 50 of the 750-pound bombs beneath her wings plus an assortment of other more exotic weapons. She could fly at 50 feet off the deck and guide herself over any intruding high terrain. Unlike her World War II and Korean ancestors, the F-111 was conceived in a test tube and had flown thousands of computer and simulator hours before her first real flight. Regardless of her studied beginning and of her capabilities, she still had her adolescent problems. She was a victim of public opinion, an outcast, a thing to be questioned, and the ugly public picture of her was inflamed and largely created by the ravings of alleged media experts.

The F-111 was taken in to Vietnam combat before she had reached operational maturity and there she experienced disastrous results, losing three of the six that had been sent. Later during that same war, after she had "grown up," the F-111 distinguished herself and was an active participant in the long-delayed bombing of Hanoi.

The F-111, now a truly combat-proven and combat-ready aircraft, still serves as one of America's front-line defense weapons.

SOMEWHERE MY LOVE

"Flutter testing" of an aircraft involves setting up an artificial means for inducing a flutter or shake in the aircraft at selected magnitudes and frequencies. Put simply (or perhaps a bit over-simply), the testing is done to prove that the aircraft has no natural shake, rattle, and roll characteristics that would destroy it or make it wear out ahead of its time.

The F-111 aircraft had four main wing positions: 16, 26, 50, and 72 degrees, each position designed for a particular area of the flight regime. This unusual characteristic made the flutter testing more difficult by a factor of four since the same flutter data had to be obtained at each of the wing sweep positions. So, combined with the many combinations of speed, altitude, gross weight, and center of gravity test points, the wing positions added this other requirement to an already long test program. To gather the data, the flight conditions had to be almost ideal—no turbulence, clear weather, and a perfectly clear view of the horizon ahead. To get the maximum data from each scheduled flight was very important.

After one of these flutter data flights, I had gone home very smug with the knowledge that we had a very successful flight and had accumulated an unusual quantity of good data. Later that evening, I got a telephone call asking me to return to the base to review and explain some of the data to

THE B-58

THE F-111

THE F-111

Model Shannon Gaughin with author and tail of F-111.
General Dynamics, Fort Worth Division, Edwards Air Force Base

THE F-111

Author Tate presenting General Jimmy Stewart with F-111 model.
General Dynamics, Fort Worth Division, Edwards Air Force Base

THE F-111

Actress/model Carolyn De Vore with early F-111 test model at
Edwards Air Force Base.

General Dynamics, Fort Worth Division
Edwards Air Force Base

DRAMA IN THE SKY

Three greats of flying history: General Doolittle, Pancho Barnes and actor Richard Arlen. Arlen was in movie **Wings**, the first to win an Academy Award. General Dynamics, Convair Aerospace Division
Edwards Air Force Base

X series of experimental aircraft at Edwards Air Force Base, California, flown by blow and go guys.
U.S. Air Force, Office of Information, Air Force Flight Test Center
Edwards Air Force Base

DRAMA IN THE SKY

Test pilots Bill Dana, Daryl Greenameyer and Fitz Fulton at a
barnstormer reunion. General Dynamics, Convair Aerospace Division
Edwards Air Force Base

The author, Ted Tate, presenting General Jimmy Doolittle with a
Golden Lifetime membership plaque to Pancho Barnes' famous
Happy Bottom Riding Club. General Dynamics, Convair Aerospace Division,
Edwards Air Force Base

the test analysts. On the data tape, there was nothing but about two hours of my terrible off-key rendition of a popular song of the moment called "Somewhere My Love." I had hummed and sung while the data was being recorded and had erased or garbled every tiny piece of that valuable data—leaving only that awful singing audio.

"What the hell is that?" my boss asked.

"It's from *Dr. Zhivago* and it's called 'Laura's Theme' or 'Theme from Dr. Zhivago' or just plain 'Somewhere My Love,'" I answered honestly.

That explanation made the boss man a bit sick, and the next week I got all of the "roller coaster" test flights—which made *me* a bit sick.

OF PLANES AND POLITICS

The governmental award for a new aircraft contract is always a hotly contested operation before, during, and after the award. The TFX (Tactical Fighter Experimental) competition was even more fierce than the average. After the smoke of battle had cleared, General Dynamics was selected to build that particular aircraft and the plane was labeled the F-111. The Democratic party was in control of our part of the world at that time, so when the rollout of the first F-111 was performed, many of the leading Democrats of the kingdom known as Foggy Bottom were on hand for the political and historic event.

The stage was set and bleachers were constructed outside of the assembly hangar where the brand-spanking-new aircraft was parked. The day was bright and sunny and the atmosphere was carnival-like. The giant hangar doors slid open and the new gleaming beast of war was towed into position before its makers and sponsors. Two pilots, not in sweaty flight togs but in beautifully tailored business suits and ties, opened the gull-wing cockpit canopies and smiled out at their admirers and the swarm of media people. These were the two pilots who would fly the F-111 on its first flight. In the lapel of each of these pilots gleamed a small golden object, highlighted by the bright Texas sunshine.

The lapel pins shining so brightly in that den of Democrats were tiny wings with a capital G in their middle—wings awarded to those pilots who belonged to the Republican "Pilots for Goldwater" movement.

PHYSICAL FITNESS

Test pilot Fred Voorhies and I were doing a demonstration drop test of a 600-gallon empty fuel tank from one of the wing pylons of an F-111. This type of test is required to demonstrate that these wing tanks can be safely jettisoned away from the aircraft onec the fuel from them is used. The test altitude was 1,500 feet and the speed was 450 knots. With everything perfectly set up, we released the tank. However, instead of dropping away clean, the tank turned in midair and attacked our aircraft. It hit between the two engines, knocked out the oil lines to one of the engines and thus rendered it useless, ruptured our aft fuel tank, and set the whole damned mess on fire.

The pilots of the chase and photo aircraft yelled for us to eject from the burning machine while those on the ground in test control were bellowing out their own instructions. Finally, we got everyone quieted down a bit and had a lucid chase pilot give us a coherent evaluation of our situation. The ruptured aft fuel tank was spraying raw fuel and it was burning but the flames remained beyond the tail of the aircraft since the fuel sprayed into the atmosphere. Structurally, the underskin of the fuselage was a bit beat-up, the right engine was spraying oil from its ruptured lines, some metal trash was dangling from the injured wing, but otherwise we were still flying and doing okay. We decided to tool around a bit to exhaust the fuel in the leaking aft tank, hoping that the fire would end when the fuel was gone, and then make an emergency landing on the dry lake bed at Edwards Air Force Base. We did all of those things as planned, landed on the lake, rolled to a stop, did an emergency exit, and ran from the smoking beast.

The aircraft was so badly damaged that it was ruled as a major accident, so Fred and I had to undergo the rigors of a major aircraft accident investigation. Although we had performed our part of the flight to perfection—on speed, on altitude, and at the precise scheduled release point—we still had to take post-accident physical exams. This involved taking about half of our blood for a centrifuge test to determine if we had been drinking booze or taking drugs before the flight or had leukemia or whatever. We were both given clean bills of health and then had a 16-page psychiatric questionnaire to answer. One of the requirements of the form was that we had to list all previous aircraft accidents in which we had been involved and all injuries received in those accidents.

After we had answered the questions for the reigning psychiatrist, he studied each of us for a long time and then asked, "Has either of you gentlemen ever considered giving up this wanton way of life and pursuing another profession? With your background of accidents, bail-outs, and injuries, you've probably used up all the luck that has been given to you by God and even any extra good-guy points you may have earned with Him."

Shortly after that we both took the good doctor's advice. Fred now has an insurance agency in Oklahoma, and I'm a runaway beach bum in Mexico.

SENATE INVESTIGATION

Prior to the development and production of the F-111 fighter-bomber, the project had been notoriously known as the TFX. This title could be applied to any aircraft of that type that was in the developmental stages, somewhat as any auto manufacturer could call his car a "touring car." It denoted a type and not an aircraft of a particular brand or design. However, because of the Pentagon battle and the unfavorable publicity that accompanied the award of the particular "TFX" contract, the resulting production aircraft, the F-111, could not shed its TFX origins, Millions of erroneous words and evaluations have been published about the F-111, many of them still referring to it as the TFX.

During the experimental and developmental stages of the F-111 program at Edwards Air Force Base in California, those of us who were participants were always in a fishbowl, with the whole Defense Department and political world watching and monitoring our every move, always minimizing our successes and maximizing our failures. We had tons of visitors and many of them in the upper echelons of power or having VIP stature. It was my lot to entertain and educate these visitors in the ways of the F-111 and to hope that I could give them the true story of the aircraft. Usually in the case of VIP's we would isolate an F-111 and use it as a demonstrator so that the visitors could touch, see, smell, and play with the real hardware of the aircraft. In the cases of really high-power visitors, we went all out to show them the total workings and virtues of our maligned little aircraft.

During the visit of one very important senator, we had movies, slides, flight reports, and all of the tools for an honest and impressive dog-and-pony show. In addition, we had electrical and hydraulic power hooked up to the aircraft so that the senator could sit in the cockpit and actually move the controls about. The wing of the aircraft could be moved from a 16-degree forward sweep to a 72-degree aft sweep, and the senator manipulated the controls and watched as the heavy wing moved from one extreme position to another. Everything went like clockwork and worked without a hitch. The senator had to be favorably impressed.

At the conclusion of the presentation of the F-111, I asked the senator if there was anything else that I could show him or do for him.

"Well, this has all been most educational and impressive," he answered, "but what I really wanted to see in detail was the *TFX*. Can we arrange for me to see it next?"

"Really, senator!

GENERAL JIMMY STEWART

Actor James (Jimmy) Stewart is one of my real heroes and certainly one of my most favorite people. He is an excellent actor and an even more excellent representative of what the human race should be like. In my opinion, he is simply an ideal man and a true example of an American patriot.

During World War II, Jimmy Stewart went through the agonies of aviation cadet life to become a military pilot and then performed brilliantly as a B-24 combat pilot and squadron commander in Europe. There was no cashing in on his star status and reputation for this man; he did it like the rest of us unknown slobs except that he did it a bit better. After the war, he stayed in the reserve forces, filled all of the reserve commitments, and, despite the protests of Margaret Chase Smith, was promoted to the rank of Brigadier General. I had the pleasure of meeting General Stewart while he was playing the part of a B-36 pilot in the movie *Strategic Air Command.*

While we were flight testing the F-111 (accursed TFX) aircraft at Edwards Air Force Base in California, I was alerted that General Stewart was coming to visit our test facility to be briefed on the workings of the aircraft. I went all out in making preparations for his visit. Special company photographers were imported, an expensive special model of the F-111 was brought from Fort Worth to be presented to him, and all of the secretaries on the base had their special viewing spots selected so that they could sneak a peek at this fine actor and military officer. News releases were written and the aircraft was polished to perfection in anticipation of the visit.

All was in readiness when the official entourage pulled up in front of the spic-and-span hangar. I had done everything perfectly except for one tiny mistake—there were two General James Stewarts in the Air Force, one a tall and elegant actor, the other a shorter and heavier career officer from the Logistics Command. Naturally, my visitor was the wrong one and everything immediately fell apart. The stage was set so we had to go through all of the motions lest we offend the unsuspecting wrong General Stewart, so we presented the model, took a million pictures, and gave him the grand tour.

After the visit was over, I was really put on the barbecue spit and roasted by everyone who had been involved in this misadventure. The guys at the home office in Fort Worth called daily to sarcastically inquire about "me and Jimmy" and they threatened to take the $750 cost for the model out of my pay. The hazing went on for weeks and it seemed that it would never die or even subside a bit. In desperation and with some motive of vengeance toward all, I wrote to Jimmy Stewart and explained the mechanics of my entire goof. I said that I knew that it was an imposition to ask that he visit the base just to help me out of an embarrassing situation, but I added that I had never accomplished anything without trying and that I was therefore trying to get him to visit our F-111 test facility as my guest.

Within a few days, I received a reply in which Jimmy Stewart told me that he had enjoyed my story about the mistaken identities and said he would indeed help me get off the hook. He added that he was scheduled for some leg surgery but that as soon as he recuperated from that he would be in touch. That was to be some months in the future so I just filed it away in my memory, felt grateful for the personal answer, figured that he would forget all about the promised visit, and hoped that the goof incident would just be forgotten by all.

Several months later, I received a telephone call from the *real* General Jimmy Stewart and he told me that he had arranged for an official visit to the base and that he would expect a personal briefing from me on the F-111 aircraft. He arrived in civilian dress, I gave him the textbook tour and briefing, enjoyed a lunch with him, presented him with an F-111 model (of lesser cost than the first one), and had a million pictures of him taken—several of him and me together. I then had hundreds of the picture of the two of us together printed and I sent copies to all of my detractors who had been giving me such a bad time. With the help of this magnificent gentleman, I had truly made a silk purse from a sow's ear.

A few years later, I met with Jimmy Stewart again at an aviation awards banquet and we had a few chuckles over the incident of the mixed-up generals. I noted to myself that he was beginning to show a bit of age and it saddened me deeply. There will never be another like him, and when he is gone the nation will suffer the loss of a great soldier, a marvelous entertainer, and a true friend.

Indeed, one of the rare privileges of my life in aviation is to have known and had General James Stewart as a friend.

THE DAY WHEN THE WHITE KNIGHT STUMBLED

Once upon a time there was an unusually bright young pilot who had been graduated from the Edwards Air Force Base Test Pilot's School with the highest of marks, the highest of achievement awards, and the promise of a brilliant career. As a result of all of these achievements, he was scheduled to be one of the main forces in the upcoming F-111 flight test project, the "hottest" and most controversial program of the time. Success in this program would mean early promotions, international recognition as a test pilot, and a secure career.

While marking time for the program to get rolling, this pilot flew several other aircraft to maintain his flying proficiency and among these other aircraft was the tiny T-38 jet. During one of these undramatic and conventional flights, he ran into a problem in the air and was forced to eject from the aircraft, breaking an arm in the process. While being repaired and questioned at the same time, he told a story of how the aircraft had suddenly become uncontrollable and of his forced abandonment of the aircraft. Sympathy and career were still his.

While all of this was going on, a farmer called the base to tell of seeing a tiny white aircraft as it buzzed about the countryside and then seeing it hit a transmission tower with one wing. He said that the wing had been torn off and that the pilot had parachuted from the broken bird. Surely, the brass thought, we haven't had another T-38 accident in the same area and just as surely our "White Knight" wouldn't be doing such a no-no as to be buzzing so low that he would hit a transmission tower. It then came to pass that there was no other accident and that it *was* the White Knight who had hit the tower.

Confronted with the evidence, the White Knight defended himself by saying that that was exactly how he had reported the accident—the aircraft was uncontrollable, so he left. He had merely failed to mention that it was out of control because it had lost a wing. Details. The pilot was allowed to recuperate from his injuries, relieved from the F-111 program, flew a brilliant combat tour in Vietnam, and later wound up out of the Air Force and as one of the Hughes Company's top test pilots.

Officials can be so damned picky about details at times.

YOU GOTTA HAVE FAITH

There is a special test that is done during flight test programs in which a chain is affixed to the flight control stick, limiting its movement in all directions. With the controls thus limited, the flight crew positions the aircraft at a specific airspeed and altitude and then violently moves the control stick to its limit in one direction. As soon as the aircraft responds to this stick movement, the stick is then popped equally as violently in the opposite direction. In the case of the F-111, these tests were conducted in the pitch (up and down) and roll (wing up and down) directions for varying flight conditions. It was my lot on this particular flight to be flying with a pilot whom I greatly admired because of his ability, his close family ties, his morals, and his devotion to his religion. I don't recall the exact speed or altitude for this particular flight but it was very fast and very low. We had been bouncing around in the cockpit doing these weird tests when the call came from the test control.

"Stop all tests, handle the aircraft as gently as possible, and return to the base immediately," was the ominous message. "Upon landing, you will be directed to an isolated parking area where the aircraft will be impounded." Nothing else, just the heart-stopping little greeting.

We did as instructed, parked in the "bogeyman" area and were driven to flight test operations. We thought that maybe the lab guys had found that one of us suffered from leprosy or something similar, but the fact that they isolated the aircraft and not one of us laid that suspicion to rest.

At flight ops, we were told that Nellis Air Force Base had just lost An F-111 and crew and that the cause was determined to be a failed weld in the rudder-servo system, a vital part of controlling the aircraft in flight. An inspector wandered in and told us that our aircraft had been inspected and that it was found to be okay but that it would stay in isolation until an inspection specialist from Nellis took a look at it. When the Nellis guy went out to inspect the suspected part, I went along to watch the operation. As he touched the part with his pointing finger, the part fell to pieces as had the one in the crashed aircraft at Nellis. Had that happened during our flight, there was no way in which we could have controlled the aircraft. I went after my fellow pilot to show him the failure and to emphasize how close we had come to losing our aircraft and possibly ourselves. He was totally uninterested.

"Had it been my time, I would have gone," he said.

"Suppose we have different time schedules?" I asked.

"I reckon that one of us would have escaped," he reasoned.

"Oh," was the best answer that I could muster.

"When I walked back to the wounded aircraft, I glanced at the cockpit and realized that it was equipped with an "escape module," one in which both pilot and copilot are rocketed out of the airplane in a single module with a single parachute. Had the part failed during our flight, it would have been a catastrophic failure and we would have both either perished or escaped together. There wouldn't have been time for some roll call of those who were fated to live or die as my friend had philosophized.

My head was already a bit befuddled from the banging around in the cockpit during the tests so I didn't try to sort out this rationale of life and death. I just left the whole matter to fate and to faith, each of which seems to work out okay, although sometimes in strange ways.

THE RELUCTANT TV STAR

Fred Voorhies, one of the best and most conscientious of test pilots, had performed miracles in demonstrating the spin characteristics of the new swing-wing F-111 aircraft and had gained a lot of well-earned respect in the test flying community because of his skill. The normal two-man crew of the F-111 was reduced to one for the spin test program, so Fred essentially had his own private aircraft. Fred was scheduled to fly an "airshow" type flight on Armed Forces Day at Holloman Air Force Base in New Mexico and it was the one-place aircraft that he used. Bleachers had been constructed on the ramp of the base so that the high-ranking military people, the politicians, aircraft buffs, and news media would have a good view of his low-level fly-by. All three of the major TV networks were there to record the show for later viewing.

The F-111 could be flown at exceptionally low speeds with the wing set for maximum lift, the landing gear down, the slats up, and the flaps down, so Fred had planned a slow approach to the field in this so-called "dirty" configuration. It was his plan to make this slow approach to the stands to demonstrate the slow and safe characteristics of the versatile craft and then to retract all of the slowdown devices, sweep the wing to a delta-shaped 76 degrees, light the afterburners to maximum, and then make a spectacular high-speed climb.

However, things didn't go exactly as Fred planned and he got a bit "behind the power curve" with a resulting high sink rate (the rate at which the aircraft is descending). He lit the afterburners but couldn't slow the sink rate and hit the ground at the end of the runway. Parts of the aircraft flew in every direction, but Fred was uninjured. This type of accident is often referred to as a "controlled crash."

After the pieces stopped falling and the dust had cleared, Fred crawled from the shattered cockpit, removed his ultra-expensive flight helmet, and drop-kicked it into the sagebrush and chaparral on the side of the runway. He then leaned against the damaged hulk of the aircraft, buried his head in the crook of one arm, and pounded furiously on the airplane remains with his clenched fist while he shouted, "Dumbhead! Dumbhead! Dumbhead!" A sympathetic ground crewman led him away and in a short while he had regained his normal composure.

Later that evening, Fred was back at home with his wife and children watching the late news on television. There he was, in gorgeous living color, on every news channel for the entire evening, banging away with his fist on the plane while shouting at himself.

His kids thought that the whole thing was quite entertaining and heroic because anybody can simply fly an airplane—but their dad really knew how to put on a show!

MORE SEMANTICS

After a cross-country flight from Edwards Air Force Base in California to Lakehurst, New Jersey, in one of the few of the ill-fated Navy versions of the F-111 aircraft, we arrived in the middle of a raging rainstorm with nothing working in the aircraft except the clock. We were low on fuel and the cockpit was filled with blinking, flashing, and steady warning lights, telling us that all was not well, or that very little was even working, much less right. Lakehurst was closed because of excessive storm damage and we didn't have fuel to reach Patuxent River, the Navy Test Base in Maryland, and in the true tradition of the distraught airman, we were running out of airspeed, altitude, ideas, options all at the same time. I went "Mayday" with anything that was still transmitting.

Some life-saving soul at McGuire Air Force Base heard my wail, allowed that he had a "skin paint" (radar image from the skin of the aircraft rather than from some electronic transmitting device) on us, and give us a big correction to put us in the pattern for an emergency landing at his base. We made the corrections, followed his radar approach instructions, hoped that there was indeed a runway in front of us, and started the business calls for a landing.

"McGuire tower, Navy number 1234 on final," we called.

"Roger, Navy 1234, what type of aircraft?" was the answer

"F-111B aircraft," I answered. The aircraft was very new at that time, there had never been one at McGuire, the radio was crackling with static, and the tower operator did not quite understand the answer. At this point we were on a near-blind final, doing all kinds of necessary things in the cockpit, and not in a loquacious mood.

"Say again, type of aircraft," the tower instructed.

"A great damn big jet!" I responded in irritation.

Surprised at the brusque, agitated answer, and a bit off-guard, the tower responded in kind. "Rog, great damn big jet, cleared to land," he stammered.

And land we did, in a river of water and a blinding rain. After taxiing in and finding the warmth and safety of flight operations, I called the radar controller and the tower operator to thank them for their vital assistance and explained the nature of the F-111B. I apologized for for my lack of patience on final and explained the somewhat extenuating circumstances. The tower operator was a real gentleman and accepted the apology after adding, "No need to apologize, sir. You were absolutely right. I just looked at your machine and it is just as you said, 'a great damn big jet'!"

FORE IS AFT AND VICE VERSA!

Can anyone imagine buying a new, expensive automobile and when it is delivered to them finding a decal on the dash that reads: TO TURN LEFT, TURN THE WHEEL RIGHT

AND VICE VERSA? Any buyer of such a vehicle would have a fit and would not rest until the situation was corrected and normalized, and no sane engineer would devise such a diabolical scheme in the first place. But just such a thing happened to one of the world's newest and most controversial aircraft—the F-111!

The F-111 was the first operational sweep-wing aircraft; its wing position could be varied from a forward position of 16 degrees to an aft position of 72 degrees. This allowed the aircraft to be flown slowly and to have lots of takeoff lift at the 16-degree position and a low-drag, high-speed capability at the 72-degree position. Logically, the selector handle for moving the wing position would be moved in the direction of the wing motion, but a philosophy of cockpit design intruded and the first batch of these sophisticated fighters had the wing moving in an opposite direction from the movement of the selector handle. Basically, to make the wing go forward, you moved the handle back, and to make the wing go back, you moved the handle forward. The logic for this scheme was that the wing selector handle should be considered as a throttle—to go fast, push the handle forward and the wing would go back, and to go slow, pull the handle back and the wing would go forward, slowing the aircraft. To try to explain this in writing is difficult and confusing, so you can imagine how clouded it was in an actual operation. Nevertheless, the idea was incorporated into the hardware and on the first of these aircraft a decal at the wing position selector handle actually read: *fore is aft and vice versa.*

This design continued until a fatal accident was caused when a pilot, in a moment of stress, selected the wrong position and the aircraft crashed. He wanted the wing to go forward to give him more lift and to slow his sink (descent) rate and pushed the selector handle forward, causing the wing to sweep back and give him less lift. The resulting loss of lift increased the rate of sink and the aircraft crashed about a mile short of the intended landing runway.

How unfortunate it is that we sometimes have to get real stupid before we get a little bit smart, but it was true in this case, and after this accident all F-111 aircraft were modified so that the directions of handle and wing were the same.

SORRY 'BOUT THAT

The F-111 was supposed to be a multi-service aircraft to serve the Navy, Air Force, and, possibly, the Marines, but that was not to be. I have always felt that any aircraft that was originally designed for both services had a terrific uphill battle for survival because each service wants to be prime in the running of the show from the beginning of design to the completion of service tests. With the F-111 that was especially true, as the Air Force was to get a large number of the aircraft while the Navy was to get relatively few. This difference in numbers made the Navy feel that whenever a difference of opinion existed between the two services, that the Air Force's viewpoint would be dominant.

Everyone went through all of the motions of a multiservice F-111 although the mood of the Navy was evident from the beginning and it seemed to be only a matter of time until the Navy bailed out of the program. A test force for the Navy version, the F-111B, was set up at Edwards Air Firce Base and test pilot Don Evans and I demonstrated that the aircraft would indeed accelerate to its downgraded performance speed of Mach 2 with four Phoenix missiles under its wings, but it took us from Edwards damned near to Hawaii to get up to that speed. Regardless of this and other favorable data, the Navy Preliminary Evaluation Team found lots of faults with the aircraft. After their final evaluation flight, they summarized their opinion and the end of their participation in the F-111 program by drawing this diagram on the briefing room blackboard:

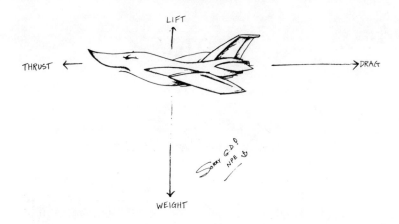

After this dramatic end to the F-111, the Navy contracted for another aircraft, similar to the F-111, that is now called the F-14 with the nickname of "Tomcat." It has always been my opinion that a more suitable name would have been "Copycat."

PART V

CARGO CREW CAPERS

Way back during those Korean days that are almost beyond recall, I was "privileged" to fly C-121 aircraft with the world's craziest practical joker of the airways. A flight never went by that this character didn't do something far out of the ordinary. The following stories relate a few of his favorite tricks, some of which he used over and over.

One time, as the assigned aircraft commander, this clown secreted himself in the cockpit of the aircraft before our load of military dependent passengers was loaded. After everyone was in their seats, he announced over the loud-speaker that the assigned aircraft commander was indisposed but that there were normally three pilots aboard so we would continue with the flight with the two remaining pilots. This caused a bit of concerned mumbling but things went well and the takeoff was made without incident. During the 12-hour flight to Honolulu, this guy hid in the cockpit and was not seen by any of the passengers. After landing in Honolulu and before the passengers were allowd to disembark, he lowered himself from the cockpit by the escape rope, ran to the nearby lanai, and soaked himself in the shower. Just as the passenger door was opened and the passengers came trooping out, he ran up to the aircraft, dripping wet and out of breath, with a palpitating heart. "My God, what a swim! I didn't think that I'd *ever* catch up with you guys," he panted.

Most of the passengers were amused, some amazed, and none convinced by his little con game, but it did break the monotony of the long Pacific trip.

On another occasion, this airborne Milton Berle had two fake plaster casts made for his arms, casts that he could slip on and off with ease. After all the passengers had boarded the aircraft, he walked up the aisle among the passengers wearing the casts. He smiled at the people patronizingly, assured one and all that he could handle things okay, and entered the cockpit. After he had closed the door between the passengers and himself, he would remove the casts and attend to the normal business of flying the aircraft, but for each of appearances in the passenger compartment he wore the casts. We had such a nervous and upset bunch of people when we landed at Honolulu that no one had the presence of mind to lodge a complaint against this joker.

Still another foolish little gimmick this guy enjoyed was to board the aircraft after all of the passengers were in place with two big bags full of beer cans in his arms. Only a few of the cans at the top of the bags were actually filled with beer and all of the others were empty. After takeoff, this court jester would toss empty beer cans from the cockpit, allowing them to accumulate in large numbers in full sight of the passengers. This went on for the full 12 hours of flight and a lot of the passengers were so disturbed that they didn't even take a nap, sure that they had a beer-soaked pilot in immediate charge of their destinies. After this caper, there was a flood of letters of protest to the Military Airlift Command and the written reprimands in the pilot's personnel file grew fatter.

A more simple trick that this jokester loved to play involved hiding a parachute in the cockpit prior to takeoff. Somewhere along the flight path, he would stroll casually through the passenger compartment wearing the parachute and would verbally console all of the distraught passengers, "Saying, not to worry, folks. Everything will be okay. I'm going for help now."

More letters and more reprimands.

Most of this man's gimmicks he got away with, but he was finally nailed after a particularly cruel and contrived little play. He got away with carrying books on *How to Fly* in view of the passengers; he got away with buying huge blocks of flight insurance while he cautioned his passengers that flying the Pacific was still a dangerous undertaking—"Look at what happened to Amelia," he would say—but he didn't get away with his "passenger jettisoning" act.

Seated among his passengers in the Honolulu lanai terminal, he had his copilot ask him loudly if it didn't prey upon his conscience that he had once been the cause of so many people having to sacrifice their lives.

"Nope," he would answer. "It was a matter of getting the load light enough after we had lost a couple of engines. A simple matter of sacrificing 36 people and saving the other 22 aboard of losing everyone. In fact, I feel somewhat heroic about the whole thing."

"Well, I can see some logic in that. But how did you choose who would go and who would be saved?" the straight man asked.

"Easy," the flighty guy explained. "First I took all of the elderly and unattractive women, then the older men, then the less attractive of the remaining women, and finally a few of the middle-aged retirees. I saved some of the pretty young officer's wives and my entire flight crew, of course."

The next act of this little melodrama was when two burly air policemen arrested the talkative pilot and hauled him off to some lockup. Two of his potential passengers who were exposed to this horror tale were the wives of general officers, so they had quietly called the authorities and had him arrested. Also, both of them were somewhat unattractive.

The last time I saw this guy, he was not allowed to get any closer to an airplane than to inspect it after it had been washed in the washrack—an operation of which he was then in charge.

MIRACLE AT DA NANG

During the Vietnam war, I flew frequent airlift missions to that enchanted place. Prior to to one of these missions, the wife of a friend, Ed Rivas, asked if I would take a Christmas cake to her son, a Marine stationed in Vietnam. The local

Catholic priest also asked that I take four large cartons of Christmas goodies to the chaplain at Da Nang, so I departed with normal cargo and these special items. The cartons I could handle because they would be turned over to the Da Nang chaplain, but Mrs. Rivas could tell me only that her son was stationed "somewhere across the river from Da Nang." It seemed an impossible task to locate her son, but I gave it a try.

The trip over was a real bear with all kinds of maintenance troubles, bad weather, and having to remove the chaplain's big boxes at each stop enroute. At Da Nang, we encountered moderate ground fire on final approach and when we landed there was a mortar attack in progress. We were advised that a burning F-4 aircraft with exploding ammunition aboard was in the path of our taxiway and that we should abandon our aircraft and take any cover of opportunity.

After we got an all clear, I called the chaplain but he was reluctant to come to the base for his boxes because there was some sort of street-fighting in progress. After I recounted the troubles that I had experienced in getting the boxes to him, he reconsidered and came to the ramp with enough troops protecting him to defend the entire west coast of the United States. He thanked me sincerely but then crossed himself in disbelief when I gave him the box with the Christmas fruitcake and the "across the river" address. An impossible task it was, but he promised to do his best with only the sparse information.

Back at home a few weeks later, Ed and Mrs. Rivas showed up one night to deliver a complete Mexican dinner to our house, one of the best I have ever tasted. Their son had miraculously received the cake and had written to thank his mother for sending it. But the coincidence of apparent miracle didn't end there. A couple of years later, while shopping for furniture, my wife and I were given a business card by the salesman who had been attending to us. The name on the card was Rivas.

"Were you ever in the Marines in Vietnam?" I asked.

"Yes, sir, I was," he answered.

"Is your father named Ed?"

"Yes, sir, he's a jet engine technician for the government at Edwards Air Force base," he explained.

"Did you get a Christmas fruitcake delivered by a chaplain a couple of years ago?" I then asked, somehow knowing that the answer would be yes.

After the salesman confirmed that he was the one who had gotten the cake and he learned that it was delivered by me, his eyes grew moist and he was profuse in his thanks. We were both surprised by the strange coincidence that had brought us together in a furniture store in California.

I also intended to one day seek out the chaplain and to find out how he had located "a marine named Rivas somewhere across a river from Da Nang." I never did, but I will always feel that somewhere in this world there is a chaplain who has a direct line to his boss.

TAKE THE EASY WAY OUT

We were headed for Korea in the C-124 and were about 200 miles from a scheduled stop at tiny Wake Island. It was so clear that Wake was almost visible from that range and there was hardly a ripple on the surface of the Pacific below us. The pilot was in a bunk asleep, the copilot was minding the store, and I was daydreaming away in the pilot's seat. I was supposed to be monitoring the performance of a navigator who was being given a routine line check. He seemed to know his business quite well so we just tooled along in splendor. The dream was interrupted when the navigator called.

"Pilot, this is Nav. Give me a 45-degree correction to the left," he instructed.

The copilot looked at me questioningly. I shrugged and we made the requested correction.

About five minutes later, the navigator called for a correction of 90 degrees to the right. The copilot and I smiled knowingly—the clown had made a big error, realized it, and was now making a correction. We cranked in the 90. After a few more minutes, the navigator called for 45 degrees to the left and I crawled back to see what in the blazes he was doing.

It was no big deal. He had spilled mustard from his sandwich on his aerial chart and was simply navigating around the blemished area. We arrived at Wake right on time and the navigator passed his flight check. He had proved himself to be very efficient—a little stupid perhaps, but he had managed to cope with the most adverse and unexpected of circumstances.

FIRST-GRADE ARITHMETIC FOR A FIELD-GRADE PILOT

Pilots, navigators, and bombardiers always seemed to have a bit of a feud among themselves and they seldom missed an opportunity to needle each other. Mistakes were magnified: the pilot makes a hard landing, the navigator misses an estimated time of arrival, or the bombardier misses the target. The mistakes live on and continue to be the subject of the friendly rivalry among the crew members. One classic to come from this frivolity was an exchange between a pilot and navigator during a long flight over the Pacific.

"Pilot, this is Nav. Give me a one-degree correction to the left."

"Nav, you're out of your bloody mind," the pilot replied. "I can't read one degree on this compass and you know it. One degree is a stupid correction to ask for anyway."

"Roger, I understand," said the navigator.

A few minutes later: "Pilot, this is Nav. Give me five degrees to the right."

"Having a problem back there, Nav? Okay, you have the five right."

Then, after a short pause: "Pilot, this is Nav. Give me six degrees to the left."

"What the hell are you doing back there?" the pilot yelled. "Make up your mind which direction you want and knock off this right and left crap. Now, there's your six to the left.''

"Thank you, *sir.*"

Another short pause, while the pilot realized how he had been duped. Then he called the navigator. "Nav, this is Pilot. I'll get you for that.''

TO EACH HIS OWN

After a week in Panama City, Panama, we were struggling home in an antiquated C-47 Gooney Bird and had just departed Kingston, Jamaica, an interim refueling spot. While on the ground at Kingston, we were all recounting our individual experiences while in Panama. Everyone except a certain reserve pilot told harrowing tales of female conquests, great financial wins at the casinos, and of the stag shows they had attended. Most of these "barracks" tales were more of fantasy than of reality but the reserve pilot became very disturbed about what he was hearing. He gave us a big lecture about morality, responsibilities to our wives and families, the dignity of our status as U.S. Air Force officers, and about our duty to our God. He did such a convincing number on us that we were all feeling a bit guilty as we tooled along toward home—not too guilty, however, since our biggest sin had been in making up the stories in the first place.

About 40 minutes out of Kingston, we lost one of the engines and made a turn back toward Kingston. As a precaution, we broke out of the ditching and survival gear and made ready to ditch if necessary. The sea was like glass and in a way we were actually looking forward to doing an actual ditching after so many years of practice. The oil pressure on the remaining engine started dropping and it appeared that ditching was imminent, so we really got busy with emergency messages, reviewing procedures, checking our position, and dragging the equipment to the door of the aircraft. With all of this activity, we had failed to notice that our lecturing reserve pilot was glued to his seat and praying out loud. He was begging for forgiveness for his behavior while in Panama, admitting that he didn't really visit churches and historical sites but had spent the entire time with a charming lady of the night at Mama Chin's Casa d'Amour. He wouldn't budge or help us get ready for the landing in the sea. He was sure that the end was in sight and he shouted apologies to us for his condemnations—it was he who was the sinner, not us, and he had accused us to salve his own conscience. Now he felt that the supreme justice was about to catch up with him.

As it turned out, the good engine and its wiggly oil pressure held up and we made Kingston safe and sound and dry though a bit disappointed that we didn't get to ditch.

The reserve pilot caught a commercial flight back to the States and never flew with our squadron again. The last thing that any of us remembered him saying was something from the Bible about casting the first stone.

SO VERY, VERY REAL

I have never understood abstract paintings and I suspect that many of those who profess that they understand them are really in the same league with me. Perhaps I equate it with the abstractions of war because few of us, if any, ever really understood what that was all about either. As a protected air crew member, I always had a rather abstract idea of the wars in which I was involved because I was never subjected to the blood and guts and gore. So war to me was an abstraction, something that was happening all around me but that I really didn't see and certainly didn't understand.

It was at some point during the Korean war, when I was on a temporary assignment with a Military Air Transport Command crew, that I first saw the reality of war with all of its ugly trappings. We had brought several caskets of dead soldiers to Travis Air Force Base and had landed in a blinding, blowing rain. During the flight, the caskets were merely cargo, identification tags, and nothing more. I walked around and among them as I had done on similar flights before. I purposely avoided thinking about what was really inside each of those aluminum boxes.

After the landing, we taxied to a parking lot on the tarmac to unload our sad cargo of noble dead. But while one of the caskets was being taken from the aircraft, it was accidentally dropped, and the body bag inside opened on impact to spill its contents onto the wet concrete. The rain washed a brown fluid from what was left of the body inside the bag and it puddled around the corpse. The wind swept over the scene as if it was all being directed by some film crew making a horror movie. We all stared in stunned silence, knowing what we had to do but hoping that someone else would attend to the task at hand. Finally, the loadmaster stooped to put it all back together and the rest of us slunk away to flight operations, easing our guilt by reciting that it was the load-master's duty to attend to such things and not ours. We all drank a lot that evening and no one slept very well.

Never again would war be abstract to me, whether I was thousands of miles away from it or within its bounds. Since that day on the tarmac at Travis, war for me has always been very, very real.

TRUE OR FALSE?

During an airlift mission in a C-124, we were carrying a large crane and a spare engine for a grounded C-124 on Canton Island. The loadmaster on this flight was a big, strong, and very intelligent black sergeant named Calvin. He and I were close friends since we both had come from the bare roots of the deep south. We kidded each other with all of the red-neck and KKK jokes that we had ever heard and agreed that living in the Depression-era south was not the ideal thing for sensitive souls, be they white or black.

After takeoff from Hawaii, Calvin and I did some weight and balance figuring to ensure that we could dump some of the heavy cargo if we ran into any kind of aircraft behaviorial problems. As navigator, it was my responsibility to work with Calvin in the event of such an emergency. After our

little meeting and checkout of procedures, I went to the
flight deck and took the empty copilot's seat to watch while
the beautiful Pacific unfolded beneath us. The pilot asked
me if Calvin and I had our procedures all worked out and I
assured him that we did and that all was well in that respect.

"Don't count on Calvin helping you if we really have to
dump that stuff," the pilot cautioned.

"Why not? He's the loadmaster and that's what he's
supposed to do," I said.

"Well, the last time that I was on a flight with him we had
a problem that required dumping a lot of cargo and Calvin
wouldn't raise a finger to help. He just sat on the edge of a
box and prayed."

"What did you do?" I asked.

"Well," the pilot said, "we had two engines that were
inoperative, a third one was a bit sick, and we were 1,200
miles out. We just couldn't hold altitude and we had to dump
everything. I ordered Calvin to help. Told him that I was a
major, then that I was the aircraft commander, and finally
that I was a direct representative of the president of the
United States and as such I was ordering him to get off his
butt and help to jettison the cargo."

"What did Calvin do then?" I asked.

"He just rolled those big eyes up at me, looked real
serious, and told me that the man he was talking to
outranked all of us and then went on with his praying."

"And then what?" I asked.

"Nothing," said the pilot. "We got rid of the cargo and
limped home on one and one-half engines. After we got
there, the engineering troops figured out that the airplane
would not fly in that condition and that we must have been
mistaken about having only that minimal amount of power
available. They even went to Oklahoma and set it up on a
simulator there and proved that the airplane wouldn't fly
under those conditions."

"So then," the pilot concluded, "we all figured that the
man Calvin had been talking to surely *did* outrank us all and
that He had more do to with our getting back safely than any
of our skills, We got Calvin promoted to master sergeant,

waited until we were in Samoa to pin on his new stripes, and had a big party to celebrate the event.''

True or false, Calvin's contact had worked a miracle, and although I didn't tell anyone, I'd called on that same head-quarters myself a few times and had excellent results.

A MILE HIGH AND OFF COURSE

As a navigator with the Military Air Transport Service, I had some of those ''not really lost but temporarily disoriented'' flights that fortunately always ended happily. Some of them even had a little bit of humor along the way.

During one such flight, the weather was horrible, the outdated radar was barely working, the pilot was grumpy about being vectored around heavy squall lines, and I was tired, worried, and lost. We had a load of young GI troops aboard, and as their ''keeper'' there was a black flight attendant from New York who knew her job better than anyone else flying the ''line.'' She saw that I was having a problem and offered a cup of hot coffee to ease the aggrava-tion but I was too busy trying to find out where we were to accept it. The flight crew bunks were directly in back of my navigation station, the lower for the pilot, the center for navigator, and the top bunk for the flight attendant. After my abrupt refusal of the offered coffee, the young lady tossed her head and climbed into her bunk for a nap.

I sweated blood and used everything I knew to try to get things organized but they seemed to only become progres-sively worse. I became more and more agitated with each failure and was soon cussing everybody and everything in absolute frustration. In the middle of all of this, the flight attendant stuck her head out of the bunk curtain and asked if it was true that I was a real southerner from North Carolina and did I believe all of those rebel sayings and superstitions about black people? My God, I had trouble enough without getting into some kind of Mason-Dixon philosophical discus-sion with her but I assured her that all of the answers were affirmative—never yes, but affirmative.

"Okay, if that's true you can just haul your butt up here in this bunk with me. According to your beliefs, you can sure change your luck and if I ever saw anybody who needs it, you do. Not only that but we're flying at 8,000 feet so you can become a member of the exclusive 'Mile-High Club' at the same time. All in one fell swoop," she challenged.

We got to Wake Island right on target and right on time.

A SMALL TRIBUTE TO A WONDERFUL GROUP

Of all of the heroes and heroines of the wars, only precious little has been said or written about the Air Force flight nurses, and there were certainly some real heroines among them. They were, and probably still are, one helluva group of ladies, and many men owe their very lives to them.

I recall one nasty, rainy, windswept day on the ramp at Tan Son Nuit base near Saigon when I watched while troops who had just been brought in from battle were loaded aboard my aircraft. They had been attacked in a surprise raid by the Viet Cong and the casualties seemed to be more than we could capably evacuate to Clark Air Base or on to San Bernardino, California. The nurses held umbrellas and IV bottles over the wounded while they themselves were soaked by the hot rain. They made innumerable trips across the bloody ramp, and it was reminiscent of the battle scene in *Gone with the Wind* where the wounded were gathered together at the train station in Atlanta. These ladies labored until the evacuation was complete, and how they managed through the long days will always be a true miracle of strengh in my book.

Other times, when the aircraft was loaded with patients with unpleasant illnesses such as the one we called "jungle rot," these same ladies worked in the ugliness and foul odor of sickness as if they were doing their daily housework in a comfortable apartment in Van Nuys. They had a lousy duty, a duty that was vitally necessary, and they always did it damned well.

I have no special stories about these nurses except those

in which they performed far above the normal call of duty and in which they did things that probably could not have been done by the strongest of men, things where they had only bloody pieces of men to work with, flew in cold airplanes in which the heaters didn't work and in an environment that would cause the faint-of-heart to be repulsed.

We often called them on the intercom as "Captain Nightingale," but we really loved them and only joked to ease the tensions of the situation. They were in fact *real* Florence Nightingales, the only difference between the noted lady of mercy and them being a different time and a different uniform.

An old vaudeville line was "give the little lady a big hand," and in the case of the U.S. Air Force flight nurses, they deserve that and the undying gratitude of all of those whom they served directly and from all of us whom they served indirectly.

I sometimes think that our flight nurses stole a line from Shakespeare and amended it to read, "Such duty as the subject owes the prince/Even such a nurse oweth to her patient." Maybe they didn't even know that line, but they sure performed as if they not only knew it but as they had written it.

Air Force nurses, here is one old, gray vet of the Pacific and Atlantic crossings in which you performed so magnificently who salutes you and hopes that your fortunes will be as generous as were your contributions.

"GOD HATH CHOSEN THE FOOLISH THINGS OF THE WORLD TO CONFOUND THE WISE"

I. Corinthians 1: 27

"Air Force 1234, taxi to the edge of the ramp, stay clear of the revetments, park the aircraft, and abandon it," the control tower guy barked. "Take cover wherever you can, the base is under a sustained mortar attack."

We put the big old bear of an airplane called a C-124 on the ramp's edge, shut everything down, exited, and looked for places to hide. I spotted a runway perimeter sandbag guard bunker and dived into it about the same time that an F-4 in a revetment took a direct hit and exploded all over the place. Inside the sandbag house was the biggest, strongest, and most heavily muscled black master sergeant that I had ever seen. He wore only the pants of fatigues and his upper body, clothed in sweat, looked like a statue carved from black onyx.

"Room for me in here?" I asked even though I was already in.

"Sure is, major. You ain't very big anyway," he grinned.

I settled into the confined space and we did a bit of fireside chatting while the bombs burst overhead. I made the mistake of telling the sarge that I was from North Carolina and then tried to rectify those legends that people from that area weren't kindly disposed to blacks by assuring him that I had no problem with people's races, religions, color, school rings, size, sex, or any of that prejudicial stuff. He laughed at my clumsy talk and after a while we were friends at ease.

The only furnishings inside the sand cubicle were the sarge's automatic weapon, a lot of ammunition, and an Igloo tin cooler can filled with warm water. The water in the can was much like a lot of the water in Vietnam, shot full of hydrogen sulfide or whatever it is that made it taste and smell like rotten eggs. For that reason, we always brought the troops some sort of stuff to mask the smelly taste of the water and on this trip we had lots of Kool-Aid and powdered chocolate. The sarge asked if we had any such goodies aboard, and when I told him that we had several cartons of Kool-Aid, he smiled a broad grin and suggested that I go and get some to sweeten the taste of the water in the cooler can.

"Sure, sarge, I'll just run across the ramp and dodge all of that junk that's flying around and get us a carton," I answered with a tinge of sarcasm. "That F-4 ammo is going off at about my eye level and there's a couple of fires on the ramp and you want me to stroll through it like a trip to the grocery store. I also have a couple of *Playboy* magazines aboard and I suppose that you'd like those too?"

"Hell, yeah, major," he replied. "It'll just take you a couple of minutes and I'll buy you a couple of cold beers tonight to repay you. However, if you don't want to go, just hold onto this little old gun and I'll go after them. Where are they in the airplane?" he asked.

Without further ado, I climbed over the bags, did an imitation of a head-down charge in a war movie, and ran to the big bird. I gathered up the goodies, ran back, triumphant and scared.

We doctored up the water, gulped down some of the sticky mess, and leafed through the *Playboy*. About four hours later, the all clear was sounded and I climbed out of the wonderful refuge. The sarge and I shook hands, promised to meet another time at another place, and I started to leave.

"Major, that was some sort of brave thing you did to get those things for me," he said. "However, like my mama once told me, they ain't a whole lot of difference between being brave and being foolish.

"He saluted a final goodbye, I returned the salute, and trudged back to the parked aircraft to get on with the mundane task of unloading cargo. Then I thought about what I had done and about what the sarge's mama had said I knew that his mama was right and that I had stepped over that line, probably having been more foolish than brave.

Oh, what the hell.

A GREAT MAN AND A GREAT LADY

We had just completed a flight from San Francisco to Hawaii, en route to Japan, and the 12 hours in the C-124 had been tiring. After hitting our estimated time of arrival within acceptable limits and entering the prescribed entry gate to Honolulu without scrambling the fighters, the next thing on our minds was to get to the Officer's Club to see a show in which vocalist Nancy Wilson was the star. The crew bus driver dropped us off at flight ops and I went in a dead run into the building to file the debriefing documents. Racing down the hallway, I ran headlong into some people who were standing in the corridor, nearly knocking one of them down. The one on whom I scored a direct hit was a rather stout man with a friendly face and only a fringe of hair. I apologized profusely, pressed on, and took the down-stairs two at a time to complete my business in the office and get on with the show at the club.

"Who were those people standing around in the hallway?" I asked the debriefing officer.

He peered up into the hallway and turned a shade of white. "My God, that's Secretary of State Dean Rusk, President Marcos of the Philippines and their wives plus some Secret Service guys. They're here for some kind of a big meeting. Didn't you see Air Force One parked out in front of ops?" In my hurry, I hadn't noticed it.

After completing my business, I went into the hallway and again apologized to Mr. Rusk and his party for my clumsiness. Mr. Rusk sensed my extreme embarrassment and he assumed all the blame for the collision by saying that they should have been in the special VIP room instead of the hallway. We shook hands and I hurried to the crew bus where the rest of the crew were impatiently waiting.

The show at the club had already started by the time we reached our quarters which were located directly across the street from the club. We didn't have time to change from our grubby flying clothes, and not being allowed in the club in work clothes, we sneaked to the edge of the outside lanai where Miss Wilson was appearing. She saw us and a couple of other "undressed" crews and asked why we didn't come and take seats at one of the vacant tables. The club officer explained that we weren't allowed in the club without being properly dressed, so Miss Wilson picked up her microphone and walked to the edge of the lanai directly in front of the huddled flight crews.

"If the working troops can't come to the show, then I'll take the show to them," she announced. We were then a front-row audience for her performance, and after the show she joined us to give each of us an autographed picture.

In two single, simple acts of understanding and kindness to a raunchy Air Force crew, two people, Mr. Dean Rusk and

Miss Nancy Wilson, achieved greatness beyond that which they had already won in the eyes of an admiring world.

THE DOMINO THEORY

At the time I was recalled to active duty for the Korean war, I was assigned to a Convair company project to construct an aircraft called the YB-60. This was an abortion of a B-36 aircraft that was an entrant into the long-range jet bomber competition. The object was to take an existing B-36, cut a pie section from the wing root, sweep the wing at a rakish angle, extend and add finesse to the nose, add jet engines and, viola, a new jet bomber. As with many things, the idea was good, the application not so good. Whatever the merits of the program, I became extremely interested in it, and after being recalled I maintained that interest.

I was stationed at Ellington Air Force Base for a refresher course in navigation, bombing, and radar operation. There I shared in a car pool with several other officers and we had a regular routine of attending classes, checking our mail, doing our assigned commissary chores, and having a few moments of relaxation at the club. On one of these days, I received a copy of a company news release about the first flight of the YB-60 and I shared it with the other officers who were in the car pool. One of these guys, a radical Boeing Company fan, showed an unusual interest in the report and read it over several times. I found nothing outstanding in the report other than that the aircraft had flown, was somewhat successful, but was not a spectacular success. The release listed the problems encountered during the flight and they all seemed very minor. Of personal interest was the note at the end of the formal report that had been added by the Convair friend who had sent me the report. It said simply, "Prissy dominoed and the number is seven." I put the report with my other mail which was mostly bills that were the result of lost income due to the recall from civilian to military life, and I forgot about the whole thing.

The following day, while in flight in a T-29, we got a call

from the tower to verify that I was aboard and after verification there was an order to land immediately. I thought that there was some emergency involving my family but was assured that it was official and not personal. Perhaps my talents had at last been recognized and I was being called in for some high-level consultation or some such idiotic thing. Those ideas were quickly dashed when we landed and I was put under military arrest and escorted to headquarters by the air police. At headquarters, I was read a list of my rights, advised that I was charged with a breach of security, and that I was subject to a fine of thousands of dollars, death by firing squad, or a combination of both. After the stern-faced Provost Marshal and the Judge Advocate cautioned me to say nothing to anyone about the matter, I was released upon my own recognizance. I was told to go home, say nothing to anyone, make no phone calls, locate the YB-60 document, and bring it to headquarters the next morning. I felt that I was about to join Benedict Arnold in the infamous hall of traitors.

At home, I couldn't find the accursed document and was reduced to sifting through the garbage can that was filled with the remains of dinner and the discarded unpaid bills where I finally located it. I slipped from the apartment under the cover of darkness to call my Convair friend who had sent the release. Like a hooded bandit, I selected a shadowed booth and left the door partially open so that the interior light would not come on. The sender was more upset than I was since he had just been summarily fired from the job he had held for 10 years, had been placed under some kind of restraining order, and was scared stiff. He had been ordered not to call me nor to talk to me if I should call. We cut the discussion short and ended with absolute confusion on both sides.

When I got home, two cloak-and-dagger types in civilian clothes were waiting for me and their visit had my wife and kids terrified. They wanted the copy of the YB-60 report and threatened to tear the house apart looking for it if I couldn't produce it. By this time, I had somewhat recovered from the initial scare and played with these J. Edgar Hoover types a bit before surrendering the paper. I made them show their identification and demanded proof that they really represented the CIA or OSS or whoever was making the investigation. I gave them the crumpled paper and I was warned that my phone was now tapped and that my house was under constant surveillance. By this time, I lost my identification with Benedict Arnold and felt more like Dillinger or Pretty Boy Floyd. My wife and I slept very little that night and waited for the searchlights to come up while a voice over a loudspeaker demanded that I come out with my hands in the air.

"They" let me sweat for a couple of days of routine classes and finally called a hearing. It was as if I was a prisoner of the North Korea and was being interrogated by some sort of high tribunal. All of my tormentors, although some were of military rank, wore civilian clothing and were introduced as Mr. So-and-So. After being questioned for hours about my activities in the aircraft industry and after finding that the "secret" paper that I had was only a copy of a company news release that had been given to all of the Convair employees, this noble group had just about reached the decision that I was not guilty of any wrongdoing and that the security-conscious Boeing fan who started it all was the real culprit. They all seemed to be a bit embarrassed by the whole scene except for one red-faced, cigar-chomping Winston Churchill type who leaned back in his chair and raked me with suspicious eyes.

"Lieutenant, you have really snowed these people with your story and are on the verge of getting off the hook, but I know that there is more to this incident than meets the eye and I intend to get to the bottom of it," he announced with assumed authority. "We know the source of the typed report you possessed and we know that it contained information already in the public domain, but we have not discussed the coded message that was handwritten on the same document."

"What coded message?" I asked the gentleman.

"*This.*" And he stood up and thrust the paper at me. "I'm referring to *this* bit that says, 'Prissy dominoed and the number is seven,' Will you be so kind as to explain this to the board?'' he asked sarcastically.

Now I was on the easy downhill side of this ridiculous mess and my natural maverick personality intruded. I sighed as though I had been really trapped, tried to look very guilty, stood and addressed the board. "Gentlemen," I said, "the man who sent this copy of the press release is a very close friend. He and I share a common interest in animals and airplanes. He has a large Persian cat named Prissy. In Texas, whenever a woman or an animal gives birth, a common saying is that she 'dominoed.' My friend is merely telling me that his cat Prissy had seven kittens."

"Bullshit!" my antagonist roared. "Now you're trying to ridicule this board! Tell us the real meaning of this note or we'll bring your friend in to explain it and hang both of you!"

At this point, another officer of the board addressed my inquisitor by name (a no-no in this type of proceeding) and told him to calm down. He went on to say that he was a Texan himself and that the 'domino theory' was correct. He than advised an aide to call the agents who were watching my friend in Fort Worth to verify that there was a cat named Prissy and that she indeed did have seven kittens. (Imagine what that agent's daily report looked like after he had spent the day checking on a litter of kittens.) After a lunch recess, the facts were confirmed, and the board was about to be brought to a close when my fat antagonist brought up another technicality. It seemed that as a 14-year-old boy, I had been arrested for disturbing the peace during a fight in a sleazy Baltimore movie house and I had not entered that on my military security clearance. He then asked about what other "criminal" activities I had left off my clearance application and why I had a special clearance when I was only 17 years old. I explained that I had worked for the Glenn L. Martin Company and part of my duties involved handling the secret Norden bombsight and that was why I had a "special" clearance. He latched onto every entry on my security clearance like a tiger and didn't let go until other members of the board quieted him down again. Finally, I was excused from the room of inquisition, the board voted me innocent of any wrongdoing, records of the hearing were burned in some sort of ceremonial urn, the case was closed, and the harassed suspect released to return to normal duties.

The civilian friend who had sent the ''mysterious'' document was returned to his job without any loss of pay and the story ended happily for all concerned.

After the hearing, I was cautioned not to say a word about the proceedings to anyone, but I did confide to a close friend all of the horrors of the probe. This friend, Capt. LeRoy Ware, had been dubbed ''the meanest officer in the Air Corps'' by war correspondent Richard Tregaskis after he had seen films of some of LeRoy's bombing and strafing raids at Rabaul. LeRoy wanted me to call the Boeing fan who had started the whole thing and ask him to talk with me behind one of the barracks classrooms and then to yell that I was being attacked by this guy. LeRoy would then come galloping to my rescue and beat the hell out of him. Others in my class volunteered to be ''witnesses'' to the attack and to verify that LeRoy was helping protect myself from the wrath of this big, athletic guy. I vetoed this idea because I had seen LeRoy in action; I believed Tregaskis's evaluation, and I already had enough trouble with the ''security'' forces.

All of this mental hell over a cat and her seven kittens! I couldn't help wondering what it would have been like if I had met with these same gentlemen faced with an assault or murder charge!

LET'S DO IT AGAIN

The Korean recall program brought together some strange bedfellows, and while I was assigned to the B-36 wing I got one of the strangest of them all. This was a young second lieutenant who had just entered active duty after graduation from the reserve officer's training program. He reported in for active duty driving a new Ford convertible equipped with all of the goodies and sporting a lipstick-red leather upholstery. On day one, he was arrested for speeding on the base and issued a reprimand. On day two, he was arrested for speeding and his car was impounded. On day three, he showed up driving a new Oldsmobile Rocket 88 convertible and on the next day that too was impounded for a speeding infraction. A couple of days passed without incident and then he arrived driving a chrome-soaked Harley Davidson motorcycle and that was impounded before the end of the day. This was the last straw for the air police and they took away his driver's license and he was forbidden to drive on the base. After this incident, he was brought to the base and picked up by a taxi—and then he played his ace.

He next showed up in a chauffeur-driven Cadillac Fleetwood and got permission for it to be on the base provided that the chauffeur always was the driver. For the remainder of his tour, this young lieutenant was chauffeured about the base in his Cadillac. He was also given permission to sell the cars and the motorcycle that were impounded. I was fortunate enough to get the Ford convertible at a ridiculously low price.

The young lieutenant, rumored to be an heir to the Johnson & Johnson fortune, performed his duties in a respectable manner, and from time to time a chosen few of us lesser lights were treated to the luxury of being transported to lunch to a chauffeur-driven limousine.

THE KIDNAPPING

Operations officers, those brave souls who faced belligerent fliers each day to outline the horrors of the day's missions, were probably one of the most maligned groups of people of all time, be it wartime or peacetime. These were the officers who would stand on a platform before the assembled group of combat crews and dramatically unveil a map or a flight plan for the day's unpleasant activities. Everyone had to hate someone and to blame the conditions of war on someone so it was quite often that the ops officers were the targets for frustration. A favorite bar room song was "Give me operations out on some lonely atoll/For I'm too young to die and I just wanna grow old."

Some operations officers really didn't want to fly combat missions but they would often close out their briefings by indicating that they wished that they too were going along on the missions. Sometimes, though, it was true, they did want to go, and many of them flew the alloted number of missions before, during, or after their ops duty. A few, who had no real desire for the flights, were the ones who aroused the ire of the combat crews when they would make statements indicating that they wanted to go along and then find excuses not to go. These were in the extreme minority and it was they who caused the writing of the raunchy songs.

A young flight officer, "Bud" Hammond, and his copilot decided that their operations officer should go along on a B-17 mission so they kidnapped him and made him a mission captive. The mission was rough as hell and when the frightened and indignant officer returned from the mission, he reported Bud and his crew to everybody who would listen to him. Bud and his entire crew were grounded and put under arrest pending the outcome of an investigation that was a dead cinch to lead to a court martial. The other flight crews on the base were in total sympathy with Bud, so one by one they went to the flight surgeon with various ailments that would keep them from flying. They complained of severe back pains, migraine headaches, double vision, cramps, dysentery, and other maladies that could not be immediately diagnosed. By nightfall, every pilot, bombardier, navigator, engineer, and gunner on the base was "too sick to fly."

The squadron commander saw the problem, inquired among the men about their various sicknesses, and wondered aloud about the incarcerated "Bud" Hammond. He "wondered," for example, if Bud and his crew were released and all charges against them dropped, if the health of the crews would improve? Never know until it was tried, was the general attitude. Charges were dropped, Bud and his crew were put back in the air, and everyone watched for a miraculous star in the east because all of the sick people who were suddenly made well. The next day's mission had a full formation of flyin' Forts.

ACCIDENT REPORTS

The most aggravating and fearsome thing about being involved in an airplane accident was not the physical injuries nor the damaged pride but the resultant written reports which were required. I recall two classic reports that seemed to be the epitome of understatement and overstatement.

When the F-86 Sabrejet was fairly new in its operational role and pilot experience in the craft was limited, a young Air Force pilot had a flameout and attempted an emergency landing on a highway. He and the aircraft wound up in a farmyard pigpen, the aircraft destroyed, the pilot uninjured. His report of the accident went something like this: "After the engine failed, I tried all recommended emergency engine restart procedures and could not get a relight. I weighed the possibility of ejection against that of a safe emergency landing and decided to try a dead-stick landing (without engine power) on the highway that was visible beneath me. The highway was actually a paved country road but it was straight and appeared to be relatively smooth. The approach and touchdown were normal, but at that point the brakes failed and I searched about for a way to slow the forward speed of the aircraft. A wire fence ran along the side of the road and I figured that I would guide the airacraft through that fence and that it would act as a restraining barrier. After hitting the fence and failing to lose much speed, I noticed a pond of water and aimed for that, knowing that the impact with water would act as an excellent decelerating device. I sort of hydroplaned across the water's surface with considerable speed and then saw a large shed of some sort in the path of the aircraft and decided to hit this rather flimsy looking building and to utilize that impact for braking. I hit the building and it shattered into splinters but the aircraft kept going. Immediately after this collision with the building I hit a large ditch and *then lost all control of the aircraft.''*

I wonder if he also lost control of having his tongue tucked firmly in his cheek.

I still have the official report of another accident that happened after a young flight officer had "borrowed" his commanding officer's personal B-25 for an unauthorized visit to his girl friend: "I couldn't see the field and the tower couldn't see us, but we did see a light-colored strip that looked like a usable runway. We were given permission to use that 'runway' and advised that there was a 20-to-30-mph wind blowing at the surface. We turned on final approach in heavy rain and very little visibility. We touched down with one wheel on the runway and one in the mud alongside of the runway. I noticed that we were veering to the left and going off the runway and the application of corrective rudder didn't help. It was then that we hit the unoccupied firehouse and some of the equipment standing beside it. The building was destroyed and the left wing and tail assembly were torn off the airplane. We shut down the airplane in the recommended manner and I evacuated the airplane to go to the dispensary to have a slight injury to my leg checked." End of report.

In reality, this flight officer, who had just destroyed half of an airfield, the private airplane of a colonel, broken his leg, and created havoc among the entire Air Force base personnel, was looking for a good place to hide and the dispensary offered a logical refuge. This same pilot recovered from the incident and went on to carve out an excellent record as a B-17 combat pilot, a survivor of a POW camp, participation in the Korean and Vietnam wars, and after that ended a beautiful 36-year flying career as a colonel.

Had he not wrecked that fancy B-25 and been a bit more conventional in his future behavior, this gentleman would surely have retired with a couple of stars sprinkled on his shoulders; but he had always had stars in his eyes, so they more than compensated for those that were missing from his shoulders. Just for the record, the gentleman involved in the above story is "Bud" Hammond, now retired and living in Hemet, California.

THE GOLDEN OPPORTUNITY

Politics and the selection of manufacturers for the military aircraft of the nation often make the proverbial strange bedfellows. The corporate officers and their lobbyists walk very softly and have rigid rules for employee behavior when in the company of ranking government officials. I did not always necessarily pay attention to these guidelines, which was one of the reasons that I was told that I "didn't hear or dance to the corporate music."

One outstanding event of this nature was when I was making a "pitch" for the manufacture of an aircraft called "The Enforcer," a modernized version of the World War II P-51. With the addition of a turbo-prop and other innovations, this airplane seemed to be an ideal ground support machine for the then-ongoing war in Vietnam. While pursuing this effort, I was granted an interview, to be of no more than 15 minutes in duration, with the Assistant Secretary of Defense for Air Guard and Air Force Reserve activities. A corporate office member was supposed to be present during this planned interview or presentation, but I had neglected to invite one and instead went alone into this highly guarded Pentagon office.

Prior to my visit, a Hungarian Freedom Fighter refugee jeweler friend had given me a ring with my initials cast in its base and a large gold nugget for a center stone. As I waltzed through my prepared speech and flipped through all manner of charts, the gold ring flashed like a diamond.

The secretary was mildly impressed with the proposed airplane, said that he would review the data, and that we would then talk again. He then asked to see the gold ring and asked many questions about it. We discovered that we both had an interest in rockhounding, the search for unusual rocks and semiprecious stones. The discussion grew lengthy and the secretary invited me to lunch to continue our informal talk. I went and we became almost instant friends— nothing to do with politics or airplanes, just friends with a mutual interest in rockhounding. In the months following our meeting, we exchanged letters and rock samples without ever a mention of the airplane.

When called to task for having been in such lofty company for such a long time without corporate counsel, I was really put on the rack. No one believed my rock story, not even when I displayed a small garnet the secretary had given me.

Future negotiations regarding "The Enforcer" were carried on by a corporate career man whose only collection of rocks was in his head.

HEARTBREAK RIDGE IN THE L.A. AIRPORT

The Los Angeles airport is always a chaotic place with jillions of people of all descriptions running about in all directions. It seemed even more active during the Vietnam War period and I was constantly flying to somewhere for some reason from this crazy airport. On this particular day, I was dressed in full Air Force uniform waiting for a commercial flight to take me to San Francisco where I would join my crew and pick up an aircraft for a cargo run to Da Nang, Vietnam. As I waited, a pregnant black lady cautiously approached me and shyly introduced herself.

"Sir, excuse me, but are you heading for overseas?" she asked.

It was a bit unusual for such a question from a stranger and I was on guard immediately. I then asked her what interest she had in where I was going and explained that the military didn't normally answer such questions.

"Well, my husband is a helicopter pilot stationed out of Da Nang and I thought that if you were going that way you might be kind enough to deliver a message for me," she explained.

Without further ado, I volunteered that I was indeed going to Da Nang and that I would be glad to deliver her message.

She then wrote a note, addressed an envelope, and gave it to me. Her eyes were running over with tears of gratitude. I told her that I would be returning in a couple of weeks and that I would call her to confirm that the message had been delivered. We exchanged addresses and as I headed out the departure gate, she gave me sort of an informal salute and a good-luck sign.

In Da Nang, I located her husband and he was overwhelmed with joy to read that the baby his wife expected was due in a couple of weeks and that his wife was doing fine. The wife had scheduled the delivery for the Air Force base at Riverside. He thanked me profusely and we parted knowing that each of us had made a new friend.

When I arraived back in San Francisco on the return from Vietnam, I called the lady to tell her that the message had been delivered and that her pilot husband was doing fine. There was a long pause at her end of the line and then she broke into sobs. She had just been notified earlier that same day that her husband had been shot down and killed. I said the things that are expected at such times, hung up with a storm of tears in my own eyes and anger in my soul.

The lady called me when her son was born and I took a gift for the new child when I visited with her in the hospital. I could not restrain my anger at such a seemingly needless loss, and the lady consoled me with quotations from the Bible. That's right, *she* consoled *me!*

A man dies and a child is born. Some sort of justice, I suppose.

"...AND THERE WAS LIGHT"

While on a short assignment in England, I was privileged to meet an RAF pilot officer who gave me an escorted tour around the countryside. We visited such places as the University at Cambridge, the race track at Ascot, the wax museum of Madam Tussaud, and the magnificent cathedral of Ely. I was so impressed with the cathedral that I returned to visit it several times. I don't remember the name or the title of the gentleman who seemed to be in charge of the cathedral, but I do remember a story that he told me about this magnificent, majestic edifice.

It was the war years of World War II and the Luftwaffe was attacking England with regularity. It was a time when the bombers of dark green with their black crosses were over the while cliffs of Dover and when there was doubt that the bluebirds would ever return. All of England was kept in near darkness at night and only the most necessary of lights were allowed to be illuminated. Near to Ely were two active Allied airfields, Mildenhall and Lakenheath, and they were sure to be prime targets for the Luftwaffe so it was especially important that they be as disguised and hidden as possible. Ironically, high atop the spire of Ely there burned a brilliant red warning light, put there initially so that friendly aircraft would be aware of the spire before it loomed up from the foggy sky as a surprise. The civil defense people and the military people wanted the light extinguished at all times, but the vicar of the church refused.

"It's a perfect target for the bloody Boche," the military argued.

"It is necessary that it stay lit to keep our own boys from hitting it and there's more of them flying in the area than there are of the enemy," the vicar countered.

The argument raged and the vicar emerged the victor— his light atop the spire remained lighted for the duration of the war and beyond. Not a single German aircraft used it effectively and it protected Ely from accidental hits by friendly aircraft. Ely was one of the only four cathedrals that were left undamaged by the cruelties of war and it still stands in its original splendor and beauty.

The light still burns and I salute it in reverence to its defender and to the cathedral each time that I pass by it in the flight pattern.

A DIRTY STORY

While in England, I met a Royal Air Force fighter pilot with the unlikely name of Flight Officer Nick Carter. He told me many stories of the wartime activities, but the one I remembered best was a rather passive story having nothing to do with airplanes or war engagements.

It was during the war and the ladies of the Royal Air Force were required to dine at the officer's mess along with the men. Most of the ladies didn't mind this arrangement but, as with most things, there was an exception. One lady officer wrote a letter of protest to the air ministry:

Sir:
We are forced to share the dining facilities of this base with the male officers and I find some of their habits disgusting. There is one condition in particular which needs the attention of your office and a corresponding immediate correction. These men enter the dining hall, go directly to the water closet, and then take their places in the serving line. I have personally timed their actions while they are in the closet and know that they do not have sufficient time to take care of their personal waste problems and to then properly wash their hands afterward. As they travel the serving line, they dip their unwashed fingers into the sugar cube bowl and contaminate it for all of those who follow.

This practice could create serious health problems and I sincerely request that the Air Ministry take corrective action immediately.
Sincerely, XXXXXXX

A few days after the lady had sent her angry message, a package from the Air Ministry arrived addressed to her. The package contained a magnificent pair of silver sugar tongs and an attached placard that read:

TO BE INSTALLED IN THE OFFICERS LATRINE
FOR THE EXCLUSIVE USE OF MALE OFFICERS
IN THE HANDLING OF PERSONAL EQUIPMENT
PRIOR TO ENTERING THE FOOD SERVING LINE.

AIRBORNE MEDUSA

While his F-100 aircraft was being refueled at Holloman Air Force Base in New Mexico, the young lieutenant pilot put his helmet and flight jacket on the ground. Refueling complete, he put on the jacket and helmet and tookoff for a base in northern California. When he was but a few miles from Fresno, California, he radioed the base there that a sidewinder rattlesnake was wound about his neck and slowly making its way down his chest. Moments later, he advised that the snake was now resting in his lap, coiled and rattling. Another aircraft in the area was advised to join up with the snake-infested F-100 and to render whatever aid that they could.

The pilot of the escort aircraft advised, "Don't make any sudden moves but turn the air conditioning as low as possible and get the cockpit as cold as you can. The snake can't operate too well in the cold and he'll probably wander about looking for a warmer spot."

"Like back under my helmet?" the F-100 pilot inquired.

"Nope, don't believe he will," the escort said. "He'll probably go to the floor. Whatever he does, you make an emergency, straight-in approach to Castle where they'll be waiting for you. Jettison your canopy during the landing roll and the fireman will join you whenever you stop. They'll shoot some carbon dioxide on the snake and remove him. Just don't make any sudden moves. Where is the snake now?"

"He's down by the rudder pedals and trying to get into the top of my boot but he's moving very slowly and so am I," was the answer.

"Roger, now hang on like you are, do it all nice and easy, and the fire guys will be waiting to take care of your passenger," the escort soothed.

"Understand, just make sure those damned fire bottles are working," the pilot replied.

All went just as planned, the landing was easy, the canopy blew off cleanly, and the firemen immobilized the snake. The badly shaken pilot was driven to the Officer's Club for a bit of post-snake-shakes tonic, but when he ordered the barman wouldn't serve him because it was during duty hours. Only the intervention of the club officer prevented a pitched battle and the pilot was promptly served after he had recited his harrowing experience.

Some folks say that alcohol is not to be taken as a cure for snakebite, but it sure seems to come in handy for recuperating from near misses.

THE LONELY SKY

An extended career in the flying business allowed even the least of us to know and walk with giants. Among those under whom I was privileged to serve was the then-Colonel John "Black Jack" Hilger, the officer second in command on the breathtaking Tokyo Doolittle Raid. We were at the time assigned to the Martin B-26 airplane and having many training and operational problems and it was seldom that our conversation, formal or informal, strayed far from the subject of the B-26.

One evening, during a somewhat quiet moment in the makeshift Officer's Club, I was a witness when Colonel Hilger answered a few questions that were asked about the Tokyo Raid. I recall only one of the questions and the answer that he gave. Colonel Hilger was asked about his emotional feelings regarding all aspects of the raid and his outstanding memory of that mission. He told little of the planning or execution but dwelled upon the loneliness that he experienced after the rest of his crew had bailed out of the B-25

Mitchell. Left all alone, in an unfriendly airspace, over unknown country, he made his way to the bomb bay and was struck by the strange loneliness of being in a bomber all alone. It was perhaps this deep fascination with these strange circumstances that caused him to jump with one leg harness of his chute not properly fastened, which later created a leg injury. As I listened to this courageous man tell his story of concern and compassion for his crew, the sadness of losing his aircraft and the loneliness of his situation, I wondered if I would ever have such courage— and I thought, "Probably not."

In later years, whenever I was faced with critical emergencies in the air, I always remembered Colonel Hilger's loneliness and his courage. When meeting with him occasionally during these years, I embarrassed him by telling him of my deep admiration for him and the remembrance of his story in the club.

His story and his actions always serve me well, for I know that no matter what situation I might be thrust into, the loneliness cannot equal that of Colonel Jack Hilger during those critical days of the unfolding of World War II.

As a part of this book, I salute the memory of Colonel "Black Jack" Hilger and thank the fates that allowed me to know him and to be privileged to be his friend.

"GIVE THEM ALL MY LOVE..."

Perhaps all men feel that within their particular professions they have the best people in the world, and it may be that they are right, but I *know* that in test flying or in just plain production flying that we have the cream of the crop of all men. They have faults and foibles and may be prima donnas at times, but when it gets to the nitty-gritty, they are the strongest and sometimes the most sentimental. They are paradoxes all.

The heartbreak of test flying was often death and destruction, and although it seemed to be stoically accepted, it was as tough on the surviving buddies and their families as on anyone else. Some people thought that I was a bit colder and aloof than most when it came to the tragedies, but I know that just the opposite was true. I kept a straight face in public and then slipped away to weep in silence. I would sometimes seek out a priest for consolation but I didn't make a public announcement of it. Sometimes I was so angry at the loss of a friend that I would draw blood from the palms of my hands from clenching my fists so tightly that the nails would dig holes in my hands.

The dilution of the fun of flying with the tragedies of flying is perhaps best told in the following excursion into reality.

A multiple-crew aircraft on a test flight was involved in an in-flight collision with a fighter aircraft, and the resulting gyrations of the big aircraft were so intense that the crew could not bail out. Trapped, they rode their stricken craft through several thousands of feet of altitude to eternity. As they plummeted to earth, the crew relayed little messages of love and condolences to their families and loved ones.

Just as one example, the pilot's final radio transmission before impact was, "Give them all my love . . ."

TO TELL THE TRUTH . . .

With all of these stories of flying, perhaps the entire business can best be summarized by a story told by Dr. Barron, a Lockheed flight surgeon.

It is Dr. Barron's opinion that all people who fly airplanes are basically dumb and that those who get involved with test flying are particularly dumb. He illustrates his point by telling of a very famous test pilot of the "old school" who was charged with the in-flight investigation of why a particular type of aircraft was experiencing so many failures resulting in losses of the airacraft. The pilot found the cause of the problem the hard way—by actually experiencing it— but the ensuing explosion, loss of the aircraft, and ejection was such a trauma that the pilot had the memory of the real cause blocked out of his mind. Dr. Barron administered sodium pentathol (truth serum) to the pilot in an attempt to revive the memory of the events of the flight. After the investigation, Dr. Barron stated that the pilot was so dumb that even under the influence of "truth drugs" he had to be prompted by the use of cue cards.

This was a tongue-in-cheek indictment for sure, but even if the good doctor was serious in his evaluation and if we were as dumb as he says, it is all the more reason to rejoice because we mostly did it "for the fun of it."

How many stockbrokers, insurance salesmen, or even corporate giants can make that same claim?

NOTHING TO IT

Among those people whom I knew in the flying business, Colonel James K. "Jimmy" Johnson was surely one of my favorites. James K. (as we usually called him) was a fighter pilot, but his other qualities far outweighed that so he can be forgiven for that small indiscretion.

James K. was small and dark with the twinkling mischievous eyes of the "When Irish Eyes Are Smiling" variety. He was soft-spoken and did not talk much about his heroic wartime achievements. He was just a plain good old guy and I somewhat idolized him. James Jabara was the first "jet ace" in Korea, and James K. Johnson was the first "double jet ace"—the first fighter pilot flying a jet-powered aircraft to shoot down 10 enemy aircraft. James K. accomplished this feat while flying an F-86 aircraft.

During a television interview one time, the interviewer rambled through a long introduction about how other pilots had the same training, had the same type of aircraft, had flown the same number of missions as James K. but had failed to score a single kill. After this prelude he asked, "What is your secret, Colonel Johnson? What is the answer to how one becomes a successful fighter pilot? How do you do it while some of your comrades fail to score? Do you do something or what is it that allows you to make 10 kills while other pilots have none?"

"Well," James K. drawled, "it is really quite simple. You

just get on the other fellow's tail, wait until the diameter of his tailpipe (exhaust) equals the diameter of your gunsight, and then you start firing. Hard to miss when you do it that way."

The announcer accepted this bit of wisdom, asked a few more little questions, and then ended the interview. He never did question the most important factor of the whole thing—how do you get on the "other fellow's tail?" And James K. didn't think that it was worthwhile to volunteer those details.

That same interview is still shown on TV once in a while as a part of big wartime programs, and although I've watched it a dozen times, James K. doesn't ever change his story nor does the announcer ever ask the right question.

COPYCAT

Lieutenant Joe Cotton, later to be Colonel Joe Cotton of B-70 fame, brought a badly shot-up B-17 safely back to home base after a bombing mission over Germany. He was called to headquarters to be complimented for such a good job in getting the badly wounded airplane and crew home.

"I don't know how you ever managed to get that junk pike back, lieutenant, but whatever you did it was a magnificent job and I'll see to it that you are suitably decorated," the CO told Joe.

"No sweat, colonel," Joe answered modestly. "Jesus was my copilot."

"That line has already been used," lieutenant," the Old Man retorted, "and someone has even written a book with that title, so don't be giving me that kind of guff." He then dismissed Joe.

Later, while reviewing some flight records of that same mission, the CO found that he had acted a bit hastily with Lieutenant Cotton. Listed on the flight report was Lieutenant Cotton as pilot and the copilot was Lieutenant Jesus Hernandez.

BOXERS IN SPACE

Sometimes we allow the overwhelming knowledge and technology of the aerospace business to dull our common sense and then we overlook the more obvious solutions to certain problems. Such was the case when the super-fast and super-high flights of the X-15 were being conducted. These flights were the ones that took us past the threshold of space and that paved the way for today's space program. The pilots wore partial pressure suits, a nylon wrap with capstan tubes wrapped around them. In case of a cockpit decompression, the capstans would fill with oxygen, draw tight, and tighten the suit around the crew member to sustain his blood until he could reach a lower altitude. The helmet that went with the suit was a giant sort of bubble with a clear glass faceplate. The suit fit so tightly that I recall having great blood blisters on my arms, legs, and shoulders after an extended flight. The faceplate of the helmet would often fill with sweat whenever the air conditioning system failed and it had to be momentarily popped open to keep from drowning in one's own sweat. The whole outfit was at best an interim answer to space flight. Along with this advance in flight clothing there had been no similar advance in footwear, and the X-15 pilots complained that the heavy GI boots didn't allow for a "feel" of the rudder pedals and requested that a suitable boot be designed.

With this in mind, a bunch of the X-15 pilots and technicians were sitting around the Desert Inn in Lancaster, California, and between girl-watching sessions were discussing the various aspects of the X-15 program. When the subject of a suitable flight boot came up, Norm Foster, a pressure suit specialist, thought the shoes that were worn by boxers—they give ankle support and yet were supple enough for proper rudder pedal "feel." The following day, after a bit of research in Los Angeles boxing emporiums, each of the X-15 pilots was fitted with a pair of high-top, soft-soled boxing shoes. In use, they worked fine and cost the taxpayers only a few dollars.

As you tour the Air Force Museum or the National Space Museum in the Smithsonian Institution, look at the photographs of the pioneer X-15 pilots lined up beside the ultra-modern and sleek X-15—each of them is dressed in the very early and complex partial pressure suit and booted in the simple shoes of a boxer.

LITTLE MEMORIES

A gigantic C-5 cargo aircraft waiting for takeoff instructions at Edwards Air Force Base called the control tower and advised that a giant desert turtle was crossing the runway. Now it so happened at that time that there was a practice of not allowing one aircraft to takeoff too soon after the one in front because of the danger of what is called "wake turbulence"—the strange swirl of air from a departing aircraft. So after a slight delay, the tower finally called, "Roger, C-5 is cleared for takeoff after turtle is clear of runway. Please utilize extreme caution and be aware of turtle turbulence on runway."

* * *

Then there was the legendary aircraft commander who bailed out of his malfunctioning craft with a farewell message to his dumbfounded copilot: "You, sir, are now in charge."

* * *

A Chinese navigator on my crew was a bit touchy about the shape of his eyes and the frequent jibes about his nationality. As we crossed the international dateline, he would always garner some measure of revenge by announcing over the loudspeaker, "Gentlemen and passengers, we have just crossed the international dateline and are now in that part of the world where *I* am not a foreigner but where *you* are the foreigner. I welcome all of you *round-eyes* to my world of oriental splendor.''

* * *

Sometime during the post World War II days, I flew into the Grumman aircraft plant in Bethpage, Long Island. The runway markings were very unusual and on each end was painted the message "CHECK YOUR GEAR, ART HALL" or words to that effect. It seems that their test pilot of that name had made a couple of "wheels-up" landings and that these messages were his personal reminders to prevent recurrence.

A guy can't be expected to think of everything without some help.

When last heard from (1983), Mr. Hall was a vice-president of Grumman and no longer has a need for such reminders.

* * *

While I was working for the Glenn L. Martin Company in Baltimore, a local newspaper ran a contest for teenagers. The theme of the letter-writing contest was "Why I Would Like to Be a Naval Cadet at Annapolis," with the winner of the contest getting two free tickets to the Navy-Notre Dame football game. I entered, won, and got a date with a pretty cheerleader and made big plans for being the "honored" guest in seats along the 50-yard line. Somehow or another, I managed to buy a new sport coat from one of the waterfront pipe rack stores and waited for the big Saturday to arrive. But fate and my love for the crazy world of airplanes intervened.

The big MARS flying boat was scheduled for official roll-out and I was selected as one of the "chock carriers," to walk alongside the airplane with heavy wooden chocks to be used for any emergency stopping that might be required.

The rollout deed was done amid all sorts of hoopla with movie cameras, reporters, and many important guests. We got the flying boat out of the hangar and into the water of the river without incident, but I missed a historic football game and lost a pretty girlfriend.

This monstrous airplane, the MARS, had experimental engines and experimental wood-laminated props that could be reversed—something very new in those days. During its first water taxi, one of the engines went into reverse at high speed, threw the blades in all directions, and the test crew bailed out into the cold waters of the river. The MARS, sans crew, ran aground. A sound that I will always remember is that of the wounded engine as ran at full speed until it burned from its mounts and fell into the river, followed by the gentle hissing of steam and a thin column of white smoke rising from the water grave of the hot engine.

It was a classic example of "back to the drawing board."

* * *

Flight crews and control tower operators have always had a lot of fun with little aerial games and try to outdo each other. At Barksdale Field, the B-26's were having so many problems and emergencies that the tower operators were a bit spooked and ready for most anything—and anything was what they usually got.

One pilot called the tower and in a somewhat desperate voice advised that he was coming in on a single engine. Visions of disaster danced in the tower operator's head, so he alerted everybody and everything on the base.

"Air Corps 1234 is on a long final." the allegedly stricken aircraft pilot then called.

Tension on the ground mounted and all emergency equipment stood at ready. The aircraft came into view and the tower operator dropped his binoculars in disgust.

"It's a damned AT-6," he said. "Some smart-assed hot-shot in a single-engine AT-6 and I never even asked what kind of airplane he was flying! A damned AT-6!"

The AT-6 pilot made a touch-and-go landing, then headed

for some training base in Texas. It was a good thing that he did, for he would never have seen Texas again had he come to a full-stop landing.

* * *

Ab Vencill, one of the notorious but excellent flying Vencill brothers of Dallas, Texas, usually gave the tower operators a fit whenever he could. He delighted in such playful things as: "Love Tower, this is Vencill, I have a problem."

"Rog, Vencill, give us your position and we'll try to help."

"Hell! My position *is* my problem. I'm lost!"

Another game he played was that he was totally dumb and that he did not understand any of the takeoff and departure procedures. After sitting in takeoff position and listening to the long drawn-out instructions from the tower, Ab would acknowledge and then ask, "Do any of you gentlemen happen to know the direction to Arkansas?"

At Tetersboro, New Jersey, Ab was getting ready to take off in a seriously overloaded Noorden Norseman when an FAA officer challenged him about his dangerously over-loaded airplane, Ab said that it was no problem and that he was taking off, with or without official approval.

"I'll pick up your license if you even look like you're taking off with that load!" the official screamed at him.

"Hey now, I'd surely appreciate it if you *would* pick up my license," Ab answered as he closed the door and started the engine. "It was pulled away from me about 10 years ago and I haven't seen the damned thing since. I'd be most appreci-ative if you would be so kind as to pick it up for me."

* * *

Another day, Ab called the Love Field tower and informed them that he was headed for Dayton and that he didn't have a copilot for the C-54 he was flying.

"Vencill, you can't do that! Where is your copilot?" was the tower response.

"Well," Ab answered, "we was having a couple of drinks in the Adolphus last night in our room on the eighth or ninth floor and a couple of those beautiful Texas ladies were our guests. Some clown knocked at the door, claimed that one of the ladies was his wife, and that he was coming in to shoot the whole damned bunch of us. He even fired one shot right through the door. Old Clyde, my right seat man, just sort of panicked, grabbed a pillow case, and bailed out of an open window. The pillow case didn't work too good and old Clyde was killed, so in the excitement I just kinda walked away from the whole thing."

"Vencill, you knew he couldn't parachute with a pillow case. Why didn't you stop him?" the amazed operator asked.

"Stop him? Hell, I thought that he could make it!" Ab answered as he accelerated, roared down the runway, and put on a one-man show in a two-man aircraft.

* * *

General Jimmy Doolittle is one of the world's greatest aviators and one of the greatest among men. After his raid on Tokyo, he was a national hero and the idol of the men of the Air Corps. His name was pure magic.

At Barksdale Field one day, a call for landing clearance came in and, as was the required, the pilot advised, "Pilot's name is Doolittle."

Pandemonium broke loose. The commander was alerted, some sort of band was hurriedly assembled, everyone who had a reasonably clean uniform was hustled into formation, and a hasty formal welcome was arranged.

The aircraft landed and one of General Doolittle's lieutenant sons crawled out of the cockpit to be greeted by a welcome befitting a national hero. He managed to hide from everyone for a while but was later caught at the club and thrown into the swimming pool in full uniform. "Absolutely no sense of humor," he complained.

* * *

To qualify for the honored title of "ace," a pilot needed to have five "confirmed kills,"—that is, five enemy aircraft shot down. How this worked in bombers I never understood because most of the crew members had gun positions and shot down enemy aircraft just like the fighter pilots did.

I do remember one B-17 lower ball-turret gunner who had it figured out to some extent. After he had shot down his fourth enemy aircraft, he called his pilot over interphone, "That's my number 4 kill, sir. One more and *you'll* be an ace."

* * *

The group chaplain went along on a particularly rough B-17 mission and when the going got unusually bad, he called the crew in interphone and consoled them, advising them to "fear not because the Lord is with us."

The tail gunner, who was besieged by enemy fighters and flak, called back. "He may be up there, Padre, but He sure ain't back here."

About the time that the gunner made this call, a "detonate on impact" shell passed through the tail gunner's position but failed to explode or to hit the gunner.

"Sir, Padre," he called, "correct my last transmission. He just walk in."

* * *

During the African air battles, one of Goering's leading pilots was shot down and taken prisoner. The captured pilot demanded to meet the man who had shot him down and was both astounded and furious when a young second lieutenant was introduced as the pilot who had done him in.

The colonel was furious. "I have shot down hundreds of airplanes, I am an ace many times over, and you, a mere boy, claim to have been my conqueror. Such a thing is impossible. How many victories do you have?" the colonel demanded.

"You, sir, are my first," the young officer answered

politely, touched the edge of his flight cap in a subtle salute, and excused himself.

* * *

The famous island of Iwo Jima sort of juts out into the Pacific Ocean and has a steep cliff at the end of the runway. Sometimes this worked as an advantage and at other times it wasn't the best arrangement in the world for operating airplanes. The sheer dropoff was a bit of an advantage for airplanes that lacked exceptional lift characteristics.

One fateful night on this lovely island, a jeep filled with aircrew officers came roaring away from the makeshift officer's club, ran by the runway perimeter guard, made a tire-burning turn at the end of the runway, and then raced full-bore over the cliff at the other end of the runway. All aboard the jeep were killed.

Even in wartime the authorities questioned such behavior, so an investigation board was formed to ferret out all the details of this horrible accident. There was a major question to be resolved regarding insurance payments and whether the accident was or was not in the line of duty. If yes, insurance; if no, no insurance.

After determining that the guys aboard the jeep had celebrated a bit after a successful mission, and finding that they had appropriated a jeep belonging to the adjutant, the board then interrogated any and all of those who could shed some light upon the bizarre behavior of the crew. When they questioned the runway perimeter guard, he told them "All that I know is that they roared down the runway and when they went over the edge of the cliff, the whole crew yelled 'Gear up!'"

The deceased crew members' survivors got the insurance because it was perfectly obvious that the crew was off on a combat mission—they had unfortunately made the slight error of choosing the wrong equipment.

* * *

Because of an accident that was blamed on a pilot taking off from the center intersection of the 15,000-foot runway at Edwards Air Force Base in California, a rule was enacted that required all aircraft, regardless of size, to start takeoff from the very end of the runway. Doc Witchell and I were in a small Stinson Station Wagon airplane that could have taken off safely from the taxiway, but when we requested takeoff from the center intersection of the runway, we got a decided and firm "no" from the tower operator. That meant that we had to taxi alongside of the runway for 7,500 feet to the very end.

Doc answered the tower with some rather obvious sarcasm. "Understand. Taxi to end of Runway 22 and wait for clearance. Would it be okay if I fly down to that end?"

The tower operator didn't think that this was at all funny and he held up our takeoff for the arrival of an incoming C-47 that was still somewhere over Denver.

OF DIPLOMACY AND PROTOCOL

Air Force protocol was usually very proper and things were done somewhat diplomatically—with a few exceptions. Whenever a base commander was being transferred to another command, he usually called all of the troops together in the base theater, thanked them for their dedication, wished them luck, and bade them farewell. One of the commanders under whom I served had been a brigadier general, but because of some political disturbance had been reduced to the rank of full (bird) colonel. We, his troops, were mostly recalled "retreads" from World War II who were being retrained for the Korean War. The colonel was having a rough time with this unmilitary group of recalled butchers, postal clerks, and businessmen and had his problems trying to convert them back in to combat crews. Many unpleasant things, most of them beyond his control, had happened and even congressional attention was focused on our base, resulting in a lot of bad publicity and press. As a result, our commander was relieved of the command and transferred elsewhere.

We were all called into the base theater for this farewell speech. We stood at silent attention as he entered and then were seated by his command. He grapsed the sides of the speaker's rostrum, looked out upon his raunchy flight crews, and thundered, "Gentlemen—and I use that salutation advisedly—we all know the usual speech of the departing commanding officer so I will not bore you with that. However, knowing the circumstances of your attitudes and behavior, my speech will be short and to the point. I know exactly what each one of you thinks of me and I want you to know I think the same of you, doubled in spades. So, on this momentous occasion, with your thoughts and mine being the same, I bid all of you raunchy a--holes farewell and leave you with this single thought, 'May God have mercy upon and help the Air Force!'"

LEAPFROG—AIR CORPS STYLE

The manufacturing plant at the Glenn L. Martin Company in Middle River, Maryland, was separated from its airport by a busy highway. Railroad crossing gates were used to keep moving airplanes and cars from arguing about the right-of-way or colliding. This was an awkward arrangement, but because most of the airplanes were kept at the airport after they were completed at the factory, it didn't cause too many serious problems. Once in a while it would create some friction between car and airplane drivers whenever a wait at the crossing was excessive, but there were no serious incidents.

One day before the big war started, an Air Corps major landed at the airport in an experimental Bell P-39. He parked at the airport and had lunch in the flight ops lunch room and then left to attend to some business at the factory offices. I will always remember him as having the shiniest shoes that I had ever seen. He declined a car and driver to take him to factory and elected instead to taxi his P-39. When he saw that the crossing gates were closed to airplanes, he advanced power, rolled a couple of hundred feet, and gently lifted the aircraft over the gates and down on the other side.

It was fascinating to watch this bit of derring-do and even more so when we learned that the pilot was Major Jimmy Doolittle, a hero to everyone who had ever heard of an airplane.

HOWARD HUGHES

One of the great tragedies of aviation is that the legendary Howard Hughes will probably be most remembered for his eccentricities rather than for his valuable contributions to the field of aeronautics and flying in general. I did not know Mr. Hughes personally but I did see him on one occasion and remember that I was deeply impressed just by his presence. Several accounts of his life have been written and most them zero in on his personal life and ignore the accomplishments of his engineering and flying genius. When the book *The Carpetbaggers* was published, Ira Reed, one of Mr. Hughes's motion picture pilots, was so angered at the picture painted of Mr. Hughes in the book that he actively sought out the author to vent his fury. He got as close to the author as the dining room of the International Hotel in Los Angeles, but the personal encounter between author and Reed did not develop into reality.

Hundreds of stories swirl about the life of Mr. Hughes and I have heard many of them firsthand from some of his earliest employees and oldest associates. The stories run the gamut from the macho stuff through some of his eccentric behavior to the softer and sentimental side of the gentleman. Many of the stories in the books where Mr. Hughes was painted as a villain actually came about whenever people tried to take undue advantage of him. I include a few of my favorite stories about him and from them I hope there will emerge a picture of Mr. Hughes that is a bit different from the lurid accounts of others.

During a cross-country flight, Mr. Hughes was stricken

with a toothache and landed near a small Texas town to seek out a dentist. The dentist he found turned out to be a very considerate and obliging fellow and did the necessary work. He presented Mr. Hughes with a bill for $8, apparently the going rate for such work at that time. Mr. Hughes, as was his habit, had no money with him and advised the dentist that he would have the money sent from his office in Culver City, California. The dentist, unaware of Mr. Hughes's identity, accepted this arrangement and the tooth repair incident was apparently closed.

While in the dentist's office Mr. Hughes noted that the dental equipment was somewhat antiquated and sparse and he was so impressed with the kindness of the dentist that he ordered a whole new set of dental equipment to be sent from one of the special manufacturers in Europe. He planned to send this new and expensive equipment to the dentist as a gift. But before the equipment arrived in Culver City, a highly inflated bill was received from the Texas dentist, and when he was quizzed over the telephone about such a change in price, he explained that he had learned the identity of his patient and charged him accordingly. The amount he asked for was sent to him without additional discussion. But when the new dental equipment arrived, it was stored in its original crates in the rafters of the hangar building at Culver City, and when I last visited there it was still unopened and gathering dust. A bit of greed and a large loss for a dentist who probably told stories of his famous patient and of how he had "nicked" him for a big bill, never knowing that he had lost a small fortune in equipment and perhaps a very good friend.

On another occasion, while one of Mr. Hughes's employees was on an overseas company assignment, the employee's small son was hit by a car and seriously injured. Upon learning of the accident, Mr. Hughes had the boy given the best of all possible medical care, brought the employee home at company expense, put him on a full-pay leave of absence while the son recovered, and reassigned the father to a Stateside job. Many years after this incident, another Hughes employee who was directly involved in the incident told me the story and his eyes glistened with tears as he told of the compassionate side of the man for whom he had worked for a lifetime. To this man, and many others like him, Howard Hughes ranked only slightly lower than God in their esteem.

If characteristics such as these are those of an eccentric, then we surely need more eccentric men like him and fewer people who seek out the ugly things in a man's life for their cheap stories.

THE OLDEST CAPTAIN IN THE AIR FORCE

I cannot absolutely swear this story is true.

A flight crew en route to a Vietnam base in 1968 had to divert to a remote island in the Pacific Ocean for an emergency landing. After landing, they were greeted by a badly worn and bearded captain who was at least 60 years old. After their astonishment subsided a bit, they all joined the captain for the cold beer which he provided. He explained that he had been the official keeper of the island since 1943 and hadn't even had a leave since that time. The curiosity of the crew got the better of them and they asked why he was still a captain when he should have been a lieutenant colonel at the very least, or a full bull colonel, or, more realistically, retired.

"I knew that you'd ask that," he replied. "Everybody does. Well, during World War II, I was a fighter pilot with a group stationed on this island. We didn't get a whole lot of rest and whenever we had the opportunity for a bit of extra sleep there was always some kind of practice or false alert. We would have to roll out of the sack, put on all of our flight gear, run to our airplanes, start the engines, and then just sit. Finally we'd get the word that it was a practice or a false alarm and we'd undo the whole mess and head back for the sack. Next morning we'd fly our regular missions, tired out from the practice of the night before, and then repeat the whole damned thing day in and day out."

"He paused for a moment. "Finally I got tired of those

false starts, so I got me an orangutang, trained him to put on my flight gear, taught him how to start and stop the airplane engine—the whole damned act," he rambled. "It worked real well for a couple of months and then one night the alert was the real thing and that damned orangutang took off in my airplane, flew a great flight, and shot down a Jap Zero along the way."

The captain's tone grew dreamy. "While he was off on that mission, the commanding officer saw me standing around and I had to tell him that another monkey was actually flying my mission. The old man took a dim view of it, he did, turned downright purple, and promised me that I'd be assigned to this island and be a captain for the rest of my natural life and, by golly, he's made it stick."

Everyone sympathized with the captain, offered condolences, and just generally tried to make him feel a bit better about the whole matter. But having some very young majors and a lieutenant colonel on the crew didn't help matters much.

Wearily, the aged captain surveyed the bunch, shook off the sympathy, and looked a bit thoughtful. Finally he said, "Well, it's really not too bad, guys. The only thing that really bothers me is that the damned orangutang retired a couple of years ago as a brigadier general!"

THE BRIDGE OVER THE RIO GRANDE

Ira Reed was a Pawnee Indian who earned the money to buy his first airplane by performing in the early-day "barnstormer" airshows. He would braid his long hair into two pigtails (pre-Bo Derek) and affix heavy hooks to the ends of the braids. During the airshow, he would crawl from the passenger's cockpit of some old war-weary biplane, lower himself to the landing gear, attach his braided hair over the axle of the landing gear, and hang by his hair. The pilot would then make a low pass over the grandstand while Ira, hanging by his hair and his arm extended to show that he wasn't hanging onto something else, would thrill the crowd with his death-defying act. With the money he earned, much of it gained by passing a hat after the performance, he bought his own DH-4 and then flew wing-walkers, parachutists, and other daredevils in the airshows.

Ira later became one of Pancho Barnes's Motion Picture Pilots Association pilots and flew in many movie epics such as *Hell's Angels* and *Dawn Patrol*. After his motion picture and wartime careers ended, he retired to Taos, New Mexico, where he operated a small flying service called the Kachina Flying Service. It was during this period when I knew Ira and I often joined him in flying fire patrol in an AT-6 or in charter flights in his modified Cessna 195.

During a flight from Taos to Albuquerque, it was only Ira, me, and Ira's boxer dog in the 195, flying low enough to be below the banks of the Rio Grande River. I was a bit concerned about the wires, cables, bridges, and other obstacles that ran across the river in our path, things that we were barely missing as we whizzed by them.

"Ira," I said, "aren't we taking a bit of a risk by flying so low through this mess?"

"Nah, no sweat, Junior Birdman," he replied. "I know every bridge, wire, and stick up and down this river. Just relax, pet the dog, and enjoy the ride.

About that time, a half-finished bridge loomed up before us and Ira had to pull the airplane up violently to miss a collision with this obstruction. We went nose-up so high and so sudden that the airplane nearly stalled. We cleared the bridge, nosed down to the water's edge, and continued the flight just a few feet above the water. Ira sneaked a sideways look at me and growled, "Well, I know them all but one." And we continued the flight.

THE STUFF OF WHICH DREAMS ARE MADE

Pete Reinhardt was one of the most interesting pilots that I had the privilege of knowing. His active stint as a pilot spanned the period of the open-cockpit mail plane to the all-jet 880 commercial airliner. Pete had a happy Santa Claus face that showed that he had enjoyed every happy or panic-filled moment of his flying career. His tales of encounters with warplanes, the elements, and passengers were endless, and his favorite story was that of a lady passenger on the first flight he made as an 880 Delta captain.

During the 880 flight, the aircraft suffered some kind of a cabin pressurization malfunction and the lady who was using the rest room was stuck to the commode due to the ensuing loss of cabin pressure. After all of the passengers were calmed down and fitted with emergency masks and the aircraft flown to a much lower altitude, one of the stewardesses turned her attention to the lady in the rest room. But no matter when the stewardess tried, the lady remained glued to the top of the pot and she was becoming extremely agitated. The stewardess went to Pete for help and guidance.

"Pete, there's a lady stuck on the commode," the stewardess whispered.

"Well, get her off," Pete said. "I have enough problems up here."

"She's really having a problem and I think you should at least take a look," the stewardess pleaded.

The idea of a young lady in distress became overpowering and Pete handed over the cockpit duties to his copilot. In fact, all of his airline life Pete had imagined some situation similar to this where he could bring his expertise into play to rescue some beautiful maiden in distress. He imagined she would be so grateful that she would offer him her all. Pete headed for the restroom with visions of a lady who would look just like the lovelies who were models in *Playboy*.

But instead of the fair damsel in distress of his dreams, Pete found a 240-pound mound of sweating flesh who started out by calling him every name in the book and inventing a few along the way. Pete's dream was shattered but he tried to appease the woman and instead aroused only more fury and antagonism. The lady wouldn't do anything he suggested; she only screamed obscenities and repeated her fear of being sucked right out of the airplane. In desperation, Pete covered his hands in liquid soap from the dispenser and quickly plunged his hands between the fat lady's thighs. The seal between the seat and flesh yielded and the lady popped free, going almost to the ceiling in the process. She was uninjured but madder than a wet hornet.

Pete returned to the cockpit to revise his dreams a bit, and the lady sued Pete, the airline, the aircraft manaufacturer, and probably God.

RAMON, ROSCOE, PANCHO, AND GILMORE

This again is one of those stories that I can tell only as a legend although the basic facts were substantiated by both Colonel Roscoe Turner and Pancho Barnes, the famous lady race pilot, when we had lunch together at the Edwards Air Force Base Officer's Club a few years before the deaths of both Pancho and Roscoe.

Actor Ramon Navarro had given Pancho Barnes a magnificent new flying outfit made of soft blue suede. To complete the outfit, she had a matching blue suede helmet and some special boots that Mr. Navarro had had made especially for her by a Brazilian leather craftsman. This was the outfit that Pancho had worn during an air race from San Francisco to Glendale, California.

Pancho and Roscoe Turner, the flamboyant race hero of the era, had taken off to settle some sort of grudge match between them. Pancho had a much faster airplane and had conned Roscoe into believing that she was to fly a different airplane in the race, but at race time she showed up in her new and special racing machine all gaily painted with shiny black and red. With her usual flair, Pancho stopped along the race route to take some movies of a football game that was being played at one of the college stadiums, Even with her dillydalling, she beat Roscoe to Glendale, and by prior arrangement she was met by a man on a motorcycle who rushed the movie film she had taken to a processing studio.

At the visitor's dinner that night when Pancho was presented with the winner's trophy and check, she let it be known that she would have won by a much wider margin had she not stopped to watch a football game along the way. The assembled crowd laughed in disbelief until Pancho had the lights dimmed and showed her movies of the game. Mr. Turner was mortified and retreated from the gathering. To be beaten by a woman pilot was bad enough, but to have her flaunt the victory in such a manner was embarrassment at its worst.

The following day, the movie newspeople were taking post-race pictures and interviewing the pilots when Roscoe's flying mate, a full-grown African male lion named Gilmore, mistook Pancho's fancy leather boots for a fireplug and saturated them. Pancho thought that Roscoe had directed Gilmore's unmannerly actions and she took a stick and started chasing the lion all over the airport. Roscoe then started chasing Pancho, cautioning her not to hurt his lion, and a real Keystone Cop routine was presented for the visiting photographers. The battle ended in a draw, but on the day when I had lunch with these two great pioneers of aviation I could detect a still-lingering bit of anger in each of them, Roscoe for having been so ignobly defeated and Pancho for having her prized boots damaged.

Gilmore the lion had gracefully passed away many years before so I didn't get his opinion.

IRREFUTABLY LEGENDARY

After dodging the authorities for a long time, my old friend Pancho Barnes was finally corralled and forced to take a "Check ride" with an authorized, guaranteed U.S. Department of Commerce flight examiner. An old narrow-bodied, narrow-geared, and narrow-minded Interstate tandem airplane was used for this memorable flight. After proving that she could cause the airplane to become airborne, that she could negotiate it in a climb, and that she understood the basics of its nature, Pancho was directed to fly from her Oro Verde ranch in the Antelope Valley of California across the mountains to Oxnard and return. She was doing quite well when the check-pilot suddenly pulled back the power and informed her that she had to make an emergency landing.

"You gotta be kidding," Pancho told the instructor, "I've had more real emergency landings than you've ever pretended to have and I sure as hell don't need to do one more just for the practice!"

"Nope, no good," the instructor yelled. "Show me where you would land, set up and approach to it, and after I'm sure that you would have made it, I'll advance the power and we'll be on our way."

Pancho then angrily killed the engine, put a ham-fisted tight hold on the fully retarded throttle, and skillfully stalled the airplane to a somewhat successful landing in the trees on the slope of a mountain. After the ground rescue troops arrived, the instructor was hauled out in an apoplectic state and reluctantly passed Pancho on her checkride. He said he only did it so that he'd never have to ride with her again. The aircraft was disassembled by mechanics and hauled out in pieces.

Pancho took a number of check rides in the years after that but the legend of that particular check ride preceded her and she was never again asked to demonstrate her emergency landing capabilities.

SECONDHAND LEGEND

During the closing years of her life, Pancho Barnes and I spent a lot of time together wandering around the Mojave Desert and trying to keep her Gypsy Springs Ranch together. Pancho was one of the first of the women pilots and was perhaps the most colorful and controversial of them all. I loved her and her stories about flying which she told with animated enthusiasm—and I suspect a bit of added color. This one she told about General Jimmy Doolittle may or may not be true. I did ask General Doolittle if it would be okay to write some of the stories that Pancho told me about him and he said it would be okay as long as I didn't make any direct quotes. With that verbal approval, I take the liberty of retelling Pancho's story.

Brazil wanted a new fighter airplane, and during that period there was a strict "fly before you buy" contract arrangement. There was also true competition in which each manufacturer built his particular airplane and then the several manufacturers had a performance "fly-off" competition. The winning airplane was then built in the desired quantity. With this concept, different contractors had built airplanes and had them in Brazil to demonstrate their capabilities. General Doolittle was the assigned pilot for one of the contractors. The other two companies and their competing pilots were of the opinion that any airplane flown by a pilot with the superior talents of General Doolittle would win regardless of the airplanes he was competing against. Just as in the movies it was said that "He could fly the crate it came in better than the other pilots could fly the airplane." With odds like these facing them, the other pilots decided to do something to try to neutralize the advantage.

It was known that General Doolittle would seldom refuse to take a dare if it was within the bounds of reason, so the other pilots zeroed in on this and after a few pops dared Doolittle to walk around the narrow edge of concrete that encircled the second floor of the hotel where they were staying. The general took the dare and almost had it made when he lost his balance and had to jump. He broke his ankles in the landing and the advantage was not only neutralized, it was eliminated. But not quite!

Pancho got a doctor. General Doolittle's broken ankles were set and cast, and the general was able to hobble about on crutches. He could get into the airplane and use his legs okay, but he couldn't articulate his ankles to use the rudder. So the seat of the airplane was lowered and moved a bit to the rear so that the rudder could be controlled by using straight motion from the knee. The general then flew the competition and he won.

True or not, I don't know—but it sure makes a helluva good story.

WILEY POST

Next to Lindberg, Wiley Post was my favorite childhood hero. He had it all, an Oklahoma boy with the dramatic appearance of a movie pilot and all of it enhanced by a black patch over one eye. Post was a "pilot's pilot" and I always heard him spoken of in only heroic and praiseworthy terms.

One of the crazy stories that I remember came from a pilot who had known Wiley Post and who had been seriously grieved when learning of his death. It so happened that this old boy had once taken refuge from the cold of the west Texas plains in a small hotel in a nearby town. As the evening grew late and after the infusion of a few heavy belts of good bourbon, the need for feminine companionship intruded and he called a bellboy for some assistance. The bellboy knew just the right girl, and shortly after he called, a somewhat shabby lady appeared at the pilot's door. She rushed in and embraced the sleepy and inebriated pilot.

"Hey, you're an old love from a couple of years past," she gushed. "I spent a couple of nights with you in Amarillo and one or two in Lubbock. You remember me, don't you, love?"

"Can't say that I do," old Bleary-Eye answered.

The lady carefully removed her blouse and slipped down one side of her black brassiere to reveal one well-proportioned snowy breast.

"Bet that you remember me now," she teased.

The old barnstormer eyed the woman's upper body for a moment and then he rushed to embrace her while tears filled his eyes. "Why, Wiley Post, my old buddy Wiley! And all these years I thought that you was dead!" he sobbed.

THE LOT OF A COPILOT

Mr. Beryl A. Erickson is one of my most favorite pilots and I find it an interesting story how he went from a career in commercial airline flying to that of being a test pilot.

Mr. Erickson was flying for American Airlines as a copilot and doing all of those things which copilots are supposed to do, but he had an added task of keeping the first-pilot's thick-lensed glasses clear of fog. The pilot had two pairs of these glasses and as one pair would cloud over he would hand them to the copilot for cleaning while he operated with the clean pair. Flying with a pilot with faulty vision is not the most conducive thing to fun flying, and at times it can be enough to concern the most lackadaisical among us. I once flew with an internationally famous test and race pilot who could not distinguish one candy bar from another in the windows of a vending machine until he put on his glasses with lenses about the thickness of the bottom of a Coca Cola bottle. To fly with him was to be more concerned about the status of one's insurance policies than with that of the mission at hand. It must have been even worse than that for Mr. Erickson since he was flying an airplane filled with passengers with a near-blind pilot in command.

The old approach to Logan Field in Baltimore was from the dark waters of the bay and over a bulkhead that separated land from sea. Normally, the lights of the landing field were easily visible on this approach. On one particularly dark night as they were approaching this runway from the bay side, the pilot handed Mr. Erickson a pair of glasses for cleaning and as Mr. Erickson bent to the task he visually checked to see if they were aligned with the runway and that the runway lights were visible. As he looked again when handing the pilot the clean glasses, he saw complete darkness—they were lower than the approach bulkhead! Mr. Erickson hauled back on the yoke until the runway was again in sight, eased the nose down, and rolled to a somewhat dramatic landing. He resigned his copilot position immediately and went into business with Consolidated-Vultee, where he enjoyed a remarkably successful career.

Commercial flying's loss was a big gain for test flying and for a nation that benefitted from Mr. Erickson's expertise during his long evaluation and test work with some of the leading military aircraft of the world.

THE STRENGTH IN SUBTLETY

Perhaps some of the most vicious ways of vengeance are the insidious things that are done with few and subtle overtones. In the flying business, these little "get-evens" were sometimes serious and sometimes very funny. A couple of such excursions into the field of vengeance that I remember seem worth the retelling.

* * *

While stationed at Roswell, New Mexico, I had a commanding officer who was continually screaming at all of us and particularly at our first sergeant. Most of the time his hollering and ranting was unwarranted, but it never seemed to ruffle our "first shirt" in the least. One night while I was officer of the day, I found the sergeant working late and asked him how he could stand working under such conditions and continual harassment. His explanation made it easy to understand. Whenever this obnoxious officer would write letters in answer to official communications, the sergeant would dutifully have the letters typed, have the CO sign them, put a copy with signature in the file, and then throw the original away. Whenever the screaming eagle CO would be called to task for not answering official correspondence, the sarge would pull out the signed file copy, show him the outgoing mail log where he had forged an entry, and let the grouchy colonel figure his way out of the situation.

The worst example of this "throw-away" mail policy was when an official letter was received advising the colonel of an impending inspection of our squadron by upper echelon officers from SAC headquarters in Omaha. The sergeant had the colonel initial the letter along with a lot of other routine papers and then filed the all-important letter. The inspectors arrived, the colonel was caught totally by surprise, and we failed the inspection miserably. A check of the files showed that the notification had been received, the colonel had duly noted the contents by initialing the border, and he had no one to blame but himself for the disastrous inspection.

Rank may have its privileges but it can also have its aggravations, especially when the one with those privileges chooses to abuse them.

* * *

During an airlift mission to Da Nang, Vietnam, we had a particularly odious aircraft commander who commanded less respect than Rodney Dangerfield but who thought that he commanded like General MacArthur. On this particular mission, he wanted to make a record time for getting there, getting unloaded, taking on a return load, and getting back to the States. His motive was personal gain and recognition and tended to be a bit dangerous so no one on the crew aided in his effort. In fact, the enlisted men on the crew plotted to ensure that this rascal would not accomplish his selfish goal. As we progressed along the way, they suffered from all sorts of maladies, headaches, upset stomachs, and so on, each illness causing a delay of two or three days at each stop. The engineers created airplane malfunctions that caused additional delays and the logbook of the airplane looked like the airplane was ready for the junkyard, although most of the noted discrepancies were actually non-existent. We did set a record in spite of all of this foolishness but it was at the opposite end of the rainbow, for the normal eight-day trip took us over three weeks to complete.

* * *

On one of the Pacific Islands where a P-38 group was stationed, there was a mandatory lights-out order at night. One pilot who had a hobby of writing lots of letters refused to obey the order and a thin beam of light could always be seen seeping from under his tent. One night there was an air raid alarm but this nocturnal writer of letters still refused to put out his light. Soon, one crew chief called to another, a little guy who always reminded me of Frank Sinatra when he played Maggio in *From Here to Eternity*: "You his crew chief, ain't you, paisan?"

"Yeah," the Sinatra look-alike answered.

"How's his airplane doing?" the first guy called out loud.

"Okay as long as I look at it pretty good," the chief replied.

"Maybe if you don't look at it so good it might not come back from a mission and then we wouldn't have this light problem, huh? Watcha think?"

Before the chief could answer, the light in the offending tent went out and there was never again a problem.

RETURN POSTAGE GUARANTEED

It isn't too often that the ground troops get to jump on the pilots and other crew members about their little mistakes and indiscretions, but they sure know how to take advantage of it whenever the opportunity arises. Their technique for twisting the knife whenever the flight crews make a boo-boo is as expert as is their expertise at nearly flawless maintenance.

At Edwards Air Force Base, the bombs for test aircraft missions had to be hauled from a "safe" weapons dump and installed on the aircraft just prior to a mission. Normally, if a mission was cancelled after the bombs were loaded, the bombs were removed and hauled back to the storage dump until the next scheduled test. Sometimes this operation took place many times before the mission was actually flown because many factors such as weather, range availability, maintenance, sick crew members and so on caused cancellations. The bomb crew would bring the bombs, install them on the aircraft, and then haul them back whenever necessary.

On one particular mission, the bomb crew had repeated the process of putting the bombs on the aircraft and then taking them off again for many days in succession. Mission after mission was cancelled and the operation became more of an exercise in futility rather than a test flight. After about nine or ten days of this, everything fell into place and the aircraft actually took off on its assigned test bombing mission.

In the aircraft involved in the test, the procedure for releasing the bombs was to first turn on a safety switch and then to depress a "pickle" switch on the control stick. As the pilot started his run in on the target, he would turn the safety switch to the armed position and then at release point would depress the "pickle" switch, releasing the bombs. As it happened, the bomb dump was in the flight path of this particular test mission and as the pilot passed over the bomb dump he turned the safety switch to armed position, preparing for an actual drop several miles ahead of him. Unfortunately, he had the "pickle" switch depressed too as he armed the safety switch and the bombs fell away and landed just a few feet from where they had previously been stored at the dump. The good news was that they were only practice duds and were used to study ballistics and separation characteristics so they did no explosive harm to anyone or anything.

The following day the pilot got a formal note from the weapons section advising him that if he did not intend to fly the mission as planned that it would be most preferable that the return the bombs to the storage area "in the approved and conventional manner." He also got a couple of weeks off without pay.

THE LOWEST DENOMINATOR

During a waiting period for the call to active duty with the U.S. Air Corps, I did a bit of "fill-in" work at Lockheed in Burbank. As a part of my job assignment, I flew as a mechanic in a Navy PV2 aircraft acceptance program. The PV2 had the same engines as the B-26 I had been flying so the transition was relatively easy.

During my first PV2 flight with a well-known test and

stunt pilot, a fuel transfer selector handle would not move. I beat on it, cursed it, used a long extension handle, and invoked the help of the Almighty. Finally the reluctant handle rotated and the necessary fuel transfer was made. After the flight, I wrote up the offensive valve as being no good and in need of replacement. The pilot read my write-up, frowned, and then asked if the valve finally worked, even with the use of pliers and such. I confirmed that it had worked after the tussle but that it didn't work like it was supposed to work. The pilot crossed out the written discrepancy, told me that the basic test was to see if something worked or not, and if it worked, that was that!

A simple enough axiom upon which to judge something and a lesson which, when used with reason, served me well throughout a long and pleasant flying career.

THE COOKBOOK SOLUTION ISN'T ALWAYS THE BEST

Regardless of the physical demands made upon the participants or victims, Survival School (or Escape and Evasion Tactics) was always interesting and often had its amusing moments.

After listening to several hours of lectures and watching countless movies, we were subjected to a question-and-answer session during which we were interrogated about what we had learned. One of the questions asked was: "What is the best policy regarding the treatment of native girls should you find yourself alone in a friendly village?"

A bright student immediately responded that the native girls should be left alone, and the instructor gave him a nice pat on the head for the corrective administrative answer.

Gurney King, a bombardier who had bailed out over North Korea during the bit of unpleasantness there, and who had taken refuge with a friendly family and enjoyed the luxury of one of the family girls as a roommate, spoke up. "And what's the second choice, sir?"

SHOW AND TELL

With all of the modern regulations and restraints in the flying business, it's difficult to believe that some of the practices of the "big war" years were so loose and unrestrained. In retrospect, it's a wonder that we survived the training phases of learning to be combat crews, much less the actual combat.

While I was a recent bombardier graduate and a student in one of the very first of the airborne radar classes, I was often called upon to fly training missions with equally as inexperienced pilots—some so recent that the price tags were still on their new pinks and greens. One flight that I best remember was with two new second lieutenants.

I was at home after a full duty day as a student and was directed by telephone to report to Williams Field, Arizona, for a night "familiarization" flight with two pilots. It was dark when we got in the airplane, a combat-equipped B-25 Mitchell bomber. Preparing for the flight was like a technical scavenger hunt, with one pilot reading the checklist while the other hunted for the various pieces of equipment.

"Flaps down," one read from the checklist.

"Wait a minute till I find them," the other would answer. "Yeah, here they are. Okay, flaps down." And so on through the list.

The skies were pure black when we finally made a shaky takeoff and the current weather was reported as deteriorating. The odds against us having a successful flight would have been about 100 to 1 if we had been running in a horse race—and they would have been correct.

After about two hours of tooling around all over Arizona and parts of California, we were rather hopelessly lost, in a heavy rainstorm and flying lower and lower to get below some real nasty weather. I managed to locate a railroad track during one of these periods when the ground was illuminated by lightning, found it on the map, and at about

500 feet of altitude we tried to locate Williams. As the weather drove us even lower, we called a Mayday and were directed to the Gila Bend Air Force strip.

We located Gila Bend but when we called the tower we were advised that an AT-6 had hit the control tower during an attempted landing and the base was operating on emergency power only. Several inches of water were running down the runway, the fire station was demolished by the fire resulting from the AT-6 accident, and all other emergency equipment was busy fighting fires. We were low on fuel, on smarts, and just about everything else, so we made a landing, skidding to a "whoa" at the very end of the riverlike runway.

An emergency call was made to Williams to tell them of the Keystone Cop activity, and after a cold dinner of left-overs, we went to bed, thanking our Maker that he did indeed look after fools, drunks, and children.

The next day was not much better, but we were directed to return to Williams, so we tried. The day was dark with a low ceiling so we had a car park at the far end of the runway as a distance marker and somehow or another got off the ground and back to Willie. We got a royal chewing from everyone on the base with a rank of corporal or higher, made out a thousand reports, and, thankfully, assumed the anonymity of other dummies.

Combat duty was looking better all the time!

THE INVENTOR

A brilliant gentleman named Phil Cummins discovered that the shaving cream from an aerosol can made an excellent insulator from heat. He also decided that it made an equally good flotation device when confined in a closed container. Pursuing this idea a bit further, Phil found that an additional quality of the cream was that it would serve as an excellent shock absorber. He continued his research and found that using the cream in the capstan tubes of the aviator's pressure suit would serve the same purpose as filling them with air or oxygen. Putting all of this data together, Phil designed a pressure suit that would be inflated with plain, old, ordinary shaving cream. A suit thus inflated would afford pressure for the flyer in the event of the loss of cabin pressure, protection against fire, floatation when in the water, insulation against the cold of water, and a good shock absorber in the event of an impact. The idea was perfect, but the mechanics were a bit troublesome.

Phil got a little bit of money to work with and, with the added heat-resistant Nomex that was being developed, had the ingredients for the near-perfect air crew survival suit. The problem of how to distribute the foam throughout the flight garment was the most pressing problem and Phil discovered that the ideal type of tubing for this purpose was that used to make contraceptive prophylactics, since it was both light and strong. For experimental purposes, he figured that he would need about 500 yards of this material and was a given a company-funded voucher for buying that much. Unfortunately, when he called his would-be supplier, he got a sassy young lady on the line.

"Ma'am, I'd like to order a 500-yard length of your contraceptive tubing," he said.

There was a long pause at the other end of the line.

"Ma'am, are you there?" Phil asked.

"Yes, sir, I'm here," the young lady said, "and I'm waiting for you to quit fooling around and get serious before I try to take your order. Are you putting me on or is this a big company joke or something?"

"No, Ma'am, I'm calling all the way from Texas and I'm very serious," Phil replied.

"Oh, now I get it," the girl said. "You're a Texan, out there where they do everything big. Well, the joke's over now—just tell me what you really want."

After a long time, Phil finally made his point and lady agreed to make out the purchase order, but not before a final dig of "Five hundred yards, Texas-sized, indeed."

The pressure suit filled with shaving cream never became a reality, but Phil and I had a lot of fun demonstrating it around the country.

THE GREAT BALLOON RACE, CIRCA 1942

During the aviation cadet program at Santa Ana, California, it seemed that the objective of the training was to keep us as frustrated as possible. We were the lowest of the low on the military totem pole and were reminded many times daily of our low and precarious status. It seemed that there was no outlet for our pent-up frustrations, so they seethed and grew beneath the surface.

Another neat little facet of the program was one that required us to take along a prophylactic kit whenever we left the base. This was the military mind at work to keep down the spread of venereal disease. No self-respecting cadet ever returned to base with his kit intact, although relatively few were probably used; the individual egos were high enough that it would be status-destructive to admit a failure at conquest and need for the kit. Regardless of this aspect, there was always a surplus of these kits around the barracks and their availability provided a small outlet for pent-up frustrations and a desire to do mischief.

Each Sunday we had a monstrous parade, sometimes as many as 30,000 cadets passing in review after standing in ranks for hours under the blazing southern California sun. Dignitaries from all over the place were often in the reviewing stand to watch this awesome display of future air-power.

As we stood at parade rest during one of these Sunday performances, one of the cadets released a blown-up prophylactic and it floated gently above the crowd, attracting everyone's attention. Soon there was another one released and then another until the sky was filled with the filmy inflated balloons. After the parade was over and all of the visitors had left, we were held on the parade ground and threatened with death or life imprisonment or both or worse if such a thing ever happened again. An attempt to find the offenders was futile, however, and all of the threats were of

250

no avail, for we had found a secret weapon, a thing of fun, a gimmick where the culprits were hidden among thousands and a way to needle those who made a career of needling us. We were not about to give up our little game or our secrets of the release to the skies, so the comedy continued. Each Sunday afternoon, just before the command of "Pass in review" was given, the skies overhead were filled with flying prophylactics.

Historically I can't prove it, but perhaps this is where the sightings of "Unidentified Flying Objects" got their start.

BUREAUCRACY THAT EVEN RIPLEY WOULDN'T BELIEVE

In the due course of men and their affairs, it is unfortunate that some of these men allow themselves to be governed by the absolutes of rules without the slightest degree of flexibility. In wartime, this often becomes more obvious than during normal times; it sometimes seems as if men's brains are replaced by that sheaf of papers known as regulations. There is a regulation for everything ranging from the exact shade of interior green that will be used for painting the latrine to the specifications for exotic flying machines. Examples of the use and misuse of regulations are endless, but there is one that I will always remember.

The PT-19 training airplane was made of wood and fabric and featured a water-cooled in-line Allison engine. It was open-cockpit, single low wing, and the body was contoured to give it a sleek fighter plane look. It looked like an airplane was supposed to look. It was a fun-to-fly little airplane and was used extensively by the Air Corps—the first airplane that a student was taught to fly. It was simple and straight-forward, but as with most things, it had its limits and weaknesses.

One young pilot trainee had the misfortune of having one of the wooden wings break off during flight and the airplane went into an uncontrollable spin. Somehow or other the student managed to bail out and land himself safely on the ground. An accident board was convened to determine the cause of the accident. The student pilot was, naturally, the star witness.

"After the airplane experienced the wing failure and went into a spin, did you implement the normal spin recovery procedures?" he was asked by the board.

The student was incredulous. The airplane had only half of a wing and that was all on one side of the airplane. No matter what he did to the airplane, it wasn't about to straighten up and fly right. Dutifully, he answered his interrogators that he had not performed the normal spin recovery actions. The questioner, who was the leader of the investigation, huddled with his cohorts, scribbled a few words on a pad before him, and announced that the investigation was completed. A decision as to the cause had been made.

"And what were the published results of the investigation? "Pilot error in that the involved pilot failed to follow the recommended spin recovery procedures, and through this lack of his actions, the airplane was lost."

Believe it or not!

THE JOKER

Every school class seems to have a class joker, someone with an irrepressible sense of humor. Military classes were that same way, but because of the regimented and military flavor of them these guys had to be a bit more subtle. In our aviation cadet class, we had just such a guy, the son of an Oregon newspaper publisher.

We were required to take physical exams at prescribed periods and as a part of these exams we had to be interviewed by psychiatrists. These interviews were very reminiscent of scenes described in Joseph Heller's hilarious book *Catch-22*. Usually, the interviews were conducted in groups of three—three cadets were questioned together and if one of them showed any "funny" tendencies, they were then questioned separately. During one of these interviews, our joker was asked if he had ever been intimate with a girl.

He gave a smug affirmative.

"How long has it been since you were intimate with a girl?" the psychiatrist asked.

"Can't tell for sure, sir. What time is it?" the joker replied, and he was passed as normal.

This same guy hated to do pull-ups during the physical training program and would run around the chinning bar when his turn came to do the required exercise. Don Budge, the tennis great, was our instructor and he finally stopped the joker as he tried to avoid the chinning bar. "Don't you miss the chinning bar when we exercise?" Lieutenant Budge asked.

"Not a damn bit, sir, not a damn bit," the joker answered, and ran off to the athletic field.

SCENIC TOUR

One of the fringe benefits of being a student aerial gunner at Kingman Air Force Base in Arizona was the frequent flights over the gorgeous Grand Canyon. When viewed from the ground, the canyon is an awesome sight of breathtaking beauty, but when seen from the ball turret of a low-flying B-17 it is another dimension of beauty altogether. Often we would fly below the walls of the canyon and then pull up abruptly to startle the tourists who were standing at the lookout points. We were also taught how to bail out of the B-17 in the event of trouble.

The bail-out procedure was that the pilot would ring the warning alarm bell, everyone would get ready, and then a final bell would advise us to jump. We practiced this procedure during each flight, all of the students lining up at the bomb bay with their chutes on and waiting for the go signal. The pilot would then advise that the exercise was complete, instructors would evaluate our emergency practice performance, and we would go back to the business at hand. During one of these practices, while the B-17 was directly over the deepest part of the Grand Canyon and the students were lined up at the bay, the copilot elected to come to the bay to use the relief tube. The student gunners, seeing the copilot heading for the open bomb bay, reasoned that it was a real emergency so they all bailed out.

This was the day when helicopters were only dreams and experiments so the gunners were stuck in the canyon for many days. Food and clothing was airdropped to them and they were eventually rescued by cowboys and burros. They survived nicely and enjoyed the scenic burro trip, a trip for which tourists now pay a handsome price to make.

BAIL-OUT

While we were in flight training at Williams Field in Arizona, we were using B-24 airplanes for radar training. The training missions for the newly installed airborne radar (APO-13 for the purists) usually had several student operators aboard who took turns at operating the equipment. Those students who were not on the scopes were assigned as lookouts for other traffic and rode at tail and waist stations in the rear. The periods in the tail were long and not particularly exciting so it was not uncommon for an observer to catch a few winks of sleep. One student was a chronic sleeper and would not wake up until someone physically shook him awake. Pilots of the training aircraft really got aggravated at this guy and threatened him with all kinds of evil things, but he just slept away.

After a mission in which this guy was riding in the tail, the pilot could not awaken this "tail observer" with normal interphone calls, so he turned on the warning bell for a bail-out to try to get his attention. This worked. Rip van Winkle awakened, checked his parachute, and bailed out of the side window. He made a reasonably good landing and suffered only minor injuries, but severe embarrassment.

The pilot had rung the alarm bell while the airplane was being parked.

EPILOGUE

An epilogue implies a conclusion or an end to a story, but there is no conclusion nor is there an end to flying stories. The foregoing stories are only the experiences and the memories of one man; hundreds of thousands of other such stories are only waiting for someone to tell them. As long as men fly, there will be "hangar flying" where new stories will be told and the old ones embellished and elevated to legends. Within my generation along, men went from jennies to jets and then to spacecraft. Stories from each of these phases have their own interesting aspects and flavor. So will the new stories as the new generation flexes its wings and reaches such faraway places as Jupiter and Mars. Instead of the "Did I ever tell you what happened to me over Schweinfurt...," it might be something like, "That last landing on Pluto was really a bear, let me tell you about it. . . ." Whatever the case, the stories from the flying troops will continue.

Perhaps the stories that we don't tell about flying are those that fill us with patriotism and love of country, for we shy a bit from the sentimental softness that is within each of us. Who can fly over this great land and not see the living verses of "America, the Beautiful" as they unfold beneath him? To see this bountiful way of life as a giant portrait of beauty, the wide and clean highways which connect farms and factories, to soar above it all and join with the eagles inspires man to a deeper love for all that he has. Flying, its history and its many stories, is a big slice of man's heritage and should always be recorded in its finest detail so that those who come after will better understand what has gone before.

Time is slowly decimating the ranks of the surviving "50-mission-crush" airmen who were the darlings of World War II and of Korea. These guys were genuine dashing heroes, and for the generations to come they will be known only as they are represented in films. Today, those brave airmen who swept the world clean during the great war are the grandfathers of the current generation. But somewhere among "grandfather's" relics the cadet picture with the soft helmet and the flying goggles framing the fresh and eager face of the romantic flier. And somewhere else among these dusty treasures of days past is the crew picture, the one of all the guys in their flying togs lined up by their airplane. Where are those men now? How many of them survived the war and the ravages of time?

Looking at these aged and fading pictures, one can almost hear the background music of "I'll Be Seeing You," "I'll Walk Alone," "When You're a Long Long Way from Home," "Praise the Lord and Pass the Ammunition," and the booming song of the Air Corps: "We live in fame or go down in flame. . ."—those were the verses we sang in a loud cacophony of off-key voices.

What was the spirit behind these splendid young men that drove them to aerial glory? I think that it was a camaraderie born of war and of the necessity to care for someone and to have someone care about them. It was the spirit of romance and of war. With these little remembrances, I hope to have captured the mood of the time and to have preserved it for times to come—the mood that led some people as children into a great war and returned them home as men and heroes.

Flying has produced many heroes, some highly honored, others unrecognized. For me, among the most outstanding heroes of flying history are General Jimmy Doolittle and his band of Tokyo Raiders; they are my favorites and I believe they are as deserving of recognition as heroes as any men in history. The heroic group of airmen who flew those land-based B-25's from the short deck of the carrier *Hornet* to become the "Doolittle Raiders" and were the first to bomb our World War II enemy are representative of the time and mood I have tried to capture in this book. Some day in the future, only two of the silver goblets which now rest in a case of goblets, each of them with the name of a Raider engraved upon it, will be left standing upright. All of the others will be turned bottom-up, signifying that the Raiders whose names are on them have died. The two remaining Raiders will then drink from a bottle of ancient brandy from those silver goblets and an era will come to a close. Never again will there be the excitement in flying such as General Doolittle and his Raiders created—and it is my hope that the good general will be one of those making that final toast.

For me, General Doolittle and flying are synonomous, and I owe them both a huge debt. As a small down payment on that debt, I hope that I have captured and preserved some of the magic of flying and of the era in which General Jimmy was indeed the best damned pilot of all.

Finally, I am grateful to the fates which allowed me to be a part of this era, the likes of which will never be known to mankind again.

The End

When a 747 jetliner falls from the sky and crashes at supersonic speed into a remote island beach sixty miles northwest of Mazatlan a relentless investigation focuses on the slow-paced village known as "Z".

Some say Zihautanejo is a place for misfits, incorrigibles and quasi-psychotics — a place for rudderless rucksack carrying Americans to live free-floating lives in a tropical paradise where the scenery becomes narcotic. They say it's a place for fugitives or simply a place to get away from yourself after a stormy marriage or a crushed love.

Whatever their reasons for being there, Mexicans and Americans alike, they seek solitude in the stillness of the palm-lined beaches and no one asks questions.

Thrust into this scene is Helen Deane, a magnet for the admiring, lusting eyes of men. Her figure is perfect, her mouth is sensuous and her teeth are splendid. She wears her raven hair long and loose over her sleek shoulders. Her skin is delicious mocha as though dipped in honey and she's a dedicated investigator for the F.A.A.

Ted Tate, a retired veteran of three wars, is one of those Americans who escaped to Zihuatanejo. He has teamed up with a Texas writer, Tom Tweddale, to bring this exciting novel to life. It has been titled, *Skyhawk*, and will be published in the fall of 1985 by Maverick.

Ted has written two other books about Zihuatanejo: *Wash Gently, Dry Slowly* and *Zihuatanejo & Ixtapa*, a travel guide to the area.

Perhaps Ted Tate's most notable literary contribution to date has been his account of the life of Pancho Barnes in *The Lady Who Tamed Pegasus* ($5.95, Maverick). Ted Tate, a good friend of Pancho's, knows as well as anyone what actually went on at that infamous high desert watering hole known as the Happy Bottom Riding Club just outside Edwards AFB. And he tells it like it was even if it is a little embarrasing to some Air Force and NASA brass.

Write to Maverick Publications, Drawer 5007, Bend, OR 97708 if you would like to order any of these books.